ALL HANDS

ALL HANDS

THE LOWER DECK OF THE ROYAL NAVY SINCE 1939 TO THE PRESENT DAY

BRIAN LAVERY

Naval Institute Press
ANNAPOLIS, MARYLAND

First published in Great Britain in 2012 by
Conway, an imprint of Anova Books Ltd

Published and distributed in the United States of America and Canada
by the Naval Institute Press, 291 Wood Road, Annapolis, Maryland
21402-5043
www.nip.org

Library of Congress Catalog Card No. 2012945844

ISBN 978 1 59114 035 1

Printed and bound by 1010 Printing International Ltd., China

The illustration on page 18 by Ken Kimberley is reproduced courtesy of
Joan Kimberley and nostalgiacollection.com

The illustrations on pages 178, 222 and 251 are from Jackspeak: A Guide
to British Naval Slang and Usage and were created by the cartoonist
Tugg. The illustrations appear by courtesy of the author, Rick Jolly.

CONTENTS

INTRODUCTION

The lower deck of the Royal Navy has made as much impact on the world as any body of men in history – and not just because of the leadership and training of its officers. The grand themes of British history – empire, industry, war and class – are all strongly represented in naval history, and class is particularly sensitive for the status of the lower deck. The lower deck seamen also left their mark on world culture, for example in vocabulary, manners and dress. One of the aims of this work is to look at how far this continues into the present day, when industry, class and empire are far less relevant than they were, and wars are distant and tend to have far less impact on British society.

As this is the conclusion of a three-volume work, it might be useful to repeat the definition of the lower deck as 'a group of men (and later women) who perform the essential tasks of any navy with little expectation of promotion to the higher ranks. This does not exclude the possibility of a minority of its members rising to officer status, but it does not include cadets and midshipmen, who are recruited in the belief that they will eventually be commissioned.'

In many ways the lower deck is a closed world – seamen naturally spend a good deal of time at sea, and for reasons of security and discipline they are not usually encouraged to talk to the press or the public during their service. Their accommodation is usually hidden well below decks in the ship – visitors are usually shown the bridge and the operations room, and entertained in the wardroom if they are distinguished enough, but they rarely penetrate the mess decks. Most of the information I have used comes from two sources: official accounts and policy, such as reports, policy documents and fleet orders; and lower deck memoirs and diaries, mostly written or made available some time after the event. I believe that between the two of them it is possible to construct a reasonably true account of the lower deck story, even if it does not necessarily match the experience of any particular individual. These two sources are occasionally supplemented by the writings of outsiders. These include the numerous, and often quite famous, people who spent some time on the lower deck in 1939–45; a few accounts by national servicemen of the 1950s; and reports by journalists and television producers in later years.

As in the previous volumes, I have not dealt with the Royal Marines in any detail but only as they affect the rest of the lower deck, because they would be better served by their own history. I have been rather cursory in the story of the Women's Royal Naval Service, as for reasons of class and type of service its members were not truly of the lower deck until near the end of the twentieth century when they began to go to sea, and the women's service was abolished as a separate body.

Writing about contemporary naval history is fraught with danger, as many of the full facts are still to emerge and a certain amount of perspective is always needed. Clearly it is too soon to write a full history of any aspect of the navy in the last thirty years or so, and particularly of the lower deck. The public records are not yet open, few memoirs have been written, and many of the stories involved are still unfolding. With massive effort it might be possible to pursue it through the Freedom of Information Act and a large programme of oral history, but that is not a realistic aim for a book of this nature, and anyway it would be far from conclusive. The last chapters are therefore intended to bring the story to the present day, to illuminate some of the lessons and tie up some of the loose ends.

* * *

When war broke out in 1939, the navy was a very conservative service, and it is worth repeating the final paragraph of the last volume:

Twenty years of peace gave the navy a breathing-space between two great conflicts, but, like British society as a whole, it had failed to carry out social reform. Starved of funds, it had used what money it had to build more ships, unlike the United States Navy, which did much to improve the conditions of its men. The gap between officers and ratings was as wide as ever, and it was still difficult for a rating to get a commission. Nothing had been done to reform the boys' training ships, which were increasingly out of step with society. Long service was valued too highly, and the three-badge AB was not always a positive force. The navy was still failing to attract the growing middle class into its ranks, and it had done little to improve family welfare. All these issues would need attention eventually, but for the moment the navy was about to be locked in a life-or-death struggle in which it would rely more than ever on the loyalty, skill and determination of the lower deck.

There had been comparatively little change in warship design since the First World War – battleships, destroyers and submarines had developed, but there were no revolutionary developments. In aviation, the one area where real change was taking place, progress had been hampered by the conflict between the navy and the RAF over control of the Fleet Air Arm. In underwater warfare, the navy tended to be over-optimistic about the value of the asdic in detecting the enemy. The lower deck was proud of its traditions, mostly established late in the nineteenth century. It was generally as conservative as the rest of the navy, despite its role in the Invergordon Mutiny in 1931. Because of strike-breaking and the navy's association with hierarchy and imperialism, young men with radical politics rarely joined. Once in, boys were trained by a brutal system that seemed out of step with the rest of society. More mature sailors tended to respect tradition and deplore careerism. Accelerated promotion was regarded with suspicion, and one captain commented, 'few men on the Lower Deck regard special promotion with any enthusiasm. Trade Unionism and an innate fidelity to their own kind limit their aim to one of general security, i.e., equal opportunity to rise steadily on a pay scale.' Many more did not seek promotion at all, and there was a glut of 'three-badge ABs', men who had served at least 13 years, to earn three good-conduct chevrons, without advancing beyond the basic grade. Such men tended to dominate the mess decks, and younger leading seamen and petty officers were often in awe of them. Though the lower deck's conduct tended to be far better than in the past, there were still severe punishments for trivial offences. The navy of 1939 was still at the forefront of British society, still the largest in the world (despite nominal parity with the Americans) and still the most prestigious of the British services. It was about to cope with its greatest tests, in world-wide war, rapid expansion and the integration of new and unfamiliar personnel and technology.

Looking back over more than seventy years since then, a great deal has changed. The Royal Navy has a knack of appearing to stand still while transforming itself radically. It still sails in grey ships, it has destroyers, frigates, minesweepers and submarines and until very recently had aircraft carriers. It still has almost the same ranks and ratings as in 1939, with very similar uniforms for formal occasions at least. Yet it lives in a very different world, in which Britain is no longer the supreme sea power, there is almost no empire left to protect and little industrial base to recruit the lower deck from. Skill with electronics is valued more than muscle power, gunnery or seamanship. Its exact role has been questioned many times, and today there are some who would treat it as a subordinate service, an auxiliary to the army. The navy still relies on its lower deck, often more than some officers care to realise. It too has had to adapt to these changes. How far has its spirit survived in these days of centralisation and rationalisation?

TRAINING FOR THE PEOPLE'S WAR

MOBILISATION

For Britain the Second World War began with a mournful radio announcement by the Prime Minister, Neville Chamberlain. The German government had failed to respond to an ultimatum to withdraw its troops from Poland, and, 'consequently this country is at war with Germany.' The coxswain, or senior rating, of the destroyer *Firedrake* reported of the crew, 'They were all crowded round the loudspeaker listening to the old boy's speech, and when he finished somebody said, "About bloody well time too." That was all.'[1] Leading Seaman John Whelan heard officially about the declaration of war with Germany while in the destroyer *Zulu* in Egypt. Was it purely coincidence that her captain used the same terminology as his colleague in the training base *Drake* had used to new recruits just three weeks earlier?[2]

> At six o'clock next morning the Captain cleared lower deck. 'Gentlemen,' he said (he usually addressed us as 'Ship's Company'), 'we are at war with Germany. We sail for England in half an hour. You may dismiss.'[3]

G. T. Weekes was a master-at-arms, in charge of discipline in the Portsmouth naval base.

> Speaking for the Portsmouth Area, R.N. Barracks, what hectic days and nights followed that announcement, we, being responsible for receiving all reserves called up, had to victual them and bed them

down, according to their rating, put them before the medical people, kit them up, via the clothing department and Pay Office, then by the time the episode was completed orders would come from the drafting office, as to where they had to go, to ships in the Dockyard, or to ships overseas, etc., etc.

This was a full 24 hour exacting period, with relief only for nature, meals were taken at the desk, where one worked, no time to think about washing or shaving, etc., this went on rigidly for four days and nights, until the intakes came in, as a mere trickle, or until reliefs could be found to relieve us.[4]

Frank Coombes was on the other side of the law, undergoing punishment in Portsmouth at the time.

Went to the cells on Thursday 31st August and the War started on Sunday 3rd September and promptly went to see the Officer of the Day with a request that I be returned to duty straight away before the war ended and I was back on board for dinner, though the Cox'n would not give me my tot as I was still under punishment, so as normal had more bubbly than my ration with all the Sippers.[5]

On the first day of the war, Winston Churchill returned to the Admiralty as First Lord, and a signal went out to the fleet – 'Winston is back' – though it was never clear whether that was a note of satisfaction or warning. One of his first jobs was to supervise the full mobilisation of the navy, which had been practiced many times, notably during the Munich Crisis a year previously, and this went smoothly. More than 62,000 out of 73,000 men in the various reserves had been called up by the end of the year. Older pensioners were given shore jobs concerned with recruitment, administration and training, while younger men joined seagoing ships. Many more men would be needed for the five battleships, six large aircraft carriers, 19 cruisers, 32 destroyers, 11 submarines and 68 escort and mine-warfare vessels that were already under construction, plus ships that would soon be ordered under War Emergency Programmes, while future needs were unpredictable. The navy would have to go a long way outside the normal range of naval recruitment.

Frank Coombes's optimism that the war would soon be over was far from universal, but very few predicted the range and scope of naval operations, above, on and under the seas and on the fringes of the land, on every ocean and every continent, in vessels ranging from a 40ft landing craft to a 700ft battleship. It was a people's war on land and in the air, and in many ways it was a rating's war at sea. Fast expansion, increased use of smaller ships and the rapid progress of new technology placed great responsibility on certain individuals. The only trained medical staff on a small ship might be a sick-berth attendant. An AB or leading seaman might be in charge of a small landing craft, putting some 30 soldiers ashore on a mined and defended beach. On a radar or asdic set or even as a humble lookout, it was usually a seaman who gave the first warning of air, torpedo-boat or submarine attack, which could develop within seconds. Even in less hazardous circumstances, lower deck expertise was often essential to cover for the inexperience of hastily trained officers, as Sub-Lieutenant John Palmer found:

> The Navy was at that time very dependent on the Petty Officers and Chief Petty Officers who knew much more about the sea than us amateurs ... I am sure it is no exaggeration to record that without them the corvettes, in particular, would have found life extremely difficult. As an example, when we sailed in *Clematis* leaving the dock in Bristol and down the Avon, I was in theory in charge aft. An order came down to get out a spring. Extraordinarily, I had no idea what the order meant and simply turned to one of the Petty Officers. I told him to get out a spring and was intrigued to watch what happened.[6]

CONSCRIPTION

The navy, like the other armed forces and the rest of British society, had faced a great war just a generation earlier. The problems in 1914 were rather less for several reasons. The navy had been expanding steadily in men and materials for 25 years and was at an unprecedented peacetime level of 146,000 men in 1913. Lord Brassey, an enthusiast for naval reserves, claimed as early as 1906: 'The Navy is in fact being maintained in peace time on a war footing.'[7] Secondly, Britain could draw its reserves from the largest seafaring population in the world. The country had 12,862 steamships crewed by more than 200,000 men, with 50,000 more in the fishing fleet. Many of these could be brought into the navy if needed. Thirdly, it was assumed that the war would be short, so instructors and half-educated trainees could be taken from the training schools on the outbreak of war. This, however, became a problem as the war dragged on and there was no supply of freshly trained men. Training courses and examinations for men of the fleet were set up in the main fleet at Scapa Flow from 1916. In all, the navy expanded to a peak of 420,301 men, or by 288 per cent during the First World War. This was not as difficult as it might have been. 46,000 men were found immediately in 1914 by mobilising the various reserves. One growth area during the war was the Royal Naval Air Service, which had 46,000 officers and men in 1917, most of whom never went to sea. They were transferred to the control of the RAF on 1 April 1918.

In 1939 it was clear that this time the navy would have to expand well beyond peacetime levels. Merchant seamen were less numerous than in the past and would be needed in their own service to face the submarine menace. But at first it was believed that the service might be able to rely on volunteers again.

The Navy got through the 1914–18 war without any recourse to conscription entries and probably could do the same thing in the present war, but, in deference to the government plan for an orderly method of utilising the manpower of the country, it was willing to adopt the conscription system. In fact, there is no reason why, provided that a controlled system of voluntary entry were maintained, the Admiralty should not equally find part of its manpower requirement from volunteers.

But in practice voluntary recruiting was confined to 'ratings required for various special services who may be above the age for compulsory military service and need not necessarily be fit for sea service'. Churchill agreed and added, 'Our policy should be to take all the volunteers who offer themselves, who are not in reserved occupations, etc., and then make up the deficiency by selected men who have been called up and have indicated a preference for the Navy.'[8]

Wartime seamen, whether volunteers or conscripts, were recruited for 'hostilities only' – they would remain in the service for the duration of the war and for a reasonable time after it to allow a programme of demobilization. These men were known as HOs and contrasted with the regulars, the 'continuous service', or CS, men who had signed on for a fixed period of up to 12 years.

There was always a voluntary element in the navy's recruiting during the war – one had to positively volunteer for it rather than the other services when conscripted, so the prestige of the navy was important. The public was enthusiastic about it in the spring of 1941. It was believed that officers and men lived close together on board ship and that 'everyone from the admiral downwards shares the danger'. Sailors were 'as always doing their job magnificently'. Every seaman was 'worth six British soldiers, and three British airmen'. Partly this was because soldiers and airmen were scattered in bases round Britain and could be overheard in pubs and cinemas grumbling about conditions and leadership. The navy, on the other hand, was mostly at sea, and sailors were rarely seen far from the naval ports. One observer commented, 'I know no sailors, but I think they are heroic.'[9] Whether or not these perceptions were true, they certainly created a favourable atmosphere for naval recruiting.

At the end of the year, the Ministry of Information found five main reasons were given for joining the navy in preference to the other services. There was the spirit of adventure – 'We have always been a seafaring people.' There was the navy's prestige: 'Near the coast, the naval uniform is taken for granted, but in an inland pub a sailor has more glamour than the RAF.' Thirdly, it was believed that the sailor's welfare was better looked after: 'While he is afloat, the man has his health and food assured, and is in a settled place.' The navy had comradeship and less drilling than in other services, as well as higher pay and better allowances for family men, while for single men there was 'nothing much to spend it on at sea'. Also there were negative reasons. The army had not outlived memories of the Western Front. Ken Kimberley was influenced by what his school teacher had told him: 'His reminiscences of life in the trenches in the First World War, freezing mud, bayonets, barbed wire and what have you, gave me the creeps. He had seen it all and had first-hand knowledge ...'[10] As to the RAF, a survey conducted in the spring of 1941 showed that the public was enthusiastic about it.

Naval expansion was slower than that of the army or navy in the first four years of war, largely because ships took time to build. But even by April 1940 men were needed for ships taken out of reserve and new construction, including the Flower class corvettes, which could be built fairly quickly. Meanwhile much larger battleships and cruisers ordered from 1936 were now approaching completion. In addition the navy had taken over large numbers of ships to serve as armed merchant cruisers and needed gun crews for them, as well as for defensively equipped merchant ships, or DEMS. This involved a fleet of 310,000 men, of which 130,000 were long-service service regulars, 60,000 were recalled reservists and 120,000 were new entrants.[11] Then, after nine months of 'phoney war', the storm broke in spring of 1940 with the invasion of Norway and France, and the U-boat war moved out from the North Sea to the Atlantic, making it much more threatening. The building programme for escort vessels was accelerated, while Churchill negotiated the transfer of 50 old destroyers from America, all of which had to be manned. A new amphibious warfare organisation was set up with a view to returning to the continent some day, while the entry of Italy to the war gave much more priority to the Mediterranean Fleet.

The numbers of conscripts choosing the navy as their first option were quite low at this point, partly because the RAF became far more glamorous in the Battle of Britain, but also because vacancies in the navy were limited, so that men feared they would end up in the army by default. About twice as many men opted for the RAF at the end of 1941 than the navy in 1940, and the navy worried that it was not getting the best men.

Initially men were selected at recruiting offices by retired chiefs and petty officers, who knew a great deal about naval tradition but nothing about modern areas such as aviation and amphibious warfare. Moreover, they were not always familiar with the education system of the country, as John Davies found:

'Education?' The rough, deep voice startled me.

'Oh! I took an honours degree in English at the University of London' ...

The arbiter of my destiny gestured briefly with impatience.

'Never mind about that. Have you got the School Leaving Certificate?

'Er – yes, of course.'[12]

Later about 300 Wren Personnel Selection Officers, or PSOs, were appointed. They gathered information on candidates and passed it to the naval recruiters. They would collect this information by a three-stage process, in which they would first of all get a group of candidates to fill out a simple form, rather like an extended application form, which would yield facts about the school and work record and leisure activities of each candidate. After 10 minutes or so spent on this, the group would go on to take a paper-and-pencil intelligence test (which, in order to allay apprehensions, was always referred to as an 'observation' test) lasting 20 minutes. Then, as the men trickled back one by one from the medical board, which saw them on completion of the form and the test, each would be given an interview lasting about eight minutes. The Wren's notes on her interview and the man's score in the observation test were to be recorded on the form he himself had initiated.[13]

Many of the navy's needs could not be planned, especially during the difficult year of 1941. The loss of a major warship with all hands, such as *Hood* in May, did not affect the manning balance, but the loss of one in which most of the crew were rescued, such as *Ark Royal* in November, would have a positive effect on the manning situation. However, there were many losses of smaller numbers of men in which the ship survived to be repaired but casualties had to be replaced. There was a new commitment at the end of 1941 as war began with Japan, though the navy's involvement was quite small for some time after the catastrophic loss of *Prince of Wales* and *Repulse*.

'You're colour blind.'

A young conscript is interviewed by a personnel selection officer.

The navy expanded to more than half a million men and women by the middle of 1942 as new ships were launched. By this time the numbers opting for the navy were beginning to overtake those choosing the RAF, and by the end of the war they were three to one in the navy's favour. By the end of 1942 the country was facing a manpower crisis, with almost everybody mobilised for war and only limited numbers becoming available as they reached the age for conscription. The war cabinet was already deciding the numbers that each service was allowed to recruit per year, but it had to cut the numbers all the services asked for in 1943. After much haggling, the navy got 85 per cent of what it wanted, while the army and air force demands were cut in half. The navy had largely defeated the U-boat by May 1943, the Italians had been knocked out of the war in September, and most of the German capital ships and cruisers had been sunk or seriously damaged. But amphibious warfare, as organised by Combined Operations, was about to come into its own as the invasion of Europe was planned. In October 1943 the navy asked for a quarter of a million more men, including 104,000 for new ships coming off the stocks, 37,000 for the Fleet Air Arm, 10,000 for landing ships and craft, and a projected 53,000 'wastage.' The navy was already thinking about a return to the Pacific, when aircraft carriers would be the prime requirement. The war cabinet cut the demand to 40,000 men and eventually it was agreed at 67,000. The navy responded by taking many of its older ships out of service.

By the middle of 1944, as the invasion of northern France was imminent, the navy reached its record level of 790,000 men – still quite small compared with the army's 2.7 million and even the RAF's million, but a huge number for a profession that involved special skills even to survive in the environment in which it was intended to fight. Though amphibious warfare and the Fleet Air Arm required a higher proportion of officers than general service, nine tenths of the force at any given moment would be ratings.

TRAINING

On being accepted, a man might have to wait for some weeks until the navy was ready for him, then he went to one of the basic-training bases around the coast. These were invariably named as ships in accordance with naval tradition, which like most traditions began in late Victorian times. HMSS *Raleigh* near Plymouth and *Collingwood* near Portsmouth were purpose-built, but very hurriedly in typical wartime style. *Royal Arthur* at Skegness, *Scotia* at Ayr and *Glendower* in North Wales were converted holiday camps. *Ganges* was the former boys' training base, now used for adult recruits and with some unattractive additions to its buildings. John Davies wrote,

> To say that the Annexe was utilitarian is to cloak its extreme and depressing ugliness in as kindly a fashion as possible. Low wooden buildings, roofed with corrugated iron, enclosed a small parade-ground within a hollow square. Around three sides of the square ran a covered way, a projection of these roofs supported upon wooden uprights, and within these tin cloisters a few unwilling celibates lurked aimlessly.[14]

The new entrants to the seaman branch included men of a great variety of background and character, as described by the actor Alec Guinness.

> My fellow sailors, if that could be the right word for us as yet, I found agreeable and simple-hearted, with only two or three exceptions. We came from every sort of background, numbering among us butcher's assistants, a housepainter, a maker of pianos, a couple of school-masters (whom I thought rather intolerable, with their condescending airs), an aggressive, foul-mouthed Post Office clerk from Manchester, who could have served Hitler well, a Scottish Laird of great distinction and a dozen or so drifters from all over. Most were great swillers of beer. When in small, intimate groups, they chatted quietly of their mothers and sisters; once they were gathered in larger groups, however, the conversation, loud and hyphenated with four-

letter words, was of football and the crudest sex. Nearly all wished to be taken for old salts within days of joining up.[15]

The men were addressed by officers and petty officers, medically examined and eventually fitted with their uniforms, which more than anything else transformed them from civilians:

> When I reached the end of a long counter I had collected two jumpers, two pairs of bell-bottoms to be known as No 1s and No 3s, two collars, two shirt fronts, one black ribbon, two pairs of socks, one pair of boots, one cap, one cap band, one oilskin, one overcoat, one pair of overalls, one housewife (pocket sewing outfit), one lanyard and one seaman's manual.[16]

The clothes took some getting used to, particularly the jumper which was separate from the collar:

> Getting into the jumper was an all-in struggle, no holds barred, a wild waving of arms followed finally by a condition of complete helplessness. Breathless and outwitted I at last stood still, my shoulders and upper arms relentlessly caught in blue serge, the extremities dangling helplessly before me. Then as though in response to an intuitive feeling that all was not well, one of the white-shirted ones suddenly appeared, ducking under the screen. Without ceremony he heaved out the collar of my jumper, which had been the major cause of the stoppage, and then he tugged industriously at my waist until jumper and trousers met, and finally, with a superhuman effort, overlapped.[17]

Sailors quickly became immensely proud of their uniform and tried to make their collars a lighter shade of blue, a sign of long wear and experience. As James Callaghan wrote,

> We were taught how to tie knots and we discovered how to launder our new, dark-blue collars so that they appeared as faded and washed

out as those of any veteran seaman. We risked the wrath of the chief gunner's mate by cutting the tapes of our collars so that they showed a U-front instead of the regulation V-front, and we made sure we had seven horizontal creases (no more, no less) in our bell-bottomed trousers. All these matters were important to us.[18]

But not everyone liked the square rig uniform, and one ex-serviceman wrote in 1946,

Abolish the pantomime uniform known as bell bottoms, and substitute a naval battle-dress or uniform similar to that enjoyed by P.Os and officers – the men are worth it. One has only to watch an A.B dress to have pity on him, with a uniform consisting of tapes and ribbons and bits and pieces, and a blue jean collar to keep the grease from a pigtail soiling his jumper – a blue jean collar that another person has to hold in place while the poor chap puts his overcoat on. Women will object, no doubt, but they do not have to endure the nonsense.[19]

The men were instructed mainly by aged petty officers recalled from the reserve. Part of the course was seamanship, which involved a good deal of knot tying:

Morbid's method of instruction was the acme of simplicity. He would ignore us sulkily for a minute or two after the class had assembled, and then contemptuously take a rope's end in his enormous hands. 'Clove 'itch,' he would mutter, or 'Carrick bend' or 'Rolling 'itch', after which he would make the hitch in slow time. His huge hands were deft and sure. Then he would hold up the finished hitch for us to see, staring at us moodily, and finally throwing it down in disgust. A pause, and then he repeated the process, this time growling words of explanation – 'Up 'ere, over 'ere, down 'ere, and up the middle. Now do it yourself'' – and after that it was a matter of making the hitch ourselves, until it was difficult to make a mistake.[20]

The men also learned to row, or 'pull', a boat either on the open sea or in a lake. They were taught how to steer a ship and to survive in danger.

> Those unfortunates who couldn't swim got no sympathy from the Clubs, the PTIs (Physical Training Instructors) ...The poor sods who showed they couldn't swim properly or not at all received poolside instruction from the Clubs who would be ready to assist with his boat hook but not always to let them get out when they tried to splash their way to the side. From there on they would be given personal attention until they were able to swim adequately.[21]

They had to learn about naval ways, and many were confused by the chevrons of the three-badge ABs who were common in the bases.

> 'Sergeant? There ain't no such things in the Navy. Them three stripes on 'is arm are good conduct badges. 'E gets one after three years in the service, another after eight, and another after thirteen. 'E gets threepence a day extra for each one.'
> 'All right, Admiral; he's still a sergeant to me.'[22]

The other half of the course was gunnery, which in the tradition of the Portsmouth gunnery school HMS *Excellent* involved much foot drill, or 'gravel grinding', as well as exercises on dummy guns. As the official handbook put it, 'The chief prop of discipline is drill, for although of itself of little fighting value, its utility as a means of exercising officers and men in instant obedience cannot be overestimated.'[23] Not everyone agreed, and one officer, writing from his wartime experience, regarded foot drill as 'a poisonous growth' which had crept in gradually under the influence of HMS *Excellent*: 'Apart from mere voice production – which I think can more cheerfully achieved *off* the parade ground – taking charge of a squad at rifle drill has always seemed to me a very stupid occupation.' Nor was it any more effective in inducting new recruits.[24] This was disputed by a group of petty officers:

23

To say that there are never any smiles of laughter during rifle training is absolute nonsense, I cannot remember one session of rifle drill passing without some amusing situation arising that is talked about for a long time afterwards …

The crux of the matter is that taking a bunch of raw men as new entries one must first ensure that each and every man is capable of carrying out the simplest of orders without question. It is the easiest, simplest and cheapest method to give them parade training.[25]

Certainly many wartime recruits found foot drill surprisingly pleasant. The poet Roy Fuller found that, 'We came to enjoy squad-drill.'[26]

F. S. Holt of the RANVR had already done some naval training and was dissatisfied with the standard at HMS *Collingwood*:

Rather impatiently we listened daily to formerly retired 'Gunners' Mates' (recalled to be instructors) continuously reciting naval gunnery drill like gramophone records. So 'parrot fashion' were they that if interrupted with a question, a dazed look would come over their faces and they would proceed to start from the beginning again.[27]

The length of the course varied according to the urgency of the navy's needs, but it lasted around two months. One officer outlined what he hoped had been achieved:

F[robisher] 88, fashioned and welded together in five weeks, was returning to its individual components, but each man was taking away with him more than he brought in. Each could look after himself and his kit; whatever his category, each could swim, and pull and sail a lifeboat; each knew enough about fighting a ship not to be a nuisance at sea. And, above all, they had a sense of belonging, a rock-bottom foundation for living together, in preparation for the time when they would be locked together for months on end in a steel box far from land.'[28]

In peacetime a boy or young adult of the seaman branch might spend years at sea before being offered training for his 'non-substantive rate' – specialising as a gunner, torpedoman or submarine detector. In wartime the demand for asdic operators, anti-aircraft gunners and radar operators was so urgent that men had already been assessed for these roles during their basic training and would often proceed with it after a short leave. By September 1943 the schools were expected to provide a quota of 240 men per month for submarine detection, 650 for gunnery, 250 torpedomen and more than 1,000 for radar, but they were finding it difficult to reach these figures.[29]

PROMOTION FROM THE LOWER DECK

Before the war the Admiralty agreed that most of the new officers for the expanded fleet should begin on the lower deck. They should be selected in the training schools and grouped in a specialist class there, then go to sea for at least three months as ordinary seamen before being selected to go on an officers' training course at HMS *King Alfred* in Hove. This was known as the CW Scheme after the commission and warrant branch of the Admiralty that issued the form by which candidates were assessed. However, it did not mean that commissioned rank was any more open to regular seamen, the 'continuous service' men. Indeed an Admiralty Fleet Order of 1940 made it clear that long-service seamen were not to have their hopes raised:

> It is necessary to man the large additions made to the Fleet in war by personnel serving for the period of hostilities only; many of the officers must accordingly be on a temporary basis. While Their Lordships' policy is to obtain a high proportion of such officers by promotion from the Lower Deck ... the grant of such commissions on these lines to continuous service ratings would normally result in their having to leave the service at the termination of hostilities instead of continuing the career in the Navy on which they have embarked ...

Moreover, the standard to be achieved for selection for promotion to permanent commissioned rank must remain one which will allow those selected to compete on equal terms with the Officer entered as a cadet. The training given to such selected ratings is thus designed to qualify them to undertake any of the duties of their future rank as required by the exigencies of the service, and to enable them to achieve a complete mastery of their profession. The period of such training must therefore be considerably longer than that for the temporary R.N.V.R. Officer who is only expected to carry out the limited duties of one special type of appointment for the duration of the war.[30]

It was possible to open CW papers on a long-service rating, but captains had to be circumspect about it. 'It is not generally desirable that a long-service rating should be informed of the commencement of a C.W. Form No. 1 concerning him, although he will no doubt acquire knowledge of his prospects in the course of time without this information being definitely disclosed to him.'[31]

A CW seaman learns navigation under an RNVR lieutenant.

The wartime army was more sincere and more successful in its attempts to level class distinctions, but the navy might argue that there were good reasons for that. In the army, every non-specialist NCO or officer, from lance-corporal to general, had to be capable of carrying out the same tasks – leading his men and defeating the enemy. In the navy, seaman officers were traditionally distinguished from the lower deck by their knowledge of navigation, which had to be based on a good general education. Perhaps this was a little outdated, and the lines had become blurred in the new kind of war – coxswains of small landing craft needed some elementary knowledge, even if they were only rated as ABs or leading seamen. The distinction was less rigid in other navies: the navigator of a German U-boat was usually an *obersteuermann*, the equivalent of a chief petty officer or a warrant officer, while the United States Navy had quartermasters to assist the navigators.

The typical naval officer did not believe that the average sailor of the lower deck was likely to make a suitable officer in any circumstances. In 1912 Winston Churchill had set up the 'mates' scheme by which selected seaman were eligible for officer training, but to qualify they had to study on the lower deck, where conditions were not encouraging. In 1937 the Admiralty had announced the Upper Yardman scheme by which candidates would be allowed time for study. But initially the success rate was rather low, and when the matter was discussed in Parliament in July 1939 MPs were given the impression that the scheme was a failure, which was denied by the Admiralty.[32] However there was a perceived difficulty because of the nature of its recruits. In the first place, lower deck entry was not generally attractive to boys with more than a minimum of education, and it did not attract 'the pick of the secondary school boys'. They were not encouraged by their headmasters, who knew that promotion to the quarterdeck was unlikely, and in any case they preferred that promising boys should stay on to take certificates, which increased the school's prestige. Moreover, after three or four years in the service, naval officers believed that a man 'had spent too long in the Service on the lower deck'; he had been 'influenced by the lower deck outlook during his impressionable years at sea' and was 'too old to acquire readily that breadth of outlook and spirit of service necessary in an officer'.[33] As in previous wars, the navy preferred to look outside its own ranks for potential officers.

As for HO men entering the training schools, only those with a good standard of education, which nearly always meant a middle-class background, were likely to be considered. John Davis noticed the class distinction:

> I couldn't help feeling a little unhappy about the method of selection, for the initial choice seemed to have been based largely on paper qualifications. In my own case, for instance, I did not see how a degree in English Literature went any part of the way towards proving that I would make a leader of men. All four members of the mess who had university degrees were among the six chosen. On the other hand the irrepressible Bert, who probably had more character and vitality than the rest of us combined, was not.[34]

The same point was made by a group of young officers who wrote to C. G. Ammon, MP, in 1942:

> No one who has not at least had a secondary school education is even considered, no matter what brilliance he may show while at the training establishment, thus many who might make very brilliant officers are overlooked. The official excuse for this is that without a secondary school education men cannot master the officers' training course. This, speaking from personal experience, is not true. Any intelligent man can easily master the course, while no matter how high his educational qualifications, unless they are linked with intelligence a good officer does not result. Particularly important is the understanding which an officer has of his men, and the present insistence on education results in a gap between officers and ratings. There is no doubt that the system as at present worked definitely

prevents the average rating from ever being considered for a commission.[35]

It is not clear if this had any immediate effect, but the standards had to be reconsidered because of the greatly increased demand for officers. In March 1943 the Admiralty ordered that

> Recommendations of ratings should not be confined to ratings in possession of some set standard of education, such as the school certificate. Intelligent men who can quickly absorb instruction and have the required character and personality are quite capable of passing successfully through H.M.S. "King Alfred", although their initial education has not been of a high standard. The essential qualities required are character, personality and powers of leadership.[36]

The policy, especially before 1943, meant that there was always going to be a large group of able but cynical men at warrant officer or chief petty officer level with very little hope of further promotion. John Whelan took perverse pleasure in the fact that it was easier to become an officer than a highly-skilled petty officer: 'Only four of us passed out as instructors. There was a shortage of instructors but (I say this with some pride) the Navy did not lower its standards ... It was possible to become a junior R.N.V. R officer within six months of joining, but it took far longer to make an asdic instructor.'[37] And when a scheme for promotion of long-service ratings was finally introduced, he was sceptical:

> The Lords Commissioners had, in fact, introduced a system of commissions for the regulars for 'the duration only' and I had toyed with the idea of applying for one. But the Admiralty warned: 'We will grant commissions only where it can be proved that the man concerned will be of more value to us as an officer than as a rating.' So I dismissed the thought. I knew the official answer: 'We can't send

you to sea as a junior watch-keeping officer when your services are more valuable as an instructor.' One or two of the optimists did apply, and were told exactly that.[38]

Continuous-service ratings were to be encouraged to seek promotion through a much slower route as warrant officers, after which accelerated advancement to commissioned rank was available in suitable cases.[39] In the age of sail the term 'warrant officer' had covered a wide range, including all non-commissioned men appointed by the Admiralty or the Navy Board unlike most petty officers who were appointed by the captain of the ship. Some were of very high status – masters, pursers, chaplains and all medical officers, including the Physician of the Fleet, who in the modern navy would probably be a flag officer. At the lower end, the term covered artisans such as coopers, armourers and ships' cooks – the cook of a Sixth Rate would perhaps be the equivalent of a leading seaman today. During the nineteenth century the higher grades of warrant officer became commissioned officers, while the lower ones became ratings. This left the middle group, consisting initially of carpenters, boatswains and gunners, to which engineers, signal boatswains, torpedo gunners and shipwrights were added.

Unlike army warrant officers, who were treated as senior NCOs, naval warrant officers were considered junior officers, though they were often shunned socially by the commissioned officers. Moreover, they had long been in decline as a class, and the inter-war years were a particularly lean time for them, sandwiched between the ambitions of their superiors and the discontent of their juniors. The lack of promotion prospects was particularly hard on men who had aspirations but no influence. During the war John Whelan

did not nurse any longings to graduate to the ranks of those forlorn and most pathetic of creatures, the warrant officers. Neither real officers nor lower deck men, they sat in their cabins darning their socks, despised by both. Ignored at ward-room parties, their single thin stripe was acceptable at celebrations ashore only if they were first-rate pianists or second-rate conjurors.[40]

As an AB, the musician and writer George Melly constantly found himself in trouble with them. They were

> martinets, sticklers for the letter of the law, hard resentful men who realised they had risen from the ranks on merit but been blocked for a commission on class grounds. Caught uneasily between the relaxed bonhomie of the PO's mess and the easy formality of the wardroom they were punctilious in their insistence on outer form, correctitude, the marks of respect as laid down by King's Regulations.[41]

The Admiralty too was aware of the strengths and limitations of the warrant officer: 'The type of officer obtained from this source may be very much "set in his ways" and unsuitable for staff appointments, but within his limits he is an extremely valuable officer.'[42]

THE CWs AND THE LOWER DECK

The presence of the potential officers or CWs doing their three-month service on the lower deck had several effects. It caused a mixed reaction among the regular ratings. Sometimes there was bewilderment. 'Well, these blokes, like Dave, come aboard, and they're just like all the other bleeding H.O.s, only worse, then just when they've started to learn how to live sensible and decent, and we've got used to 'em, they go and leave the ship.'[43] Sometimes there was downright dislike, starting on HMS *Tynedale* when some 'men dressed as seamen' appeared on board: 'Numbah twooo mess. Six of us hev to report to numbah twooo mess, the other six are going to numbah one mess.' 'Guns' was 'verging on apoplexy', which only increased as the newcomers sipped their rum – '"Knock them blasted tots back," growled Guns. "The messdeck's taking on the atmosphere of a blasted cocktail party.'" And when the men poured the remainder of their rum into a bucket, 'Guns was out for murder.'[44]

Geoffrey Ball was nervous as he joined the destroyer *Duncan*: 'Not only was I a Grammar School boy but also a "C.W. Candidate" ... Would I get all kinds of jibes, taunts and insults from the other seamen who, I assumed would mostly be from lowly backgrounds and very anti-officer? Worse still, would I, as a future potential officer, get beaten up regularly by a gang of them?' But he soon found that the only standard by which he was judged was whether he pulled his weight in the mess.[45]

Actor Peter Bull believed that the lower deck was tolerant of the CWs but was put off by the attitudes of many of them.

> They were not a bad lot, with one exception, but were out of place in such a crew. To break down the ill-feeling which is bound to exist in the mind of the average matelot towards the favoured few is not a very difficult job. But so many would-be officers conducted themselves in such a ludicrous way that the barrier was never removed. It was their constant washing and airing their knowledge that got the permanent residents down.[46]

The Culture of the Lower Deck

Another effect of the CW scheme was that several of the candidates recorded their experiences and revealed the culture of the messdeck as never before or, perhaps, since. John Davies published *Stone Frigate* about his time in training, and *Lower Deck* about his service in a destroyer. S. Gorley Putt wrote *Men Dressed as Seamen* with illustrations by the great stage designer Roger Furse. But the most successful was *Very Ordinary Seaman* by J. P. W. Mallalieu, who wrote it under extraordinary circumstances while waiting for a place on an officers' course.

> When I got back I found that I had been appointed Commander's Messenger which meant that for eight hours a day, five days a week,

I sat in Commander Reid's office, facing a blank wall and typing myself dry. There was no question of hanging about waiting for inspiration. There were no pauses for artistic temperament. I was under 'naval discipline'. I wrote.[47]

It is not easy to tell how much of the book was fact and how much was fiction, but it provides a detailed and accurate impression of lower deck life.

In addition, several men who later achieved fame served as CWs and their biographies are equally revealing. James Callaghan, prime minister from 1976 to 1979, came from a naval background. His autobiography, *Time and Chance*, was rather brief about his experiences in training and with the Patrol Service, but it provides some insights. Alec Guinness was already quite well known as an actor when he joined HMS *Raleigh*. His autobiography, *Blessings in Disguise*, deals with that in some detail, along with his service in landing craft, while he also kept diaries that have been quoted by his biographer.[48]

From the lower deck itself, Petty Officer Writer Robert Burgess and Leading Writer Roland Blackburn appeared regularly on the radio programme *Make and Mend* as part of a discussion group called *The Briny Trust*, based on the more philosophical but surprisingly popular *Brains Trust*, and they published *We Joined the Navy* in 1943. It was a more official and less lively account that Mallalieu's book, but it gave some insight into naval vocabulary and customs. They provided a useful guide to the naval mess deck vocabulary of the day:

I heard the Sky Pilot taking to Jimmy the One and the Custard Bo'sun the other day, and they all agreed that it was too bad of the Sloshy to unhook the Crusher's caulker from the cooler to get his head down. The Chief Buffer has got a howl on now because he got a blast from Torps, as so many of the part of ship hands were doing a never on the messdecks instead of working the main derrick.[49]

Using the glossary provided, this might be translated as:

> I heard the chaplain taking to the first lieutenant and the warrant cookery officer the other day, and they all agreed that it was too bad of the ship's cook to steal the regulating petty officer's blanket from the cells to get his head down. The Chief Boatswain's Mate is complaining because he got a telling-off from the Torpedo Officer, as so many of the part of ship hands were loafing on the messdecks instead of working the main derrick.

In addition, seamen were rarely known by their real names.

> For instance we have 'Shiner' Wright, 'Dusty' Miller, 'Pincher' Martin, 'Nellie' Wallace, 'Topsy' Turner, 'Pusser' Combe, 'Hookey' Walker, 'Smouge' Smith, 'Paddy' Walsh, 'Nobby' Clark, 'Bungy' Williams, 'Jack' Hilton. All Thomases are 'Tommo', and all members of the Day clan are 'Happy'. Tall men are alluded to as 'Lofty', short men as 'Stumps', 'Sawn-Off' or 'Shorty'.[50]

But it was the outsiders, especially Davies, Putt and Mallalieu, who gave the most intimate picture of the lower-deck seaman, at home in its messes rather than on the streets and in the pubs where middle-class writers had seen him in the past. The law prevented them from using swearwords in print, and Mallalieu got round that by using 'flicking':[51] 'Nobby was certainly not ashamed of his own swearing (another occupational disease, if you like).'[52] But there were limits: 'He swore more than anyone on the ship. Almost every third word was unprintable and yet he never meant anything by it. He would say, "Yes, I know it's silly. I never do it at home. It's just a habit on the ship."'[53] The seaman in his mess was witty, as when quoting *Psalm 23*:

> 'He maketh me to lie in green pastures.'
>   Wet hammocks, more like.
> 'He leadeth me beside the still waters.'
>   STILL waters? O, flicking yeah!"[54]

Religious seamen were usually a minority and sometimes mocked by the others: 'It's all troipe. Oi know. Oi used to go to church. Oi was in the flicking choir ... Troipe. All religion is troipe.'[55]

The seaman was protective of his few possessions. '"Ye robbers," wailed Jock. "Somebody's took ma shaving brush. Somebody's took my soap. Come round, ye flickers, and ah'll give ye the razor. Then ye'll have a complete set."'[56] Going ashore the seaman could be vain: 'Whatever warm rags a man may choose to wear during the night watches and however caked with grease and salt his "No 2" clothes may be, he will always preserve inviolate his "Number ones" for shore leave.'[57] He had his superstitions, either collectively or as an individual: 'A bet thi' summat'll 'appen to t'ship before t' week's art. Tha should nivver chuck a rat overboard.' The seaman complained constantly – 'Sweeping the flicking iron deck. I no sooner sweep the flicker than some dockyard matey drops a pile of muck all over it and I have to do it again.'[58] But if he complained too much, 'A rating who takes a delight in "dripping" (expressing his disapproval of everything and everyone) is usually dubbed "Appy Day", "Famous Crimes" or "Acid Drop."'[59] His reading tastes were not sophisticated: 'the luxury of reading in "bed" was universal ... Youngsters of "unhair'd sauciness" and elderly three-stripes who had grown grey in service could be seen curled up in their several nests, conning photographs of "cuties" or thumbing the pages of a juicy paper-backed murder story.'[60] Some regular ratings were orphans who had not yet established a family of their own, but many were married, and home was especially valuable to them because of their nomadic life. 'I wish I was at home sitting in the armchair, by the fire, with my carpet slippers on and the missus handing me a cup of tea and the nipper squitting all over the floor just to make it home-like.'[61] One man received news that his house had been bombed, and his messmates asked after his wife:

'No, she's all right ... in a shelter when it 'appened. But the 'ouse is gone, and all the bleeding furniture, not that she 'ad much. Every bleeding thing, by the look of it!' After the first shock of the news his face flushes with anger. 'I'll be glad when we've finished mucking about 'ere and get another crack at them bastards!' he says.[62]

Some men, especially those who were 'gooey' over their girlfriends, wrote obsessively. 'He used to say, quite frankly, "If my girl told me to stay home, I'd desert tomorrow," and he used to bring out pictures of his girl whenever he could get anyone to look at them.'[63] But for most, shipboard life was all-consuming: 'At sea, where there was nothing to remind them of women, they forgot them all except the gooey boys, and lived the ordinary life of the ship without suffering any discomfort from their natural instincts.'[64]

Above all, the CWs had to share with the continuous service men, the reservists and the HOs the experience of constant danger in a grossly overcrowded ship:

After the meal, all the irritations of overcrowding seemed to be

An overcrowded messdeck.

intensified. Every mess was 'washing up' at the same time; men carrying cans of hot water bumped into one another and into the ironwork; scraps of food mingled with fugitive potato peelings on the deck ... On these occasions, when mugs and spoons and boots and books were likely to be flung to and fro by the ship's crazy movement, when the narrow air between jumbled bodies and ammunition hoists was filled with steam and tobacco smoke, when shouts churned the thickening atmosphere ... a poor effete old gentleman in his late twenties may be forgiven for wandering off to sit on a depth-charge ...[65]

Only a small minority of CWs failed at this stage, often for becoming too close to the lower deck. They remained in square rig during three months' officer training at HMS *King Alfred* distinguished only by a white band round the cap and the designation 'cadet-rating'. Failure rates now were still quite high, as many could not absorb the technical information of the course, or failed to show 'officer-like qualities' or, even worse, showed evidence of 'lower deck attitudes'. In that case they went back to the naval barracks to start again, now some way behind their colleagues in basic training who had learned useful skills by that time.

> Uniforms were cancelled; white capbands were immediately removed. The rejects had to mess separately from the other cadet-ratings and were generally declared 'unclean'. Then came the depressing journey back to barracks. The arrival there was like receiving a bucket of icy water full in the face. The cadet-rating chrysalis had been on the point of bursting into the officer butterfly when it had been rudely stamped upon. Now one had to revert in a flash to the manner, habits and thoughts of a rating.[66]

The 'failed CW' became a recognised type on the lower deck, perhaps as a class leader in a training school. He added to the increasingly unstable mix as the war went on.

The Continuous Service Man at War

Whatever happened, the traditional long-service man was still the king of the mess deck, even when he was greatly outnumbered by HOs. He was the guardian of naval tradition, not that of the officers or the historians but of the lower deck itself. In the circumstances one might have expected the continuous service man to be swamped and his culture suppressed or greatly modified. In fact the opposite happened, as HOs aped the regulars in dress and custom. As Captain Oram put it of the cruiser *Hawkins*,

> In effect the ship was steamed and defended by a cross-section of British provincial life with a handful of South Africans thrown in as leaven. The Jolly Jack of peacetime was a rare bird indeed, so rare that one was tempted to pipe a tear of affection for the breed, now a practically extinct prototype. The wartime sailor, faithfully modeling himself upon his glamorous predecessor, was conscious of the ready-made aura which attached to his own interpretation of the part. He was often dismayed to find that the dazzling mythology surrounding this sea business did not quite come up to expectation. There was much to be said for the 'new boys', though. The model set for them to follow was good and by his exacting standards we were able to run our complicated machines on a very weak mixture of RN spirit! [67]

Recruiting for the regular navy or continuous service was carried on throughout most of the war, as the navy looked to the long-term future even as the nation faced its greatest crisis. Tristan Jones was in one of the last boys' courses in *Ganges* before it was turned over to adult recruits:

> Life for a boy trainee at HMS *Ganges* was one long harassment from dawn – when the bugler sounded 'Charlie' – until lights out at nine-fifteen p.m. There was hardly a minute of the waking day when we boys were not on our feet and doubling, or sat at attention in a classroom, being yelled at. Even when the 'working' day was over,

our time was taken up hand-sewing our names on to our uniforms (red chain-stitches, each not longer than the rest). Some of the class were still busily engaged in this pastime, even though they had been in Ganges for ten weeks. There was always something to be done, and never enough time to do it. The boy who could find five minutes to sit down and write a letter home was lucky indeed.[68]

After that, boy training was concentrated in HMS *St George* on the Isle of Man, away from enemy action. It was another holiday camp, near the capital of Douglas with room for 600 boys in chalets. Discipline was a strict as in the older bases, and life was 'a constant round of parade ground, seamanship and gunnery instruction'. Recruiting for boys was closed for a time, but when it was re-opened early in 1943, more than 6,000 enquiries were received at the Admiralty within a week.[69] For the boy who was anxious to do his bit for the war, the navy had the advantage that he could join at an earlier age – though he had to sign on for twelve years' adult service to do so. But they remained a very small proportion of naval recruits. In 1942–3, 2,302 boys were taken on 'on normal engagements' compared with more than 55,000 volunteer HOs, 5,000 potential officers and technicians who had done some pre-entry training as part of the Y-Scheme, and more than 82,000 conscripts.

Three-badge ABs, who had competed at least thirteen years' service without promotion, were naturally a smaller proportion of the fleet than in peacetime, but the recall of pensioners swelled their numbers. In 1939 the Admiralty was trying to make sure that no man over the age of 48 was sent to sea, but their presence was still noticeable on the decks of many ships.[70] Three-badgers, according to Mallalieu, 'had all the privileges of Leading Seamen and most of the privileges of Petty Officers … they were elder statesmen who gave advice but were under no obligation to see that it was followed.'

A Stripey would always do his whack in the mess. When he was cook he always did his share of peeling potatoes, taking the food up to the galley, fetching it back again, and dishing up the plates afterwards. When a three-badge man was cook, he didn't get his head down like Price. But if he was not cook, nothing would induce him to lend a hand – 'It just encourages the real cooks to shirk.'[71]

One of the heroes of Dunkirk was Able Seaman Samuel Palmer, who had passed for leading seaman in 1927 and earned three good conduct badges and the Long Service and Good Conduct Medal but was not promoted, perhaps because his initiative and independence were not valued in the peacetime navy. He took a 30ft motor boat across the Channel, rescued some French soldiers and made many ferry trips to craft waiting offshore. He had to deal with engine failure and lack of charts before he took some British troops back to Ramsgate.[72]

2

THE BRANCHES

As he joined his first seagoing ship after basic training, the new seaman was already aware of the lower end of the naval hierarchy. He was rated perhaps as ordinary seaman or stoker second class, and he could look forward to promotion to able seaman or stoker first class within a year or so, provided his performance was satisfactory. Officially the first level of authority above him was the leading seaman or stoker, distinguished by an anchor, the 'hook' or 'killick' on his left arm. The killick lived in the mess with the seamen and wore the same uniform. Above that were the petty officers, who lived in a separate mess and wore the 'fore and aft' uniform with peaked cap and collar and tie after a year in the rate. The chief petty officers were still higher, with extra privileges after long service.

The new entrant had probably seen very little of the commissioned officers in his training base, except when welcomed by the captain or assessed by the lieutenants as divisional officers. He would probably see more of them now, on the bridge, in the engine room or on deck. He had been taught the significance of the rank stripes on each officer's lower sleeve. The single stripe of a sub-lieutenant almost certainly signified inexperience, though not necessarily youth in wartime conditions. A lieutenant had two stripes and was more seasoned, probably in charge of a watch in a corvette or destroyer, or the captain of a small vessel of coastal forces. The first lieutenant of a ship was often a notorious figure, though he did not necessarily hold the rank of lieutenant. The lieutenant-commander, with his 'two and a half' stripes, was often encountered as the captain of a medium-sized vessel, where he was a figure of great authority – in a battleship or cruiser he was merely another cog in the machine. The full commander was best known as the head of a department such as engineering in a large ship, or the second-in-command, where he was the leader and organiser of the crew. Those who wore four stripes and held the rank of captain, as distinct from the courtesy title, were usually on staff duties or in command of the larger ships. Above them was a hierarchy of admirals, mostly remote from the lower deck even in their own flagships.

The navy had seen much service overseas in the past, as one of its primary roles was the protection of the British Empire. This was pleasant in peacetime, especially for the single man who wanted to see the world. In war, the favourite exercise area of the Mediterranean was hotly and violently contested, while the North Sea, like the English Channel, was a no-man's-land where both sides ventured out at night or under heavy air cover. The navy found itself devoting more attention to the North Atlantic than it had ever considered necessary, and with the onset of the Russian convoys it had to operate in even more inhospitable and dangerous waters in the Arctic Ocean.

It did not take long for a new hand to find out that service in the navy was often hard and unremitting. The bulk of the army was disengaged from the enemy for four years after 1940, preparing to resist an invasion of Britain or planning its own invasion of the continent of Europe. The RAF had a policy of rotating aircrews in operational situations, withdrawing fighter squadrons from the most active areas after a few months in action, or resting members of bomber crews if they survived for 30 missions. The navy was continually in action and had no policy of rotation. On escort duty in the North Atlantic, for example, one convoy would follow another in quick succession, apart from gruelling training in between. Leave was granted according to the needs of the ship rather than of the men when it went into dock for a refit or its boilers needed cleaning.

The new sailor soon became aware that each ship was a collection of specialists, each of whom was essential to keep it operational. As well as its vertical division by rank, the navy was divided laterally into the branches to which both officers and ratings belonged, such as seamen, signalmen, stokers, domestics, writers (or clerks) and artisans. The seaman branch was the largest, with about a third of the navy, followed by the stokers, who formed about 20 per cent. Marines formed about 10 per cent, while smaller but vital branches, usually with about 3 per cent of the fleet each, included the highly skilled engine room artificers and the signalmen. Domestic, medical and administrative ratings formed about 6 per cent; they were distinguished from the others in that even junior ratings wore a version of 'fore and aft rig', with peaked cap and collar and tie.

GUNNERY

Most members of the seaman branch went on to qualify for a 'non-substantive' rate as gunner, torpedoman, submarine detector or eventually as radar plotter. This brought extra pay but was distinguished from a man's 'substantive' rating as able seaman, leading seaman, petty officer and so on. For most of the war the gunnery branch consisted of four main sections. Quarters ratings were the most general; they operated the guns with the assistance of non-gunnery ratings, and those of second class rating and upwards might take charge of turrets or groups of guns. The layer section included the men who would train and lay the guns and, more importantly, the directors. Those in the control section were mostly responsible for operating rangefinders, and inclinometers, which measured the angle of a target and assessed its changes of course. Finally there was the anti-aircraft section, which would become increasingly important during the war, with such subdivisions as the AA Gunner (Light Craft) who only learned to use the smaller guns to be used in coastal forces, landing craft and so on. In addition a gunnery rating might train as the gunnery lieutenant's writer, or become 'qualified in ordnance' as the assistant to an ordnance artificer mostly working on hydraulic machinery. At the top of the tree, as always, was the gunner's mate, a chief or petty

PHONE MAN
SPOTTING OFFICER
CONTROL OFFICER
DIRECTOR TRAINER
DIRECTOR CHANGE-
-OVER PISTOL
RATE OFFICER
DIRECTOR LAYER
CROSS LEVELLING OPERATOR

A director showing the seats occupied by the ratings:
the director trainer, director layer, cross levelling operator
and phone man.

officer. In 1944 a new group of radar-control ratings was added, to
supplant the old rangefinders.[1]

The heavier guns of battleships and cruisers were still directed by
methods that had evolved before and during the previous war, now
with the assistance of radar to determine the range. The senior ratings
of the gunnery branch still had a vital role to play in this. According to
the *Gunnery Pocket Book* of 1945,

> On the Director Layer, more than any other individual, except
> perhaps the Control Officer, depends the success of a gunnery action.
> He works alone and unobserved and he must make himself worthy
> of the responsibility imposed on him. He must practice in all
> weathers and especially at night, because he is the eyes of the guns

and unless he has practised at night and in foul weather he will not be able to see when the enemy is met. If his opponent in the enemy ship is quicker and steadier than he, by virtue of drills and practice, his ship will be sunk instead of the enemy's.[2]

But with smaller guns, far more depended on the individual gunlayer. In *Motor Gunboat 658*, the captain ignored all gunnery qualifications and took his men to the rifle ranges to find the best shots.[3]

The 20mm Oerlikon gun, developed by the Swiss company of that name, was fitted to almost every type of ship. There were 55,000 of them in service by the end of the war, each with a crew of two – 110,000 men, or about a seventh of the strength of the navy.[4] Any success could make an Oerlikon gunner a hero, or at least redeem his reputation. Ordinary Seaman Fitzgerald of the destroyer *Fortune* had accidentally fired a flare off Gibraltar, but when he shot down an Italian Savoia bomber there were 'loud cheers from everybody'.[5] Likewise with AB 'Happy' Day in *MGB 658* during an attack by a Focke-Wulf 190: 'As he banked, A/B Day in the twin Oerlikon turret had him exactly in his sights and gave him a long searing burst which ripped down his fuselage. Splinters flew and the tail of the aircraft seemed to hang drunkenly down. As we cheered wildly, the plane plummeted into the sea.'[6]

The navy had failed to develop an adequate director system for anti-aircraft fire and instead it relied heavily on 'eyeshooting'. The gunlayers used sights with two or three rings, each representing 100 knots of an aircraft's speed:

> The method of using the sight is very simple. Look at the aircraft, note its direction of flight and estimate its aim-off speed. Point the gun so that the aircraft is flying towards the centre of the sight, with its nose the distance from the centre corresponding to your estimate of its aim-off speed. As the attack develops and the aim-off speed increases, bring the nose of the aircraft further and further out from the centre, always adjusting direction of aim-off to keep the aircraft flying towards the center of the sight.[7]

Aircraft recognition was a key factor, and it often went wrong:

> The challenge by our signalman went ignored and by this time the
> plane was right above us, slightly perhaps to our port side, so that I
> had an excellent view of it. The sound of our klaxon horn told us to
> open fire, and we did. Two Shells from our two-pounder on the
> fo'scle, manned by Taff Johns and two others, hit the plane, and my
> machine guns raked it from nose to tail. Only then did the crew of
> the aircraft come to life, and a somewhat angry signal was radioed
> to us stating that the aircraft was British ...[8]

But it was more common for gunners to open fire too soon and empty
their magazines before hitting the enemy.

TORPEDO AND ELECTRICAL

By 1939 the torpedo branch had become increasingly concerned with
electricity. Its men maintained the low-power electrical equipment on
board ships, operating radios, lighting, sensors and signals – the
'brains' of the ship – while the new electrical artificers maintained the
high-power equipment, operating gun turrets, winches and so on – the
'muscles'. It was not a natural division, and it was recognised that a
real electrical branch would have to be set up some day, but no one
wanted to grasp that nettle in wartime. Since much of wartime training
was done on board ship, the need to include torpedo work in the
training of a man who was essentially an electrician posed some
difficulties, for battleships and cruisers often had no torpedoes.
Leonard CharlesWilliams describes successive jobs in HMS *Hood* from
1939 to 1941:

> My job was at the Main Switchboard, although my action station was
> in the engine room attending one of the dynamo supply breakers. It
> was not a comforting thought to realize that the switchboard was
> well down in the bowels of the ship, and directly over the forward

15˝ magazines; and that in order to get out, one had to squeeze through numerous manholes …

At that period I had recently been promoted to Leading Seaman and was put in charge of all the electrical emergency circuits, which included those auto lanterns, temporary circuits, sick bay operating lamps etc. I had an assistant and it was a full time job, for we had some seven hundred of these auto lanterns to check over and maintain. These had to be kept charged up and periodically tested to see that the relays did not stick.[9]

Other kinds of electrician were introduced. Wiremen were also members of the torpedo branch; they had worked as electricians in civilian life and took on leading rate after a two-week course in ships' electrical systems. The Electrical Artificer was one of the most highly skilled men in the navy, and a psychological survey showed that his standard of intelligence and ability was equal to most officers.[10] The Electrical Mechanic was the 'diluted' version of this, a Hostilities Only man chosen for training by his good education without necessarily having any previous technical experience. The structure of the Torpedo Branch became very complex. By 1943, no less than 131 different courses were offered in the torpedo schools, including 71 for ratings.

SIGNALLING

Naval signallers came in two types. Wireless telegraphists were skilled in Morse code, as voice transmissions were not considered reliable, while visual signallers used flags, semaphore or flashing lights to signal to ships at close range – still a useful facility because the enemy could not intercept the signals. Either as regulars or HOs, signallers were usually selected from among the intelligent or well-educated boys and men in basic training, though they had to compete with other branches and with potential officers. On being made a CW candidate in his training camp, John Davies was initially disappointed to leave the telegraphists' mess:

'A telegraphist no longer,' I said with as much melancholy as I could muster. 'The Brains of the Navy no more. From now on just a poor bloody down-trodden, over-worked, under-paid, much abused ordinary seaman.'[11]

The novelist and wartime naval officer Nicholas Monsarrat liked working with the visual signallers:

> If you want an example of alert intelligence in the Navy, a young signalman, interested in his job and keen to get ahead, is probably the best specimen. From the very nature of his work, he knows more about the ship and her movements than any other rating; and he has the opportunity of learning much more besides. He sees almost every signal that comes in, on a very wide variety of subjects ranging from the First Lord's anniversary greetings to the provision of tropical underwear for Wrens. He spends long hours up on the bridge, in the centre of things, where he has the best opportunity of talking to his officers and of picking up fresh ideas.[12]

Occasionally there were suggestions that the signalling and the telegraphy branches might be merged, but the two groups worked under very different conditions. According to one telegraphist,

> Radio, or wireless, was an oddball branch in the Navy, with very little of the ship's routine applying to it. Radio, or wireless, offices were tucked away in odd corners as if by an afterthought. The visual half of the branch worked in a completely different environment on the bridge. There, the signalman was under the constant scrutiny of the captain and the deck officers; many of whom may not have been conversant with the mechanics of flag hoist and the Aldis lamp, but repeated observation would give them a fair understanding of the art. The working of the radio office, however, remained a closed book to the majority of officers.[13]

Sometimes the telegraphist did not even have contact with his own divisional officer, who was often the navigator when there was no specialist signal officer: 'Like his predecessor, *Manchester*'s new navigator ... never entered the radio office or made himself known to the staff (except, perhaps, our chief) ...'[14]

In 1942 the Radio Mechanic Branch was established, partly to service delicate radar installations in ships and aircraft. This freed the Wireless Telegraphists and radar operators to concentrate on operating the sets.[15] Radio Mechanics were selected from new entrants who had School Certificates, and men who already had radio skills. Roy Fuller had been a solicitor before the war as well as a poet, and he had a School Certificate with credits in maths and physics. He volunteered because 'a spell in a civilian technical college ... greatly appealed'.[16] Trainees learned radio theory and workshop practice during 17 weeks in civilian colleges such as the Technical College at Cardiff, Robert Gordon's College, Aberdeen, and Battersea Polytechnic, followed by 18 weeks of practical work on service radio and radar sets. On completion, a man was quickly promoted to Leading Radio Mechanic, and petty officer after a year's service.[17] Radio Mechanics wore the 'fore and aft' uniform and lived in the artisan's mess on board ship.

The new branch took some of the best of the new entries but there was no time to give complete training:

> It is the intention that the Radio Mechanics shall eventually be capable of maintaining all W/T and R.D.F equipment, but in order to meet immediate needs training must be specialised in certain directions until circumstances admit of complete training. Advancement will not be prejudiced meanwhile, though ability to maintain all types of equipment will be a qualification for advancement to Chief Petty Officer.'[18]

Thus it was concluded in 1944, 'The war has unfortunately given the branch a rushed start and poor training.'

Voice radio, known as radio telephony to the navy, was increasingly developed during the war, for example for convoy escort work, and it changed the role of the signalman, who no longer had to send messages in Morse in ships fitted, for example, with the American voice radio system known as TBS or 'talk between ships'. One escort group commander, Captain Donald MacIntyre, was enthusiastic about it: 'The transformation the TBS worked in the cohesion of the group dispersed around the sprawling convoy was wonderful. Instead of the tedious process of call-up by lamp and the laborious process of spelling out an order, or the shorter but insecure communication by HF radio, each ship was in immediate touch with the others simply by speaking into a telephone handset, the message coming through a loudspeaker on the bridge.' It did have drawbacks, as when 'the differing accents of two signalmen on TBS could produce moments of misunderstanding which would have brought the house down as a music-hall turn'. But in general, 'the efficiency of the group as a team rose tremendously'.[19] One escort group commander regarded TBS as a 'regular goldmine for a Group Leader, especially with a remote control "telephone" at his elbow on the bridge. All we need now is for all V/S ratings and all officers of the watch to grasp the RT procedure and become loudspeaker conscious. Rather too much devolves on the RT operators at present.'[20]

ASDIC

Despite the almost fatal threat posed by the U-boat during the First World War, the navy became complacent about it in peacetime. The asdic apparatus, which detected submarines by echoes, had been developed at the end of the war. Anti-submarine officers were happy to exaggerate its virtues, while other branches, including gunnery, had no wish to divert scarce resources away from their activities. As a result there was undue optimism that the submarine menace had been conquered, so the branch had to expand rapidly in wartime. The situation became far worse when the Germans occupied France and set up bases from which the U-boats could have easy access to the Atlantic. The anti-submarine school at Portland on the south coast soon moved north due to the threat of bombing, and new asdic operators were trained at Dunoon and Campbeltown on the Firth of Clyde. After years of neglect, the branch had 1,200 men at the start of the war, rated as submarine detectors, higher submarine detectors and submarine detector instructors. This rose to 7,600 by the end. In the destroyer *Fortune*, Sub-Lieutenant Roderick Macdonald noticed, 'Our anti-submarine expertise depended entirely on the skill of the H.S.D. [higher submarine detector] ... sensible, careful Leading Seaman Clark. Poor Matthews, the nominally responsible officer, knew little of the technique, and nothing of the tactics. This was the Navy's fault.'[21] Sometimes a ship would delay its sailing if such a key man were missing.

An escort vessel usually had six asdic operators to cover three watches. In normal circumstances two were on duty: one listening on the set while the other rested or carried out other duties nearby. Half an hour was considered long enough to maintain concentration. The operator might use the 'pings' of the set and listen for an echo, or he might listen passively for the noise of a submarine – this allowed one to be detected at a longer distance but gave no indication of range. If something were heard, it was the operator's duty to classify it as 'submarine', 'non-submarine' or 'doubtful'. 'Non-sub' echoes might be obtained, from the bottom, from rocks and sandbanks, from wrecks, tide rips, shoals of fish and whales. The operator would report any contact to the officer of the watch, who usually had far less knowledge of the matter but could take into account other possibilities such as the presence of ships or rocks nearby. Operators were warned not to cover themselves by reporting everything as 'doubtful'. It was a process that could easily go wrong. When the higher submarine detector of J. P. W. Mallalieu's destroyer kept his shipmates up all night because he believed he had a contact, they complained about being 'fetched out of bed for a lot of bleeding mackerel'.[22] But the risk of underestimating a contact was far greater. Able Seaman James Hasty and Ordinary Seaman Edward Millichope of the frigate *Tweed* classified an echo as 'non-sub' in January 1944. Their officer quickly queried this, saying, 'That is a good trace.' The alarm was sounded too late, and a torpedo broke the ship in half. An enquiry concluded 'That blame for the torpedoing of H.M.S. "TWEED" must rest with the cabinet crew ... in that they did fail to report the suspicious echo in time for the officer of the watch to take effective action.'[23]

Having made a definite identification, the ship would normally steer towards the submarine to attack it. The crew would be called to action stations, and the most skilled submarine detector would take his place at the set, training the beam and reporting the 'cut-offs' that marked the edges of the target. The range operator beside him would press the button on the range recorder, and the bearing operator on the other side of the cramped compartment would keep a record of the submarine's bearing, from which her course and movements could be calculated by the plotting team below. John Whelan tells the story of an asdic attack, as described by two of his fellow operators, Jock Campbell and George Norris:

This is it, thought George. This is it. Automatically, confidently as the result of all his years of training and experience, he made a quick calculation and measurement ...

'Target moving very slowly right,' Campbell shouted.

'Range nine hundred yards,' added Norris. 'Hold it ... Bearing Steady ...   Extent of target three degrees ... Range eight hundred ... Bearing steady ... Extent of target two degrees.'

The submarine was bows on. 'Range eight hundred.'

'Estimated course two-seven-oh,' sang Norris. 'Submarine's speed five knots ... Jock, the target's been steady over the last hundred yards ... Careful, careful!'

Ahead of them, three hundred feet below the surface, German asdic operators were sitting at a similar set, listening to the merciless high C notes feel outwards and bounce back. Out and back, out and back – the length of the notes growing ominously shorter as the range narrowed.

'Hold him, Jock.'

PING ... ing ... ing ... ing GOOP!

'Target going left.'

'Range four hundred.'

'Estimated course two-six-five degrees.' Curiously, a picture of the canteen flashed in Norris's mind, then went again.

'Hard a-starboard,' ordered the Captain. The compass card spun swiftly. A distant 'Steady as you go ... Stand by depth charges ... All guns follow director.'

'Two hundred yards.'

'One hundred yards!' screamed Norris.

The range was so short that Ping and Goop merged into a wildly hysterical P'yoop ... P'yoop ... P'yoop.

'Here it is!' shouted Campbell.

'Fire one,' roared the Asdic Officer.[24]

The submarine was indeed sunk.

In later sets, the asdic might be linked directly to the steering during an attack, to leave the captain free to concentrate on broader aspects of the situation, so the senior asdic rating (rarely more than a leading seaman) was in effect conning the ship.

RADAR

Unlike the anti-submarine branch, radar training had to be built up from nothing – only two ships were equipped with it (then known as RDF) when the war started. Early radar sets were primitive and needed a great deal of skill to tune. Ordinary Seaman Lindop describes his initiation:

First impressions were that it appeared to be of bewildering complexity with a mass of coloured knobs, dials, meters, switches, co-axial cables, handles and cathode ray tubes. It was the size of a bulky wardrobe and the transmitter, buried in the basement, the size of a small room. The Instructor gave details of how the instrument was switched on and gave a practical demonstration with the CRT [cathode ray tube] light up with a vivid emerald green tinge, on the left side a large blip caused by the ground returns and the top of the trace, an 'A ' trace, looking like grass, which was the term for it, this was the equivalent of noise in a radio set plus odd returns from mountains and the like. Turning a large wheel in the front of the set rotated the aerial so that it was pointing at the mountains of the Lake District some 60 miles away and on the CRT appeared a large blip on the 60 mile range; our first echoes.[25]

Fred Kellet found there were other difficulties once at sea in a corvette:

> Our training as RDF operators had been minimal and because the equipment was only just out of the experimental stage, no firm rules or procedures had been established; we simply made our own and learnt from our own experience.
>
> The aerial could be swept through 180 degrees on either side of dead ahead but not through a continuous arc or 360 degrees, and due to the position immediately in front of the funnel there was always a 'blind spot' astern of the ship. Signal quality became a problem out in the Atlantic where the sea rarely cooperated with any of our activities; the firm green trace on the tube became fuzzy, we called the result 'grass', and a small signal, such as the one produced by a U-boat's conning tower, could be obscured and easily missed. A slower and more careful sweep was called on in such conditions and demanded more concentration; it became almost impossible to retain the positions of the convoy's ships in the head.[26]

The radar branch did not have time to establish the normal hierarchy of leading seamen and petty officers, so the path to promotion was wide open in 1942. Examinations were waived for leading seaman and petty officer, and captains were allowed to promote men to leading seaman after six month's service – 'the only requirement is the

Commanding Officer's recommendation as being a reliable and safe *operator* on such set (or sets) that he is required to *operate* in his own ship, and able to take charge within his own department.' After another year and a ten-week course at Portsmouth they would become eligible for promotion to petty officer.[27]

Radar ratings had even greater responsibility than asdic operators, as aircraft attack could develop very quickly. They could also take the initiative in identifying surface targets.

In March 1945, in perhaps the most important assertion of authority by a junior rating in the whole course of the war, Ordinary Seaman Norman Poole of the destroyer *Venus* insisted that he could see a solid shape in a rain cloud 34 miles away as his ship sailed through the Strait of Malacca. This was well beyond the normal range of a Type 293 radar set, but he asked the bridge if there was any piece of land he could possibly be picking up and was answered in the negative. He called for his fellow operators, the leading radar operator and the radio mechanic, who pushed Poole aside and re-adjusted the set, losing the echo in the process. Poole struggled back into his seat and found it again, and it was noticed that the target was behaving like a ship rather than a cloud. At last the officer of the watch began to believe Poole, though the captain of the ship and of the destroyer flotilla still had to be convinced. At last, after an hour of debate, the flotilla began to prepare to attack the target. It turned out to be the 13,000-ton Japanese cruiser *Haguro*, which was sunk in the last destroyer action of the war. For his persistence 'almost to the point of insubordination', Poole was awarded the Distinguished Service Medal.[28]

ENGINEERING

The ratings of the engineering branch were divided into two main classes. The engine room artificers were highly skilled men, trained by apprenticeship inside or outside the navy. When fully qualified they were rated as chief petty officers, the highest rating in the navy and equivalent to a staff sergeant in the army. In the merchant navy they would probably be engineering officers, but in the Royal Navy it was not considered seemly for officers to handle tools.

The stokers did not necessarily have any particular skills when they joined the navy. Unlike the boys of the seamen branches, they were recruited at the age of 18 and upwards, because originally it had been believed that they needed physical strength to shovel coal. But in fact they rarely had to do that now, nearly all ships being fuelled by oil, and the stoker became a semi-skilled mechanic. He had fairly good promotion prospects to chief petty officer, or he could train as a mechanician, which made him almost equal to an artificer in skill.

The engineering branch of the navy did not have to deal with any new kind of engine, but it had to learn to operate a greater variety. The reciprocating steam engine had powered almost all major warships until the *Dreadnought* introduced the steam turbine in 1906. By 1939 the reciprocating engine was still common on merchant ships, but it was only used in a few old warships. It was found in many trawlers and other vessels that were taken up for naval use, and it was revived for the new corvettes and frigates for convoy escort. Petrol engines were used on motor torpedo boats and gunboats, while diesels and electric motors were used on submarines. The branch also faced other challenges. ERAs (engine room artificers) and stokers were more at risk than other members of the crew if their ship sank: 'It is evident that casualties to men in sunk or damaged ships is affecting the number of higher Engine Room ratings available, as the proportion of casualties is usually highest in the Engine and Boiler Rooms.'[29]

Looking to the long-term future, the navy continued to take engine room and electrical artificer apprentices at the rate of about 300 a year during the war, even though they would not be available for service for some years. Mechanicians were also trained and were regarded as 'the elite of the stoker entry … usually men of considerable intelligence', but the supply was limited and clearly did not meet the needs for immediate expansion, so large numbers of direct-entry artificers were wanted. However, skilled younger men in engineering trades were in short supply, due to restricted numbers of apprenticeships during the Depression of the 1930s, and were in great demand for industry and the other services. At the end of 1940 the Ministry of Labour decided that the navy had lower priority and that its demand for skilled men would be cut by half – and even that would not be allowed unless it found ways of 'diluting' its labour force with slightly less skilled men who did not have the extremely thorough training of artificers and mechanicians. As a result it set up the trade of engine room mechanic, 'selected from likely recruits either having some previous experience or a sufficient standard of intelligence and mechanical aptitude to enable them to be trained'. Training was concentrated at Hounslow, near London, with about a thousand men undergoing a 24-week course in 1942. Schools were also opened at Watford and Pontefract, but the latter proved unsatisfactory: 'Probably the worst feature of the conditions under which they live is that they are on lodging and compensation allowance. In the case of men living far from their homes for the first time and having to live in a very unattractive industrial town on a small wage, it is not surprising that they will save on their food in order to pay their fares during the week-ends to their homes.'[30]

The navy also needed a new trade of motor mechanic for the internal combustion engines of coastal forces. Again they were recruited from civilians with experience in the motor trade until September 1941, when the supply began to dry up. Men were then chosen 'from Stokers or Seaman entry whose general intelligence is high, but who have no previous knowledge of the [internal combustion] engine'. It was found that the most adaptable men were joiners, bricklayers, plumbers and policemen. They were given a six-month training course at places such as Andrew's Garage in Bournemouth and the Pears' Soap Factory at Hounslow. Like the engine room mechanics, they soon reached the rating of petty officer if successful.

An enquiry led by Sir William Beveridge identified the methods the navy used to find its engineers:

> There is an organised search for talent in the Navy. At each of the home ports officers of the engineering branch make a systematic investigation of all men at the general reception centre with a view to discovering men who can be trained for technical work. They find in this general body of seamen and stokers appreciable numbers of men suitable for training for every grade up to Engine Room Artificer, that is to say men possessing qualifications which for one reason or another had escaped notice at an earlier stage and with less expert enquiry. This search for talent is conducted not on paper, by examination of forms, but by interviews making possible a real judgment of personal skill and capacity.[31]

But the situation was not always so rosy, especially in the selection of stokers, who were usually allocated to the branch before entry and had separate training bases from the seamen. According to John Gritten, 'In over four years on the Lower Deck I never came across another stoker who had an office job in Civvy Street. Professionals called up into the wartime Navy were considered "officer material" and did their six months obligatory lower deck service, usually as seamen ...'[32] Albert H. Jones noticed this with his class of stokers: 'We all came from working class backgrounds, no toffee noses or upper class types here.'[33] This was the opposite of the diversity that Guinness and others found in the seaman's training bases. For the navy it created a problem that men of education were rare in the branch. In peacetime men often became stokers rather than seamen because they were too old for boys' training, but in war they were the result of a process of selection. The best men from a 'rather thin cream' were often selected to become engine room or motor mechanics. But, according to Admiral Ford, 'The stoker under modern conditions has a difficult to job to carry out. He requires intelligence, mental alertness and a reasonably high standard of education, if he is to watchkeep on machinery with understanding.'[34]

Stokers rarely had to shovel coal except in requisitioned merchant ships and trawlers, but they did a variety of jobs according to skill and experience. After Len Perry joined the destroyer *Beagle* in 1943, his first job was to clean the bilge pumps, 'plunging your arm into freezing, filthy bilge water'. Then he was assigned to boiler control, 'moving like a gazelle when the bridge called down for "Full Speed"'. Next he was promoted to keep watch on the fresh-water distilling plant, and he had to lash himself against a pipe in rough weather. Finally he joined the elite throttle party that adjusted the speed of the engines. They 'moved like finely honed and superbly trained athletes, moved as one team, instantly responding to every instruction from the bridge'.[35]

Tristan Jones thought the life of a stoker compared well with that of a seaman:

> I looked down through the iron gratings and saw Stokes calmly going about his business. The Stoker POs were usually humane and friendly, with very little disciplinary bullshit about them. Often, if things were steady and quiet, the PO would be reading a cheap paperback under the forced draft fans, and his mate, the stoker, would be making cocoa or tea. They appeared to be completely isolated from the world we knew topsides, and the most comfortable ratings in the ship, with no officers to oversee them directly. They certainly seemed the most content, even though they and we knew that only a quarter inch of steel plate stood between them and sudden, excruciating death.[36]

But it was far more hectic for the ERA or stoker in action:

> If the *Afridi* increased speed beyond 30 knots, the lungs of the furnace craved more air and the huge fans revved up with a roar which drowned out most other sounds. If there was a call from the bridge, Stoker Petty Officer Cock Kent had to put a finger in the ear that was not glued to the voice pipe. Then, because it was almost useless to shout, he would mouth at Jimmy: 'Up one!' simultaneously

holding up a finger. Or: 'Up two!' holding two digits at which Jimmy would repeat his balletic leaps to turn on the appropriate number of sprayers. But the duffle-coated figure on the bridge, who we knew was pitting his skill against that of the Nazi pilots and bomb-aimers by trying to anticipate their moves, might suddenly order SLOW or even DEAD SLOW on the telegraph when *Afridi* was steaming FULL AHEAD. That was the real test in the boiler-room: how speedily could those sprayers be turned off and steam reduced after the turbine throttles had been shut down? It was a race against the needle.[37]

An even greater test was to remain calm while the ship was under air attack, for the men in the engine room knew very little about what was going on, as Perry found:

> We never knew if the people on the bridge of *Beagle* were having a bit of fun to relieve the boredom, or were about to drop depth charges, launch torpedoes, or take desperate avoiding action to dodge 'tin fish' or bombs. We were certainly under no illusions that nobody would tell us if a large hole was about to be ripped in the side of *Beagle*.[38]

There were around 8,000 ships in the navy by 1944, and every one needed an engineering staff of some kind, from the single stoker of a landing craft to the engineer commander of a battleship. Large ships always had fully qualified staff, while the smallest ones – landing craft and coastal forces – rarely spent more than a few days away from bases or mother ships, so most of the servicing could be done in harbour. The greatest difficulty came in the middle, with the increasing numbers of escort vessels, which often had to make ocean voyages lasting for weeks. A chief ERA might be the senior engineer of a corvette making regular voyages in the rough and dangerous waters of the North Atlantic. Nicholas Monsarrat describes how the chief artificer and his staff had to carry out a major repair while the ship was stopped in mid-ocean.

I remember going down to the engine-room to see if I could hurry things up at all, finding a ring of engine-room ratings, stoker petty officers and the Chief gathered round the offending crankshaft, and withdrawing again without saying anything. Anxiety was excusable, but it was obvious they were doing their utmost without any chivvying from the bridge.[39]

MEDICINE AND WAR

The ratings of the medical branch, the sick berth attendants, wore the red cross insignia as required by the Geneva Convention. Since 1885 they had undergone regular training in the main naval hospitals at Chatham, Portsmouth (Haslar) and Plymouth (Stonehouse). The branch expanded to a peak of 12,000 at the end of the war. When trained, an SBA was considered 'normally capable of routine nursing, changing dressings, elementary dispensing, first aid, cookery for the sick, sterilisation of instruments, and dressings, and elementary diagnosis of injury and sickness; administrative and clerical duties'.[40] But some were very hastily trained in the early days of the war. William Stanmore of the destroyer *Foresight* was 23 years old and had worked as a butcher's boy before being conscripted in 1939. He had had a few lectures on first aid at Haslar Naval Hospital but spent most of his time filling sandbags. According to his officer, his intelligence was limited and he was very seasick, but he distinguished himself helping the survivors of the torpedoed *Eskimo* during the Norwegian campaign of 1940.[41]

The duties of a wartime sick berth rating could vary considerably. He might work as a nurse in a shore hospital or in a relatively large ship, a frigate or above, as an assistant to a medical officer. In a corvette he might be the only medically-trained member of the crew, with great responsibility during a voyage of up to three weeks, not only for his own crew but also for survivors from sunken merchant ships and warships.

In the early stages of the war, peacetime practices were still used in treating battle casualties:

In larger ships this consisted of evacuating the Sick Bay to
Distributing Stations situated in protected positions, which acted
merely as places of refuge for medical stores and personnel. Pending
a lull in the action casualties could receive only minimal first aid
locally ... When the action was over the Sick Bay, if still serviceable,
reverted to its ordinary function; otherwise, some upper deck space
had to be chosen where the casualties would be given more
methodical treatment.

By 1943, first-aid posts were to be set up round the ship, each with
either a medical officer, a sick berth rating or an especially well-trained
first-aider, plus a less skilled assistant. First aid was the concern of all
the crew – 'Everyone must accept this as part of his duty, realising that
the treatment of casualties cannot always be left to the Medical
Department alone.'[42] People who learn first aid are usually looking at
remote possibilities, but when a seaman studied his *First Aid Manual*
in 1943 he must have known how close it was to reality. He was
informed about the penetrating wound to the chest ('Remember that
as well as the danger of sucking air into the chest there are also the
dangers of fractured ribs and internal bleeding with this kind of
wound.') or how to help a man in flames ('When a man's clothing is
on fire, the flames ascend and burn his neck. By laying him down, his
head and neck are protected').[43] He might well see his friends suffer
these wounds, or perhaps suffer them himself; most preferred not to
reflect on that.

The Second World War brought a greater variety of weapons than
ever before, producing many new types of injury. Shell-fire and bullet
wounds were already familiar to experienced SBAs. They knew that
the blast of a bomb or shell between decks would kill everyone within
about 20 feet, often disintegrating the body – beyond that distance
there might be slight injuries or concussion. Ships had been sunk by
torpedoes before, but in the middle of the Atlantic or in Arctic waters
the problems of exposure were greatly increased. And intensive
bombing might last for many hours, severely damaging morale. A

young rating was observed during prolonged air attack during a Russian convoy in 1942:

> During one attack today, I carefully observed a sailor at the back of the bridge, whose job was to telephone the orders for the gunnery officer. I must say the attack was very heavy, and the general noise and confusion were unbelievable ... I have never seen anybody quite so terrified as this sailor. His head, body and limbs were trembling, and he transmitted his orders in a high-pitched squeak. Nevertheless, he continued to do his job, and managed somehow to keep himself from breaking down completely.[44]

A magnetic mine might explode under a ship causing fractures in the lower part of the body, and far worse injuries in the immediate vicinity. In 1940 the Medical Officer of a destroyer reported, 'a scene of indescribable horror met me. Men were cut in two, internal viscera strewn about and intestines wrapped around the mast which was visible when I looked up through a large hole in the upper deck.'[45]

In land warfare the numbers of wounded usually exceed the dead by a considerable margin, but the figures were reversed in the navy, where many men were likely to be lost if a ship went down. In the 1939–45 war the Royal Navy had 50,758 men killed and 14,663 wounded, with the relatively low figures of 820 missing and 7,401 made prisoners-of-war. Roughly one in twenty of those who served was killed. But most sailors seemed to be undaunted by figures such as these. As a medical officer wrote in December 1942, the seaman's attitude was, 'I am a British Sailor. The British Sailor has always been the best seaman, the finest fighter, the hero of the people. Therefore, I am a hero.'[46]

DOMESTIC AND ADMINISTRATION

Naval cooks were still divided into two classes, for officers and 'ship's company'. After their disciplinary training they were normally sent to the barracks at their home port, to spend eight weeks learning the trade under the supervision of the cooks there. They studied the

Manual of Naval Cookery, including chapters on cooking for a general mess as used in most ships, spices and condiments, invalid cookery, field cookery for landing parties, bread- and cake-making, and subjects such as cleanliness, serving of meals and the dietary values of various foods. Cooking was considered a menial trade rather than a high art in Britain at that time, so naval cooks had low status. And life could be very difficult at sea in a small ship:

> Chef had one of the hardest jobs, I would think, on a corvette. No doubt about it. He had a very small galley – if he's got three pans on top of the range then this was as much as he could do. A very small oven. And most of the times we had hot pot. We always had something on top there, a massive great big receptacle. We were limited to what we could carry, like meat. About four days and that was that, veg the same thing, about three or four days and that was gone. So then you went back to the old tinned stuff. And chef used to do miracles with some of these tins – his own concoctions.[47]

Naval clerks were traditionally known as writers. Alan Brundett found the training at HMS *Demetrius* in the north of England was strangely relaxed. There were no captain's rounds, he was able to order a daily newspaper and, 'All in all, it has more of the atmosphere of a college then the navy.' He learned the basic duties of a writer. 'The course is divided into two sections, the first being devoted to the captain's Office including Administration of the Navy, whilst the second covers the Ledger. Each lasts four weeks.'[48]

Not everyone liked the work.

> I was placed in the Accountancy Branch as a supply Assistant, much to my chagrin. The uniform was a cross between that of a taxi driver and a Workhouse inmate. Despite the advice from the PO in charge of our class I made two requests to transfer to some other branch. Stoker, Wireless Tel. etc. The requests were refused.[49]

'Divisions' or morning parade in HMS *Collingwood* near Portsmouth in 1943. (IWM A18929)

A batch of new entrants is welcomed to HMS *Royal Arthur* in Skegness by a warrant officer in February 1940. They are rather more mature than peacetime entrants. (Getty)

Above: A class in HMS *Royal Arthur*, with the leading seaman instructor just behind the lifebelt. (Royal Naval Museum)

A "Tiddley" Sailor

Left and Right: Naval uniform as the authorities believed it should be worn, and as adapted by a 'tiddley' seaman with all its features exaggerated.

Trainees learn rowing or 'pulling' in a boat on shore, under a petty officer.

(IWM A3141)

A gunnery class at HMS *Raleigh* near Plymouth in 1941. (IWM A3144)

An Asdic operator in HMS *Anthony* puts his head out of the cabinet on the bridge to report to the anti-submarine control officer. (IWM A22617)

Radar operators at work. One looks into the screen and turns the handle while the other plots the results. (From *Radar Manual*, 1945)

A stoker at work in HMS *Inglefield*, supervised by petty officers or ERAs. (IWM A15408)

Stewards worked most closely with the officers:

> We were also taught how to address an officer, when calling him in
> the morning. A cheerful 'Good-morning, Sir', tell him the time and
> what the weather was like, then ask him what uniform he would be
> requiring. A good valet soon came to know the officers, and also, just
> what to say to them.[50]
>
> I now learned the art of mess waiting, such as:– pushing
> condiments, butter, etc., in easy reach of an officer and advising an
> officer on the menu; also to push the side plate in front of the officer
> as he finished his sweet – then serve cheese, without the officer
> having to ask. These little points soon gained you respect from the
> officers.

They also learned about wines:

> Reynolds taught me a lot on the storage of wines, wine accounts, the
> care of wines and the mixing of drinks. If you could mix a good
> cocktail, then you were highly regarded by the officers. It was useful
> to know what each officer drank, as some officers would just nod to
> you – you then served him his drink.

But the gap between officers and ratings remained huge. 'I had now
formed an opinion of naval officers; they loved to be made a fuss over,
but I found it hard to trust them as there was a barrier in regard to the
Service; the W.R. [wardroom] mess. One had to be careful when
choosing a friend.'[51]

Despite the evident devotion of men like Brown, some officers
were not satisfied with standards. According to Nicholas Monsarrat,
'The allowance of three stewards for twelve officers seemed
inadequate by any except hash-house standards: in harbour it meant
one dishing up, one ashore on liberty and one to serve the meal on
his own.'[52]

In action a steward, like any other member of the domestic branch, had to take a humble and often dangerous place in the ship's battle organisation.

> One night when we were closed up [at action stations], I kept looking at the bulkhead [ship's side] wondering what would happen if a torpedo hit us; and thinking of the cruel sea outside, I was brought to my senses by a slap in the face by the Royal Marine sergeant in charge of the magazine. His name was Webb; a name I will never forget, as he had done me a good turn. I never let my imagination stray again.[53]

THE WRENS

After service towards the end of the First World War, the Women's Royal Naval Service was reformed in 1939. This time the acronym 'Wren' was adopted as the official title for ratings, which gave the force a strong sense of identity. It was always more popular than the other women's services and had no difficulty in attracting a high standard of recruit, often from varied backgrounds. Stephanie Batstone describes the members of her course:

> Into the melting pot we all went – conscripts, volunteers, engaged, married, widowed, single, Zara from Brazil, Rita from Balham, Cathy from Anglesey, Marianne from Barclays Bank in Aberdeen, Joy from Sainsbury's cold meat counter in Birmingham, Clodagh from milking her father's cows near Kinsale in County Cork, Maureen from being a hotel chambermaid in Dublin, with the bright lights and butter and German embassy, Joan from helping her mother run a boarding school in Skegness, Judy straight from school, Pauline from an estate agents in Wood Green, Celia from the Prudential in Exeter, Vivienne a second year nurse at Leeds General Infirmary, Patricia from a repertory company in Belfast, Betty who thought life was fun, Irene who wore glasses.[54]

By early 1942 nearly 7,000 women were in traditional roles as steward-esses and cooks, and 5,000 more were clerical workers. But in addition

3,800 worked in naval communications and many more in ground-breaking categories such as Recruiting Assistant, Night Vision Tester, Cinema Operator and Exercise Corrector. There were Aircraft Checkers and Fitters, Radio Mechanics, Range Wardens and Machinists, all jobs unthinkable for women before the war.[55] They found a vital role in Royal Naval Air Stations. Rear-Admiral Ford was impressed:

> Reports from Naval Air Stations show that these girls are producing astonishing results. Their energy and intelligence put the men to shame, as does the fact that on an average they 'qualify to sign' in a month, while the average man takes three months. Naval Air Stations are clamouring for more and it will be disastrous if, due to the manning situation, the training of these women must cease ...

But there is doubt about whether Wrens could be considered true members of the lower deck at this stage. It was not just that they did not normally go to sea, or that some of the early recruits were 'immobile' Wrens of upper-class background:

> These particular Wrens were not volunteers for any job but only the one which was near their home. They therefore lived at home in splendour, knowing they could not be posted to Singapore, Colombo or Scapa Flow. Their mums were keen that they should meet a good cross-section of Fleet Air Arm officers. There were therefore plenty of party invitations for us. We played tennis and croquet outdoors and various other games indoors.[56]

More important, many Wrens had a tendency to regard themselves as superior to ratings. After his ship was sunk, Tristan Jones waited in line for hours at Chatham Barracks.

> Being in front of a counter, only three feet or so from a Wren, was the closest that almost all of us matelots had been to a woman for months. For them, the ones in that office at Chatham, we might just as well not have existed. Men who were reporting from their second

or third sinking in the past eighteen months were treated like unwanted intruders, and made to stand silently in line, forbidden to smoke by a big notice in six-inch letters on the yellow-painted wall, while the split-ass mechanics, maybe twenty or so, puffed away at their Black Cat corked tips and retouched their lipstick in little mirrors they kept in their desk drawers ...

It never ceased to amaze us matelots, who were by no means the stupid people we might have appeared to be when on parade, how a few of the transformed shopgirls and some of the jumped-up office-secretaries could suddenly be stuck up stars, behaving as if they had, as Nobby put it, never been for a shit in their lives.'[57]

Even in the galley of a shore base, George Melly found that a Wren working with him paid little attention to the male ratings – she was waiting for 'Lieutenant Right'.

THE SHORTAGE OF PETTY OFFICERS

The leading seaman occupied a precarious position in the hierarchy. Unlike a petty officer, he did not have any legal authority – disobedience of his orders was only 'conduct prejudicial to good order and discipline' rather than disobeying the orders of a superior officer, which was a court martial offence. Nevertheless, he had to live in the mess with those under him.

On joining his first ship, the journalist Godfrey Winn believed that 'the lord of the mess was always a leading hand, and always called (like *The* Commander) *The* killick. Go to him for everything that concerned your mess: obey him absolutely: never answer back, or you'd be emptying the gash-bucket for the rest of your sea-going days.'[58] But reality was rather different, as John Whelan found:

For as soon as the furled anchor was sewn upon my sleeve above my good conduct badge, its weight bowed down my shoulders and bowed my head. I was now a leader of men, a setter of examples, a figure of authority – yet I still had to live with Dusty. I lost weight. My cheeks became sunken, my eyes red-rimmed.[59]

Tristan Jones joined the armed merchant cruiser *Cameroon* and soon found that the petty officers were a very different breed from those he had known as a boy in *Ganges*: 'It was a shock to me to be addressed in the least bit so civilly by anyone over the rank of Leading Seaman. The PO's voice was almost gentle, and there was a welcoming gleam in his eye. He was dressed in his Number Three blue serge uniform, but unlike the barrack bullies', his was worn and greasy in patches, and his shoes looked as if they had hardly ever been polished.'[60] George Melly also found that petty officers were decent men:

> Long association with the sea and its ports had given them a certain tolerant sophistication, part cynical but certainly affectionately so. They had learnt to mistrust the moral imperatives of any one place because they had seen them replaced by others, often equally rigid and ridiculous, elsewhere. The [sic] made allowances too for us temporary sailors. We were there because we had to be. One day the war would be over and the Navy its old self; a machine for sailing in.[61]

In 1941, an American observer noted that the inexperience of many wartime officers meant that extra responsibility was placed on petty officers:

> The officers rely on the petty officers much more than do the officers in our Navy. For example, the signalmen not only read but interpret the signals. They always tell the OOD [officer of the deck] the meaning of the signal and not the signal itself. The officers were not concerned with such matters, except the captain who knew the meaning of all the signals. Other petty officers perform their duties in the same manner as the signalmen. There is no officer assigned to the plotting room during action. With the exception of the engineer officer and the two gunners, the officers (in observer's opinion) did not have even a working knowledge of the equipment they worked. They did not seem interested in such matters. This is no doubt due to the great reliance placed on their petty officers.[62]

In 1943 Captain Pelly advised new officers:

> You should bear in mind that the responsibilities of the higher rating are more important now than they have ever been. They should be made to feel that they are in your confidence, and they should be made to feel that they really are the men that matter. Bring them into any discussion of a job of work, drill, improvement or amenity. Not nearly enough is done by officers to encourage the status of Higher Ratings.

Promotion could be fast in wartime:

> I was passed for Leading Seaman on the 7th February 1941 and I saw the Two and a Half Ringer that day too, who after asking me when I joined, where I had been, and when, sent me up to the Joss man to join the Ship's Commanding Officer to be rated up. I was sent to the ship's office, details taken, given a couple of Duck Suit Killicks to sew on and sent back to my own boat …
>
> I progressed through these rates: temporary acting leading stoker; acting leading stoker; leading stoker and petty officer within two years. Escapades of mine during that period would, had they happened in peacetime, surely have deprived me of any one of these tentative steps. How I escaped the delicate hold on the first is an indication of the scarcity of senior ratings.[63]

Junior officers were warned to be aware of the problems of fast promotion: 'Do not expect too much of your higher ratings. You cannot expect their standard to be a high level one, as large numbers are at present being made and many of them are of very limited experience.'[64]

Even so there were not enough experienced men. By early 1943, as the expansion programme finally moved into top gear, the Director of Personal Services was becoming seriously concerned about the shortage of suitable men. 'From the latest statistics we are 18% short of Leading Seamen and 8% short of P.O.s. ... With next year's expansion to face, this situation cannot be allowed to go on.' In a sense the navy was paying for past mistakes – the failure to develop a class of men of above-average education, as might have been done with the Advanced Class scheme of the 1920s, the poor status and heavy duties of the leading seaman as established early in the century, and the failure to develop men's qualities and fit them for promotion.

Large ships had a master at arms as the senior rating in charge of discipline. Destroyers and smaller ships each had a coxswain, whose duties were much broader and who had a more intimate relationship with the crew. He was known as 'swain' to the lower deck and was not to be confused with the other type of coxswain who took charge of a ship's boat. To D. A. Rayner the coxswain was 'the third most important man, as far as the happiness of the ships is concerned', after the captain and first lieutenant.[65] Nicholas Monsarrat recognised his importance:

A good coxswain is a jewel ... The coxswain can make all the difference on board. As the senior rating in the ship, responsible for much of its discipline and administration, he has a profound effect on producing a happy and efficient ship's company. Usually he is a 'character', to use an overworked but explicit word: that is, a strong personality who would make himself felt in any surroundings, and who is, in his present world, a man of exceptional weight and influence. He keeps his eye on everything, from the rum issue to the cleanliness of hammocks, from the chocolate ration to the length of the side-whiskers of the second-class stokers. It is his duty to find things out, however obscure or camouflaged they may be – a case of bullying, a case of smuggled beer, a case of 'mechanised dandruff' in the seaman's mess – and either set them right or else report them forthwith to a higher authority. In the majority of cases, as might be expected, he is fully competent to set them right himself, and can be trusted to do so.

He is the friend of everyone on board, and a good friend too – if they want him to be, and if they deserve it: failing that, he makes a very bad enemy.[66]

The importance of the coxswain continued after the war, as battleships and cruisers were scrapped and aircraft carriers became increasingly rare, so he is now a key figure in most naval ships.

3
NAVIES WITHIN THE NAVY

THE BIG-SHIP NAVY

As well as the conventional division into branches, the wartime fleet was divided by the type of ship in which a man served – the big-ship navy, the destroyers, the escort vessels, landing craft and coastal forces, among others, all had very different standards of discipline, length of sea time, hazards, cultures and proportions of regular to hostilities-only ratings. Once a man had been allocated to one part of the navy, it was unlikely that he would ever transfer to another during his war service.

The battleship and cruiser navy remained the preserve of the regular seaman longer than any other, as Cliff Smith found at the end of 1940: 'When I joined *Nelson* as a sprog writer (HO) hostilities only, the majority of the ship's company, 80%, were regulars (RN). I recall vividly that the full-time sailors considered themselves to be far superior beings to us lowly part-timers, and we were informed that we just had to learn the Navy way – chop chop!'[1]

Anyone who believed that up to 15 inches of armour plate surrounding a battleship gave it any kind of immunity from damage was soon disillusioned. Early in the morning of 16 October 1939 the old battleship *Royal Oak*, left behind at Scapa Flow, was hit by torpedoes from *U-47* which had penetrated the defences of the base. Eight hundred and thirty-three men out of 1,424 were lost. Many survivors had horrific experiences as the ship turned over:

A door slammed behind him, crushing the head of a man who was trying to get through it. Batterbury saw his eyes and tongue sticking out, then came the sound of the third explosion, and the lights failed. He ran on. The anti-flash curtains in the battery aft were aflame and people were pouring up from the stokers' messdeck below, 'hollering and howling about men being on fire down there'. This new scrum of men, many of them dazed with horror, scrambled for the ladder. It was, said Batterbury dryly, 'survival of the fittest'. The fear of being trapped inside the heeling ship was overwhelming. Batterbury himself was frantic to get a foot on the ladder.[2]

The big-ship navy had its first triumph when three cruisers found the German pocket battleship *Graf Spee* off the coast of South America in December 1939. Able Seaman Len Fowgill was in *Exeter*:

I was in the after control position and relieved the man on look-out who told me that a ship had been sighted on the port quarter. Just at that moment the challenge lights on the mast lit up and I turned my glasses on the sighted ship. ... Then there was a flash which I took to be the flashing light in answer to our challenge. There were flashes all round us and then the sound of guns. This was no friendly ship.'

Exeter was heavily damaged in the action largely due to a direct hit in the chief petty officers' mess. Fowgill found a new role as the captain's eyes were damaged and he had to keep him informed of the enemy's position.

After a while the captain told me to take over as his messenger and I had to run from place to place, delivering messages to all parts of the ship. It seemed as if I bore a charmed life because all the time I was going about, my shipmates were being killed ... There were bodies everywhere and some of them were in a terrible condition. A piece of shrapnel took the back of our sub-lieutenant's head off. I'd never seen anyone die before. We were a young ship's company; a lot of us were in our teens and early twenties. This was our first action although most of us had been together for nearly three years

… We were trained to do our utmost and I'm sure we were doing our duty automatically.[3]

Exeter had to retreat to the Falklands for repairs, but *Graf Spee* was forced into Montevideo from where she was scuttled. The men of *Exeter* were treated as heroes when the ship eventually got home.

The main duty of the Home Fleet in the early stages of the war was to keep an eye on the great German battleships *Bismarck* and, later, *Tirpitz*. When the former escaped, the beloved and venerable battlecruiser *Hood* and the brand-new battleship *Prince of Wales* were sent in pursuit and caught up with her in the Atlantic. Leading Sick Berth Attendant Sam Wood was at his action station over 'B' turret in *Prince of Wales*, where he had 'a smashing view, better than being at the pictures':

> I was watching the orange flashes coming from the *Bismarck*, so naturally I was on the starboard side. The leading seaman said to me, 'Christ, look how close the firing is getting to the *Hood*.' As I looked out, suddenly the *Hood* exploded. She was just one huge pall of smoke. Then she disappeared into a big orange flash and a huge pall of smoke which blacked us out. Time seemed to stand still. I just watched in horror. The bows pointed out of this smoke, just the bows, tilted up and then this whole apparition slid out of sight, all in slow motion, just slid slowly away. I couldn't believe it. The *Hood* had gone.[4]

Able Seaman Ted Briggs was on the compass platform of the *Hood* when it happened:

> There was no panic – it's uncanny, but everything seemed to be in slow motion. We tried to get out of the starboard door. The Gunnery Officer was just in front of me, and the Navigating Officer stood to one side to let me go through. I had got half-way down the ladder to the admiral's bridge when we were level with the water. We were just dragged under. I do not know how long it was, but I got to the

stage where I just couldn't hold my breath any more. It sounds silly but there was a cartoon of Tom and Jerry where Tom is drowning, and he had a blissful smile on his face. I was just like that – a calm acceptance – and then suddenly I shot to the surface ... I came up on the port side, even though I had gone out of the starboard door – I don't know how I got there – and I was roughly 50 yards away from the ship. The ship was standing on end from B-turret up – that was the most terrifying sight you could see. I swam away as fast as I could, so that I wouldn't get sucked down again, and when I looked back the ship had gone, but the oil on the water had caught fire. I panicked and swam away again, but when I looked back again the fire was out.

He climbed on to a raft to join two other survivors, Midshipman Bill Dundas, and AB Bob Tilburn. 'There wasn't a sign of anyone else – we couldn't see any bodies or anything. I think those below decks would not have stood a hope in hell, and those on the upper decks were killed or wounded before the ship went. I just couldn't grasp it. We could see the *Prince of Wales* disappearing, still firing, and when she had gone I could see in the distance the tops of three funnels – one of the cruisers, but I didn't know which one. And that was it. I remember Bill Dundas was singing Roll Out the Barrel, like he was conducting a band – he was just keeping his circulation going, because it was bitter cold.'[5] After four hours they were picked up by the destroyer *Electra*, the only survivors out of 1,421 men on board. But the Royal Navy had its revenge a few days later when *Bismarck* herself was sunk. These were not the last losses of capital ships: *Barham* was torpedoed in the Mediterranean, and *Prince of Wales* and *Repulse* were sunk by Japanese aircraft. One in four of the 20 capital ships was lost during the war.

The big ships found a new role in 1941, in covering the convoys to Russia, and had their great moment in December 1943 when they sank the *Scharnhorst*. But naval warfare, like most forms of conflict, was a combination of a few hours of intense action with many weeks or months of boredom. This was felt just as intensely at Scapa Flow as in the previous war:

> Harbour routine at Scapa was the same day after day: clean guns; clean ship; watch-keeping; divisions; evening quarters; store parties and sometimes a day on the Island of Flotta doing military training and fraternizing with the local crofters and A.-A. gunsite crews based on the island. Their lot was more monotonous than ours. I remember tombola, the odd film show. Someone leaves the ship under observation – suspected mental case. I wonder there were not more.[6]

By 1944 Italy was out of the war and nearly all the larger German ships had been sunk or put out of action, so the battleships and cruisers found a new role in shore bombardment, mostly in support of the invasions of Italy and Normandy.

DESTROYERS

Destroyers were the most versatile and therefore the busiest ships in the fleet, 'always on the go' according to Joseph Wellings of the US Navy. Apart from their duties with the main fleet, the more modern ones served in the convoys to Malta and Russia, where air, submarine and surface ship attack threatened constantly:

> As the war goes on it has thrown up a marked snobbery about being present at the right battles. Actually those who have done both the early days' Russian and Malta runs several times – especially the destroyer crews – all agree that there is, or rather was, no comparison. Though the Malta run at its worst was hell, it was hell that lasted days, not weeks, and the water was comparatively warm – compared, that is, with the Arctic seas. Moreover you had a good chance of being picked up, whereas in the waters of the Barents Sea, where visibility is more often than not down to zero, even if you escape with your life, when your ship goes up, you won't [end up] with all your limbs.[7]

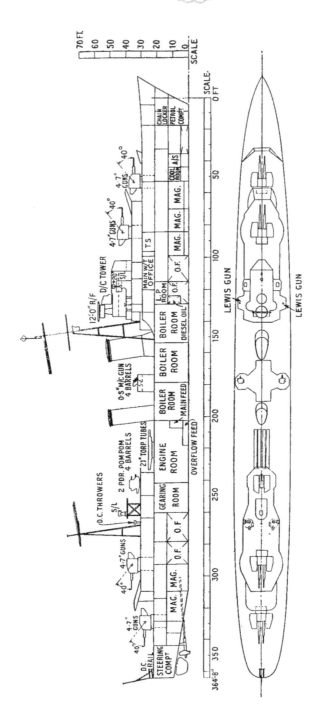

The layout of a Tribal class destroyer, one of the most glamorous and versatile types of ship during the war.

Torpedo attack, one of the original purposes of the destroyer, was comparatively rare by this time, but it was used against *Scharnhorst* in 1943 as described by Tristan Jones:

> Our stern went down, the bow shot forward, then we went ... like staghounds at last, at long bloody last, off the leash ... Faster and faster, plunging and swaying, pulsing with strain until her whole hull screamed in protest ... All we could see of the nine other destroyers were their pale wakes, until Captain (D) in *Onslow* opened up with his four-inchers. Crash after crash shook our hull ... and how the Torps got the tinfish away in any semblance of an aim I'll never know. Out slid the tinfish, long and sinister, and splashed into the darkness.[8]

Convoy Escort

The convoy escort force in the North Atlantic was one of the greatest growth areas in the navy, as the U-boat campaign proved far more deadly than predicted. Escort vessels were mostly small- to medium-sized ships, from converted trawlers at the beginning of the war to frigates towards the end, with a number of older destroyers.

Continuous Service men were to be found in escort vessels, but mostly in the senior substantive rates, especially as coxswains and gunner's mates. Atlantic escorts worked up at Tobermory under the eye of the legendary 'Monkey' Stephenson, as described by Cyril Stephens of the corvette *Orchis*:

> Tobermory, oh my God, it was murder. We had this Commodore Stephenson, 'Monkey Brand', they nicknamed him. He used to have two little tufts on his face. And he was about seventy odd and [he and his training staff would] come aboard at any time of the night ... It was him who used to sort us out in the working up trials and he had some quite funny tricks he used to do. He'd allocate a ship to raid another ship during the night and pinch anything they could find, like the log books or gun off the bridge or something like that, and woe betide the officer next morning ... You'd come on board and

you'd have exercises: 'abandon ship', 'collision at sea', 'fire in the galley', 'fire somewhere else', pipes and wires all over the place, but in the finish we knuckled down.[9]

The Atlantic forces had settled into a regular routine by the end of 1940. The ships were based at Londonderry, Liverpool and the Clyde. They sailed on two- or three-week trips across the Atlantic, to Gibraltar

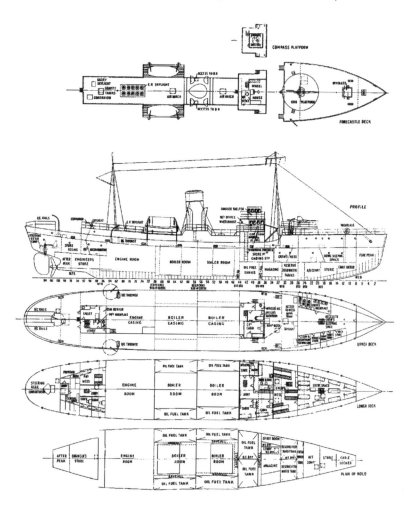

The layout of a Flower class corvette.

or to Freetown in West Africa, then returned a few weeks later. One of the biggest single problems was the pitching and rolling of the corvettes, which had been designed for war in gentler climates and to be manned by experienced merchant seamen rather than hastily trained landsmen. After two ten-day voyages in September and October 1940, Lieutenant Commander Robert T. Bower of HMS *Fleur de Lys* noted:

> The rolling was incredible. In over twenty years in the service in every type of ship, I never encountered anything like it. Officers and men on duty became rapidly exhausted by the mere physical effort of holding on. Accurate navigation was impossible owing to the gyrations of the compass cards and the inability of helmsmen to keep the ship anywhere near her course. At times she was yawing 60 to 70 degrees.
>
> The plight of the numerous seasick members of the crew and of some of the older men became pitiable … Under such conditions sleep, or indeed any kind of rest is impossible, as it entails considerable physical strain even to remain in a bunk … neither ships nor men will be able to stand up to prolonged severe winter weather in the Atlantic. It is not that the men lack courage or resolution; merely that the physical strain is insupportable.

Improvements were made to the corvettes, but they were never comfortable in heavy seas:

> Meal-times were a test of tenacity and endurance for them, nowhere more so than in Number One mess up in the point of the bow where every movement of the ship was most exaggerated. Five men packed the tops of the four lockers outboard of the narrow mess table, and were faced by four more jammed together on the form opposite. With a greatly reduced air circulation, the atmosphere was oppressive, and all too often the sight of the unattractive food was the last straw.[10]

Life was especially gruelling in the support groups, which moved from one convoy under threat to another and might see constant action:

> Thus ensued an epic 25 days continuously at sea hunting and attacking U-Boats which had come back in force into the Atlantic. Action stations more ON than OFF – refuelling 5–6 times in heavy seas: stopping (not recommended) to pick up 2 survivors from a U-Boat and attacking with new weapons called 'hedgehogs' which projected small bombs ahead of the ship.
>
> My enduring memory of that time is of feeling so very tired even at age.[18] Gretton drove everyone week after week in his relentless pursuit of U-Boats. He got the medals (Bar to his D.S.O.) … we, the seamen, did all the hard work.[11]

There was little rest between convoys as the escorts carried out further training:

> Before leaving on each escort duty, two or three days and nights were spent exercising off the entrance to the River Foyle, working with submarines, firing at targets and carrying out the multitude of jobs which might fall to a convoy escort. In fact, the men sometimes complained that they felt more tired after the pre-convoy exercises than after the convoy itself![12]

THE FLEET AIR ARM

The navy had built up a very large Royal Naval Air Service by the last year of the First World War – though much of its work was nothing to do with the sea and only a small minority of its aircraft were launched from ships. All this was merged into the new Royal Air Force in 1918, and it was 1937 before the navy won back complete control over its air arm. Inter-service rivalries in Whitehall meant that Britain had lost its lead in naval aviation to Japan and the United States.

The great majority of naval pilots were officers. Although the navy had disputed with the RAF over its plans to recruit rating pilots, in practice it took on very few once the Fleet Air Arm became independent. Instead it recruited hundreds of young men 'from the shore' and trained them as officer pilots. Likewise the rating of observer's mate never really got going, for the navy demanded a high standard of education and officer status for the men who would navigate its aircraft. Unlike the RAF, the Fleet Air Arm had very few aircraft with crew of more than three, so it did not need an array of specialists such as air gunners, wireless operators, flight engineers and bomb aimers. Two of these tasks, at least, were combined in the naval rating of telegraphist air gunner, selected from young men who were fit for flying but who did not have the education needed to become a pilot or observer.

Unlike the RAF flier, the TAG's uniform had little to distinguish it from the ordinary naval one and it seemed less glamorous ashore. His rating of leading hand was equivalent to a corporal in the RAF, whereas from 1940 all RAF aircrew (including air gunners who were less skilled than the TAGs) were at least sergeants. Since nearly all naval pilots and observers were officers, the crew was naturally divided by rank and did not have the comradeship of an RAF crew. The TAG probably flew in an obsolescent biplane, for more modern three-seaters like the American Grumman Avenger only became available later in the war. The TAG was hardly ever invited to the briefings and did not necessarily know the purpose of a sortie. He usually sat facing backwards. He had to trust the skill of his pilot, even in a dangerous deck landing. Unlike the observer, he had no influence on the direction of the aircraft. And there was no real promotion path for him, for there were few petty officers and even fewer warrant officers in the branch.

The TAGs missed out on the Fleet Air Arm's most famous action when the Italian fleet was seriously damaged at Taranto, for they were left behind to allow for extra fuel. But Les Sayer describes the torpedo attack on *Bismarck* in mid-Atlantic:

Gick told us over the speaking tubes that he wasn't lined up and that he was going round again. So we went out to about 25 mile and came back again all on our own; all the others were on the way back. So we came right down at sea level. I'm standing up looking forward at the Bismarck and she's getting bigger and bigger and still they didn't see us. I thought to myself, well, they've only got us to aim at, they're bound to hit us, this is your lot anyway, so forget it. But we went in and dropped the fish and turned away and it was only then that they saw us and they let us have everything … When they started firing their heavy stuff at us we had to count from the time they fired and take avoiding action. Another hazard was the huge waterspouts made by their shells. You could go through the splashes and get pulled down. We did fly through one of these splashes. It came up underneath us and ripped all the underside of the aircraft out so it was a bit draughty! We kept about ten feet above sea level.[13]

The steering mechanism of *Bismarck* was seriously damaged, though it is not clear whose torpedo did it. Donald Bunce took part in a far less successful attack, on *Scharnhorst* and *Gneisenau* during their 'Channel dash' of 1942:

In came the FW 190s. I don't know how many there were. I was just concentrating on those that were on our tail; it seemed endless. As soon as one peeled off another was in its place, with its tracer speeding towards us. After a while they lowered their under-carriage and flaps in an attempt to reduce speed and prolong the attack.

I began swearing away and at the same time fired as much of the feeble .303 tracer in front of the 190s as I could, stoppages permitting; all drill in this respect went overboard, as indeed went any malfunctioning magazine. There simply wasn't time for anything else. From my backward viewpoint, it was developing into a practice shoot for FW 190s, and we were the drogue target; they were coming so close, as they peeped off to the port I had a clear sideways view of the pilot.[14]

The German ships escaped and the Fleet Air Arm lost six Swordfish.

Before the war the navy had provided deck-handling parties for naval aircraft, but practically all the skilled maintenance work was done by RAF personnel. There were few volunteers to transfer from the RAF to the navy, though some technicians served aboard aircraft carriers in RAF uniform for most of the war. The navy had to build up its own force of technicians. The navy's plan for training air artificers by a 3½ year course was clearly long term. In the meantime it reluctantly had to rely on the RAF to train maintenance crews for aircraft carriers and Royal Naval Air Stations. Potential air fitters went to HMS *Medina* on the Isle of Wight for initial naval training, and by the time they left for RAF stations for technical training they had 'an almost excessive regard for the Navy'. In the squalid huts of the RAF stations they tended to lose the sailor's pride in his mess deck. They resented being under RAF instructors, but there was much praise for the RAF's standards of instruction. In huge bases like RAF Hednesford near Birmingham, where up to 4,500 naval men might be training at once, 'The equipment is sufficient and almost lavish and the numbers of instructors enabled classes not exceeding 15 trainees to be maintained.'[15] Air fitters (airframe) and (engine) had a course of 25 weeks and wore the fore-and-aft uniform.

Maintenance of naval aircraft poses many problems that do not present themselves on land. It is done in restricted space on a moving ship, often when rough weather prevents flying. Every carrier is self-contained, and it is rarely possible to bring in expertise or spare parts at short notice. Not all the ships carrying aircraft were big fleet carriers – there were smaller escort carriers and even converted merchant ships with complements of about four aircraft – so servicing crews were often spread thinly and operated in isolation. Naval aircraft have to endure particularly harsh conditions at sea and in deck landing. They often have to switch rapidly from one role to another, as did the famous Fairey Swordfish, which was designed for torpedo attack, spotting and reconnaissance work but took on many other roles including radar patrol. Despite all this, the Fleet Air Arm usually followed RAF procedures in its servicing, with four main types of aircraft inspection – before a flight; daily; a 'minor' inspection after every 40 hours flying or else quarterly, whichever was the shorter; and a major inspection after eight minor ones.

Handling parties were regarded as 'unskilled work on the flight deck and in the hangar' at the start of the war and were drawn from general service ratings, a dozen men for each squadron plus about 30 more from the complement of an *Illustrious*-class fleet carrier. The Americans in the Pacific showed that far more aircraft could be handled with well-trained working parties, and from 1943 permanent groups were allocated to the duties, 90 men in a large carrier.

AMPHIBIOUS WARFARE

The British services had neglected amphibious warfare in the 1930s, and at the start of the war they still believed that the alliance with France made it unnecessary. This all changed in May 1940, and Churchill set up a Combined Operations Organisation to plan and develop techniques and material for an eventual return to the Continent. The first base was at Inveraray in Scotland, where Ordinary Seaman Rowland Draper was trained:

> The Majority of Inveraray's population of about 450 lived in stone houses gathered on each side of the one short main street. There was one shop, two hotels and a cafe. One house slightly larger than its neighbours sported a flagpole from which flew the white ensign; this was the admiral's house and naval headquarters. It was a peaceful scene with snow still hanging on the tops of the hills, but it was all due to change. Soon a naval camp was going to be built further down the loch, and camps to house troops which would be sent for training in combined operations. [16]

The Combined Operations Organisation grew from practically nothing until there were more than 50,000 men in landing craft alone by mid-1944. Many different types of landing ship and craft were developed. The landing ship infantry was a converted passenger ship. It needed its own crew, including engineers and anti-aircraft gunners, plus crews for up to two dozen minor landing craft that could be lowered from its sides, and also carried perhaps a thousand soldiers on board. The tank landing ship had quite a large crew of up to 190 men. Unlike most ships of its size, it could do the whole voyage, landing the tanks on a beach itself rather than putting them in smaller landing craft for the last stage of the journey. John Holden was an Able Seaman in *LST 418* and describes his training:

> We were constantly wet through with rain and sea spray, doing endless landings on the beach from early morning to late evening. The worst part was if we lost our kedge anchor wire by dropping the stern anchor too soon. Apart from the skipper losing face in front of the other LSTs, it was a cold, wet job for a boat to fish for the cable with grappling hooks. The practice paid off, however, as we never lost our kedge anchor during operations in the face of the enemy.[17]

The tank landing craft (as distinct from the much larger 'ship') was commanded by two officers and had a crew of about 20 men, of whom the coxswain was an important figure. Gavin Douglas describes one such group in 1944:

> The crew of my own craft were all little more than boys: the eldest was twenty-five, and only three out of the ten hands carried were entitled to draw a rum issue, which means that only three were more than twenty. My Motor Mechanic, in charge of the craft's machinery with two assistants, was a fair-haired, boyishly smooth-faced expert of nineteen, and the First Lieutenant was a happy-go-lucky New Zealander of twenty-one. At the age of forty-five, I felt the complete horny-handed old sea-dog in such company.
>
> Only one or two of the hands had been at sea before. The coxswain had seen most of the Mediterranean landings in minor landing craft and was a fair seaman, but none of the others was much advanced from the landsman he had been not many months before.[18]

The assault landing craft, the only one that was fully developed at the start of the war, was crewed by four ratings – a coxswain, stoker and two seamen. Ideally the coxswain should be a leading seaman, but the navy was always reluctant to lower its standards and many remained ABs until they had passed the examinations. The coxswain had great responsibility. He was probably carrying a platoon of soldiers with at least a lieutenant in command, but he had to assert himself as commander of the craft. He also had to find his way to the right beach though all the opposition and obstacles that the enemy might put in his way.

Probably there was no time in history when the lower deck of any navy took on more individual responsibility than at the beaches of Normandy on 6 June 1944. The American landing on *Omaha* Beach was in danger of failing, in which case the one at *Utah* would have been isolated, so everything depended on what happened on the three British and Canadian beaches, *Gold*, *Juno* and *Sword*. The swimming tanks that were supposed to spearhead the invasion mostly failed, so the first wave consisted of specialist engineer tanks landed from LCTs. Behind them came about four hundred assault landing craft, carrying infantry and engineers and each with a rating or marine as coxswain. Those of the 506th Flotilla, launched from *Duke of Wellington,* were given orders to use their initiative and to act independently among the beach obstructions. They landed their men safely. Petty Officer Motor Mechanic A Robb was with the 518th LCA flotilla that morning:

> With about a quarter of a mile to go word came that H-Hour had been put back 30 minutes to 8.30 a.m. as the LCT(R)s which were to blast a mine-free path up to the beach were late in arriving. So there we were, right on Jerry's doorstep, circling round and round for half an hour with mortar shells being lobbed at us and under machine-gun fire. But again we were lucky with no craft or men hit, then in we stormed, weaving our way through obstacles and on to the beach. Down went the door, a shout of 'Good luck!' to the

sergeant in charge and within 20 seconds the troops were off and away up the beach.

Now I had to get off that beach and it turned out to be quite a job. I asked for both engines astern and the wheel amidships, but there was no response from the starboard engine (when the craft was hoisted aboard ship later I found a lifebelt jammed solid round the propeller). Realizing I could not control the craft astern on only one engine, the bow and stern men and myself went over the side and we pushed her clear and around from the beach, then it was all aboard and full-ahead on the port engine alone.[19]

Efforts like these turned the tide in the most ambitious military operation in history.

COASTAL FORCES

The Royal Navy had neglected the development of light, fast coastal craft before the war, partly because it did not like the idea that such a small vessel armed with torpedoes could sink a battleship, and partly because British industry did not develop a suitable high-speed diesel engine like the Germans had. The main German coastal craft, the so-called E-boat, was a highly effective vessel, and it became more dangerous as the two navies faced each other across the English Channel as well as the North Sea. Coastal forces employed motor torpedo boats, motor gunboats and motor launches to fight an intense war there and in the Mediterranean. It expanded rapidly to more than 20,000 men in 1944. It was said that Coastal Forces was 98 per cent Hostilities Only.

The coxswain was a key figure on a coastal forces boat and was often the only regular on board. In *ML 216* Petty Officer Sharkey Ward was 'an outstanding seaman, completely devoid of fear, but also very understanding towards those of us who lacked experience'. He was also dedicated – 'The [ML] 320 was his pride and joy, it was as if he was married to it; it was more than a boat to him, it was his life, his world.'[20] The coxswain's medical training was very brief. Each was 'put on a crash course of perhaps two hours with a Killick sick Berth Tiffy (sick-berth attendant), to qualify them as Ship's Doctors'. To Fred Coombes, 'it was a young man's war in the Coastal Forces. Ted Barber thought the new Cox'n joining them on *621* was an old man being a veteran of three years war. Ted was 18 years old, the next Cox'n 23 ...'[21] At sea there was no room for recalled pensioners, but experienced men were needed ashore for maintenance and administration. At 60, Able Seaman Lamont was described as 'the oldest rating in Coastal Forces'.[22]

Coastal forces craft could be very unpleasant even in moderate weather, and their designer admitted that 'the motion of a corvette in a seaway is positively stately in comparison with the motion of a coastal force craft in the same seaway.'[23] The engine-room staff got the worst of this, down below with the smell of petrol. They had to open and close the throttles of engines very quickly, for the propellers might race while they were out of the water in rough seas. A large boat had a skilled motor mechanic and two stokers. In the early stages of the war their training was largely done by the makers of the boats or engines, until special schools were set up, but it was not until the last two weeks of a ten-week course that trainees went afloat. 'During this period they begin to get their sea legs, are seasick and learn how to handle their engine.'[24] This was not always successful, and some men had to be relieved because of chronic seasickness.

Sometimes coastal forces operated like bomber aircraft, leaving bases in the evening for a raid across the water and returning next morning, but in other cases it involved the escorting of slow convoys. Practically all warfare involves some combination of boredom and excitement, and in coastal forces it could be particularly intense. Fred Coombes remembered 'the boredom of the endless hours we spent patrolling or rolling around, stopped and waiting for "E" boats to close our Convoy Routes', and in similar vein John W Davies wrote, 'It was not all action though. The largest part of our operations were often boring and dull, also very uncomfortable.' On the other hand, 'The loss of life among Coastal Forces men was very high. It was inevitable with the risks they had to take. Our officers in the main were dare devils; they were not called "death or glory boys" for nothing'.[25] Describing close combat, LC Reynolds of *MGB 658* unconsciously echoed Nelson's famous dictum that, 'No captain can go far wrong if he places his ship alongside one of the enemy.'

> Once any action had begun, the results achieved depended on the crews, not the officers. What the S.O. and each C.O. did was to place the ship as close as possible to the enemy; from that point on the aim and the continuous shooting of the gunners was all that really mattered, and finally accomplished the results.[26]

THE PATROL SERVICE AND MINESWEEPING

The Royal Naval Patrol Service had served throughout the First World War, largely manned by fishermen operating trawlers and yachts in coastal patrols. The service was maintained in peacetime, and it was boosted in 1939 as the Admiralty planned to take up a hundred trawlers, a number that increased to 3,000 small vessels and 60,000 men by the end of the war. It had its depot in the fishing port of Lowestoft, reflecting its origins in that industry.

The Patrol Service's connection with the regular navy was even looser than other branches. Most of its officers were Skippers RNR, fishermen who as warrant officers had none of the education or social graces of regular naval officers. Under them, the mate of a small vessel was rated second hand, equivalent to a petty officer. In the early days they were all fishermen with a Board of Trade certificate. In *Euclase* at Great Yarmouth in late 1940,

> the most important individual as far as we were concerned was the Mate – Tom ... Sometimes we used to call him Snow White, because there were seven of us seamen, although he, to be sure, was the dwarf. He was a weather-beaten old fisherman, nearer fifty than forty I should guess, and he had swept mines in trawlers all through the

last war ... Tom was a man of deeds and not words, and deeds was what he liked in his seamen too. He had a sharp-featured face, and his ill-fitting false teeth gave his mouth the pointed look of the muzzle of a fox terrier.[27]

Such men were soon augmented by others who had experience in other kinds of small boats and were rated as Second Hands (Small Craft Only). HO seamen from general service began to enter the Patrol Service soon after the start of the war, attracted by its reputation for being less formal than other parts of the navy. 'The Patrol Service, rightly or wrongly, was considered a quiet number compared with service in the Mediterranean or on Atlantic convoys ... No pussar's flannel, no Divisions, or standing to attention as you came in and out of harbour. Free and easy and you were always coming in and out of harbour, too.'[28]

At first all the Patrol Service engines were old-fashioned steam reciprocating, tended by skilled enginemen who were equivalent to ERAs, assisted by stokers. In 1940 the Patrol Service took over the running of motor minesweepers, but it had no experience of this type of power. About 600 ratings with some experience of diesel engines were enrolled soon after Dunkirk and given training by the manufacturers. By the end of the war the Patrol Service had 17,000 engine room ratings, more than a quarter of its total numbers, including nearly 7,000 enginemen and chief enginemen.[29]

There were different opinions about the quality of Patrol Service men. Combined Operations Headquarters was concerned about the numbers who failed officer training and suggested that candidates who were above average in the Patrol Service 'do not compare favourably with candidates from other sources'. But at almost the same time it was found that Patrol Service submarine detector trainees learned the operation of sets much more quickly: 'Almost certainly the P/S gets a better quality of rating, since someone at Lowestoft looks after their interests.'[30] In fact the Patrol Service man was often a highly skilled seaman but without the qualities that the Admiralty, rightly or wrongly, saw as necessary in an officer.

The Patrol Service carried out much of the navy's minesweeping effort, but they did not man the ocean minesweepers that went with the main fleets. The fishermen were used to the handling of ropes, paravanes and otter boards that conventional sweeping demanded, though not the more scientific work needed for new types such as the magnetic mine.

SUBMARINES

Originally all submarine ratings were volunteers, but that was abandoned in wartime. The submarine service was another preserve of the regular seaman in the early part of the war; then in January 1940 it became necessary to draft in HO engine room artificers, followed by increasing numbers of HO ratings from January 1941.[31] Some ratings believed they were within their rights to refuse duty until an Admiralty Fleet Order was issued in 1942 making it clear that 'any rating may be drafted to submarines as and when necessary'. Some men enjoyed submarine work so much that they were prepared to give up higher substantive rates to stay in the service. For others it was the reverse – they deliberately got sentenced to detention to be taken out of the service, until the rules were changed.

Stoker Arthur (Tancy) Lee describes his experiences as his submarine worked up in the Firth of Clyde:

Doing the rounds ... Deep dives in Loch Long, Scapa, Tobermory where we held out 'Uckers' [ludo] championship (under the clock) ... Dunoon ... Campbeltown ... Where a churn of Ideal Milk was purloined, trying to get it back to the boat ... Stoker Regan falling into the 'oggin' while eating his fish and chips in the blackout ... Yes Campbeltown was always 'lively', what with Jan Pearce taking on half the crew of a destroyer, Billy Brown doing his 'noble art' turn, yes it was extremely lively at Campbeltown.

Surviving an involuntary ramming which snapped off the periscopes we returned to *Rothsey* alongside *Cyclops*. The lads were quite thrilled to get a run ashore there, as the Ivy Benson ladies band was performing at the local. Being duty watch that night I was assisting the ERA ... Later the boys returned from their shore leave all merry and bright and recounting their experiences ashore, apparently half the crew of submarines alongside had been 'tapping up' the Ivy Benson band although not very successful. Anyway PO Jordan (what a helping SPO he was, couldn't do enough for the lads) brought me fish and chips from ashore, so the evening finished off nice and quietly ... All creeping off to their billets and kipping it off. [32]

Submarines had not been designed to be lived in for long, but voyages were extended increasingly to more than several weeks, especially after the war began to move to the Pacific. Submariners were supposed to have the comfort of a depot ship between voyages, but that did not work out well in practice:

Submarine depot ships are popularly supposed to be floating palaces where submariners rest after patrols whereas in actual fact, rather than suffer the conditions on this depot ship they prefer to go to sea ... There are no baths or showers aboard, and washing facilities are practically non-existent. In my mess, which should accommodate 30 men, there are 97. It is absolutely impossible to find a vacant space in which to sling a hammock and even mess tables are used for sleeping on ... Finally the whole ship is over-run with cockroaches ...[33]

SHORE BASES

The traditional naval bases were at Chatham (including Sheerness), Portsmouth and Plymouth. Every 'general service' rating (excluding those in the Fleet Air Arm, coastal forces and the patrol service) was attached to one of these bases and was expected to return to it when between ships or on a training course – though in wartime many ratings were outside this system, part of the Fleet Air Arm, the submarine service, coastal forces or a smaller branch such as the boom defence service. The old bases were all in the south of England and were difficult to use because of the threat of bombing. However men still lived in the overcrowded barracks there. To Alec Guinness, Chatham Barracks was

> the nadir of my lower-deck experiences where thousands of men slept, snored, or vomited – their hammocks slung three-deep in a cavernous tunnel which served as dormitory, bomb-shelter and lavatory. Chatham, where to get a meal you had to fight your way to the food – which sometimes I refused to do. If it hadn't been for kind, tough messmates who took pity on me, I think I might have starved.[34]

Dozens of new shore bases were set up in all sorts of places, including converted holiday camps, requisitioned schools and factories and purpose-built hut settlements. HMS *Nimrod* at Campbeltown in Scotland was one of the least comfortable:

> The squalor of H.M.S. *Nimrod*, situated in a commandeered local school, was dreadfully depressing after *Osprey* ... Appallingly overcrowded, it was devoid of even the pretence of comfort ... Iron stanchions and strengthening bars had been fitted from floor to ceiling to take hammocks, and each matlow [sic] was allowed fourteen inches of sleeping space. There was still insufficient room, and at night men slept on and under tables and stools, and hammocks were slung three deep down the stanchions.[35]

This contrasted with its counterpart, HMS *Osprey* at Dunoon farther up the Firth of Clyde:

> I doubt whether the navy has any establishment equal to it even at the time of writing [1957]. It boasted putting and bowling greens, and tree-lined walks. I had my own private 'cabin', fitted with H. And C., bed, wardrobe and bedside table. The petty officers' mess had

been a nursery, and the walls were still covered with coloured silhouettes of animals from popular nursery rhymes. The only creature missing was one that would have been most appropriate: a pink elephant. There were billiards and table tennis, a bar – Ye Olde Seagull's Nest – and deep armchairs in an arc round a large red-brick fireplace. We ate at white clothed tables which overlooked a beech edged sward sweeping down to a stream ...[36]

There were 48,500 men in the three naval bases in February 1944, a number that caused Churchill to question the efficiency of the system. Some were permanent staff, some were undergoing courses, and about 12,000 were seamen awaiting posting. Despite the squalid conditions, some of the older men aspired to become 'barrack stanchions', who avoided sea drafts for as long as possible. George Melly soon found out how easy it was to become one. Arriving at Chatham near the end of the war, he was greeted by a petty officer who said, 'We'll have you out East before the fuckin' week's out', but he stayed for over a year:

> Wings filled me in on many useful dodges. For example he advised me never to attend the regular pay parades in the barracks. At these parades suspicious marines stalked about seeking out ratings who might be posted to ships about to sail East. Far better to attend the miss-musters parade when those who had been on watch duty drew their money, and only a bored officer and an equally indifferent Petty Officer were present.[37]

DISCONTENT AND MUTINY

The Royal Navy had seen many mutinies over the years, including the inconsequential but famous affair of the *Bounty* in 1789 and the Spithead and Nore mutinies that rocked the state in 1797. More recently it had seen several quite important revolts at, and after, the end of the First World War, followed by the highly-publicised Invergordon Mutiny of 1931, when the government had been forced to modify pay cuts and come off the gold standard. Many politicians and officers were also aware of mutinies in foreign navies, such as those at Keil and Kronstadt, which had eventually led to the overthrow of the German and Russian governments in 1917–18. They were extremely wary of the possibilities.

In March 1944 new Second Sea Lord, Sir Algernon Willis, observed, 'We have seldom got through a major war without some breakdown of morale varying from serious mutiny down to vociferous expressions of dissension and dissatisfaction.' In addition to general discontent, there were specific problems if the war in the Pacific continued for a long time:

> Some of the ingredients which go to make trouble of the type referred to seem likely to exist when the Germans are defeated and the full realisation that for the Navy this will mean an even greater effort in order to defeat Japan is brought home to the personnel. We shall no longer be fighting for our existence, the homeland will no longer be in danger, many of the other two services will be released to industry and at the same time personnel of the Navy, which must be kept at full strength, will be required to do more foreign service than ever.[38]

He wanted all officers to be 'mentally prepared' for that, and a booklet was written to give guidance. It was often quite alarming, with instructions such as, 'Shooting *to kill* should only be resorted to as a last extremity.' Admiral Horton of Western Approaches Command objected to it and claimed, 'No ordinary ship's company will resort to mass indiscipline unless they are labouring under grievances which a reasonable investigation will prove to be well founded.' In addition, the pamphlet itself was misconceived:

> I feel that if they are generally distributed in their present form and at the present time there is a grave danger that they will not achieve their object and may indeed help to bring about the contingencies which they are designed to prevent. We have now serving a very

large number of officers, even of Commander's rank in the Reserves, with relatively short experience of the traditional principles and methods of naval discipline and leadership. I feel strongly that the effect of these instructions in their present shape on many such officers, and on the even less experienced officers to whom it is intended to be circulated, is likely to be very unsettling and to produce in them a state of anxiety and distrust which must invariably arouse similar reactions in their men.

This was accepted, and the pamphlet was only distributed to senior officers. But there is no doubt that the mutiny was a growing problem in the fleet. HOs who made up the bulk of the navy can be assumed to be as politically knowledgeable as the rest of the population; men like Mallalieu and Callaghan would soon begin careers as Labour politicians, but they had suspended political action for the duration. There was no major party for a lower deck movement to look to. The Labour Party was part of the coalition government and in power in its own right by the end of the war with Japan. It took the trade union movement with it, and, despite a rash of unofficial strikes from 1944 onwards, any lower deck politician would have been advised to use official channels. Britain was allied with Stalin's Soviet Union, which was enormously popular in the country at the time, so the Communist Party would oppose anything that might undermine the war effort. In addition, the fleet was far more diverse and dispersed than it had been in 1918 – in April 1944 there were 11,000 ratings in North America, 78,000 in the Mediterranean, 45,000 with the Eastern Fleet and 19,000 in defensively equipped merchant ships.[39] There was no organized lower deck movement as there had been in 1918. The continuous-service seaman recruited between 1919 and 1939 was probably less political than his predecessors. By the very act of joining he had accepted the fact that the navy was a main prop of the Empire, and that he might be called out for strike-breaking. He might have some memory of how the last movement had fizzled out against official opposition, with a great deal of effort and little to show for it.

Nevertheless, and although there was no central organisation of any kind, there were a remarkable number of single-ship mutinies in 1942–5, without any apparent connection between them. Indeed, when the men of the headquarters ship *Lothian* refused to sail from Panama in 1944, they believed that their mutiny was 'the first in the navy since Invergordon, as far as anyone on board could tell ...'[40]

In fact, there had already been many small-scale mutinies. Tristan Jones describes how the crew of the destroyer *Obstinate* refused duty in 1942 in 'the nearest thing I ever saw to full-scale mutiny on board one of His Majesty's ships'. Roderick Macdonald tells how the men of the destroyer *Fortune* refused duty in what was undoubtedly 'Mutiny as defined in the Naval Discipline Act' until the first lieutenant went round the mess decks and read extracts of the act to them. A chaplain had to go to Ipswich to mediate in a mutiny among landing-craft crews there just before D-Day. A. H. Cherry described a revolt by the crew of the destroyer *Braithwaite* in which the marines from another ship had to be used as a threat. When the crew of the cruiser *Mauritius*, having already spent many months in the Mediterranean before emergency repairs at Plymouth, were told that they were to go back without the chance of leave, they refused to sail despite attempts to persuade them:

> First the padre came down to the mess-decks to talk to us; he was not liked and soon left without getting any replies. Then the commander, who selected the CW candidates sitting worried at their mess table. They had been told to turn to if ordered to, but no one else did. After the Commander, came Commissioned Gunner Mr Mole, who was very popular, but could not shift anybody.

Eventually the ship sailed after the officers and petty officers raised the anchor with great difficulty; no one was punished for the affair, after the crew had a show of hands and agreed to follow the captain 'through thick and thin'.[41]

In other cases the mutiny simmered but did not quite break out. A taut new captain told the crew of the destroyer *Laforey* that 'the Mediterranean War was a two-penny affair and wished to take the ship into the far east where the real war was going on', which did not go down well with those who had been fighting there for some years. He also expressed a thought that was perhaps in the minds of many regular officers – that the regulars were 'the scum of the back streets of the industrial cities, glad only to be in the service for a feed and good clothing'. As a result, the lower deck was 'on the very verge of mutiny'.[42] Mutiny could also involve the refusal of certain duties. One destroyer was commanded by Australian volunteer reservists who lacked leadership skills: 'By the time we reached Algiers there was real trouble, almost mutiny. We refused to turn to for part of ship, no extra work or cleaning duties. We manned the guns and took the ship to sea, nothing else. The Australians did not know what to do and nobody was charged.'[43]

Practically all of these stories are based on anecdotal evidence, and the *Mauritius*'s log, for example, says nothing about mutiny. It seems likely that there were many more, perhaps hundreds of cases in the later years of the war.

THE BRITISH PACIFIC FLEET

The British practically abandoned the Pacific naval war to the Americans after the catastrophic loss of *Prince of Wales* and *Repulse* early in 1942. By 1944, with the Battle of the Atlantic won, the Mediterranean secured and the Allied armies landed in France, the government wanted to build up a new Pacific Fleet to restore honour and take on the Japanese – though they were not wanted by the American authorities, and the project was likely to strain material and personal resources to the limit. Men who had volunteered in 1940 to defend their homeland against the Nazis would be kept on to fight what many regarded as an imperialist war far from home. There were early signs of trouble when an ill-conceived and badly organised force was sent out in August 1944. When they knew where they were going, one Liverpudlian seamen remarked, 'They can stuff the Far East right up the Drafting Jaunty's arse. Buggered if I wants to be stuck up some jungle creek. Leave it to the effing Yanks – they was in no bloody 'urry to 'elp us.'[44] After passing through the Panama Canal, the seamen staged a protest against appalling conditions on their mess decks and even sang *The Red Flag* – though most of them did not know the words. Some of them stormed the gangway and went ashore, where they were confronted by armed marines. A hard core of 17 men still resisted, and were eventually tried by court martial. Three ringleaders were each sentenced to a year's hard labour, while the 14 others got 90 days' detention, and those who had left the ship but returned when the marines arrived got six months' restricted leave and extra duty.

When the bulk of the BPF reached the area, comparison with the conditions on American ships also provided a flashpoint:

> I remember we tied up alongside a Yanky cruiser. I couldn't help comparing it with ours, as about half a dozen American cooks were lined up in whites being inspected by their Officer of the watch, their hands held out while he looked over them.
>
> I was sitting on a Fan Shaft with my dhobi bucket and standing by the guard rail was our cook. He had on a pair of marine boots which hadn't seen polish since they left the Guss (Devonport), a pair of shorts one would never call sparkling white, his body was covered in heat rash, and he was holding a Gash Bin on his shoulders gazing down at the inspection. 'Christ Taff,' he said, 'They are fussy …'[45]

The Pacific was becoming increasingly dangerous as the Japanese stepped up their kamikaze attacks. One hit the carrier *Indefatigable* in the spring of 1945:

> There was a terrible scraping sound. The kamikaze had missed going down the funnel, but was scraping down its side. It hit the deck near the doorway in the island, but did not penetrate. The blast went

straight in the doorway where it blew a huge hole, and up the stairwell causing death and destruction. The 279 [radar] office was largely destroyed and did not operate again. I lay on the deck amongst the ruins and not able to see a thing. Where were my colleagues? Pete White had got his head through the porthole overlooking the flight deck when the Jap hit. I shall never forget what I saw of him after the event. Ken Onion died later in the Sick Bay.[46]

In *Lothian*, now treated as a pariah ship by the authorities, there was stunning news as they prepared themselves for a possible invasion of Japan:

Above the row came the unusually excited loud cry from one of our quartermasters as he thundered down the ladder. Barely able to get the words out quickly enough he yelled: 'Pin your ears back lads I have some effing great news ... the Yanks 'ave just given the Japs an effing big 'ammering ... right in their own backyard ... some effing secret weapon ... killed thousands according to Aussie radio.'[47]

This, of course, was the atom bomb attack on Hiroshima, which ended the Pacific war almost instantly and every seaman could now look forward to going home at last.

The lower deck could look back with a sense of achievement, having endured up to six years of extreme and often constant hardship. Though the RAF took most of the credit for preventing an invasion of Britain in 1940–1, there is no doubt that if the air force had been defeated the navy would still have provided an almost insuperable obstacle, and the enemy knew it. The Royal Navy, with its Commonwealth allies, had done the lion's share of the work in winning the Battle of the Atlantic, defeating the greatest single threat to Britain's survival and allowing American armies to be brought over to Europe. It did the greatest part of the work in landing these armies in North Africa, Sicily and, most famously, Normandy in 1944. It had suffered losses and defeats, but none on the scale of the army's defeat in France in 1940. None of its actions was as controversial as the RAF's bombing of Germany; the nearest naval equivalent was the elimination of the French fleet at Oran/Mers el Kébir in 1940, but that was imposed from above, and orders were only reluctantly carried out by the navy. The navy and its lower deck held its head up high as it entered a new era of relative peace, in which it would face new problems and its past efforts would not always be appreciated.

4

THE AGE OF AUSTERITY
1945–1955

ADJUSTING TO PEACE

The government had been planning the demobilisation of the armed forces ever since the defeat of Germany came into sight, and in the autumn of 1944 the Admiralty took good care to explain the scheme to the lower deck. Learning from the experience of the last war, it gave priority to length of service and age, letting the needs of civilian industry and commerce take second place. Class A men would be assessed according to a simple sum, two months of service being equivalent to one year of age. Class B, a much smaller group, consisted of men and women whose skills, mostly in building or education, were urgently needed at home, while priority was also to be given to married people and those over 50. The lower deck reacted very favourably to this at meetings in various depots, and also to a pay rise of a shilling a day for an AB. In the Patrol Service depot at Lowestoft, for example, it was 'very well received' and considered to be 'fair and just'. At Portsmouth the reaction was similar, though some men expressed fears that unless the scheme were rigidly applied there was the possibility of 'pulling of strings' to get selected men out. There were various anomalies: for example, the men who had joined with the militia scheme in 1939 did well on length of service but might be kept on due to their younger ages.[1]

The dropping of the atom bombs ended the Pacific War while the election of a Labour government promised the kind of social reform that had been lacking after the last war. There was no general revolt, as the admirals had feared, but the wave of mutinies did not end with the war; indeed more of them came before courts martial and could no longer be kept out of the press. In the destroyer *Javelin* in the Mediterranean during October 1945, the men 'objected to a return to peace time routine and refused to fall in at an early hour'. The captain, who was not respected by his crew, picked on Leading Seaman Leverett, who was held in great regard. The seamen barred the rest of the leading seamen from the messes and they went forward to confer with the petty officers. For once the petty officers did not stand aside, as their officers often accused them of doing: instead 'they decided on the desperate step of themselves refusing to fall in, whatever might be the cost'. It was easier for them, as most were time-expired or HO men who had nothing more to expect of the navy.[2]

Demobilisation proceeded more slowly than many had hoped. One problem was that, in order to keep it completely fair, men overseas had to get back, usually in a slow passage by troopship, before the equivalent men on home stations could be released, and in the meantime many were kept in idleness or employed upon futile tasks. Educational programmes to keep them occupied soon fell into chaos as one officer at Chatham recorded: 'I recall ... starting a large mathematics class ... at the third meeting, its size was no less, but the personnel entirely different. I have visited a language classroom, and found everyone absent – picking sugar beet.'[3] But eventually the men did go home, to face a changed world, children who did not know them and all the traumas of war veterans, largely unrecognised by medicine in those days. Bill Bates, a survivor of the sinking of HMS *Goodall* in the last days of the war, suffered from what became known as survivors' guilt: 'Here I am in the bright sunshine, everything's nice and clean, I've had a good evening, and my mates are laying out in the Kola Inlet. And I might have been with them.' He began to tremble as soon as he was discharged in November 1946, and continued to suffer from agoraphobia and anxiety neurosis, one of many thousands who were expected to suffer silently after their experiences.[4]

The navy tried to persuade HO men to stay on after the war, for it would be desperately short in radar, submarine detection and aviation, which were almost entirely manned by them. It had a great deal of success with the officers. Up to December 1945, 6,727, or around 80 per cent, of those affected volunteered; but only 1,694 ratings, or two per cent. 'Stoker' Edwards, the Civil Lord of the Admiralty, tried to explain this by claiming that, 'Most men are war-weary, and are anxious to return to civil life ...', but that did not explain the huge discrepancy between officers and ratings.[5] The journalist Hannen Swaffer published an article called 'Wanted, a Naval Inquiry' in *The People* newspaper in December 1945, and the response far exceeded his expectations. 'For to-day, if hundreds of witnesses are to be believed, the Royal Navy is ridden with a caste system that has been abolished in our civilian life; its lower-deck is ruled with a discipline that is out of date; and its traditions belong to that age of Squiredom when the villagers bowed and curtsied if the landlord passed on his way.' Swaffer cited hundreds of letters in his book *What Would Nelson Do?* in 1946. Even if the picture was exaggerated, it did nothing to aid naval recruiting.

There was a serious shortage of men, the effects of which could be seen in practically every ship. According to David Phillipson,

> Trained Boy Seamen were often employed to fill adult billets; this was the case in *St James*, which was at that time losing several of its ship's company every week to demobilisation. A significant proportion of the upper-deck hands – forecastle, maintop and quarterdeck – were boys, as were the gunner's and boatswain's parties.[6]

THE POST-WAR WORLD

There was no question now of Britain resuming her place as the world's greatest sea power, as the Americans abandoned their pre-war isolationism and moved on to the world stage. A new conflict with the Soviet Union and her satellite states in Eastern Europe had begun by 1948, but that did not automatically restore the position of the navy in the public consciousness. The Soviet threat would take the form of possible nuclear attack, of internal subversion, of supporting independence movements in colonies throughout the world and of a land invasion through Europe, and for now the navy was not the primary defence against any of these. Far more than in the 1920s, the navy was no longer the main shield of the country. Furthermore, from 1949 Britain was part of an alliance, the North Atlantic Treaty Organisation. The Royal Navy made a strong contribution to this, but it was always going to be overshadowed by the vast American fleet. In sum, a cut in the British naval budget would have a far less immediate effect on national security and prestige than at any time in the past.

The admirals continued to dream of a navy to cover all possible needs, but they were constantly disappointed. Britain was heavily in debt after the war, while the politicians in power and the public supported an expensive programme of social reform, including the National Health Service and nationalisation of key industries. In the meantime naval power had become vastly more expensive, largely because it demanded the very latest technology in electronics and aviation, a trend that would accelerate over the years. There were regular reviews of defence spending, with titles such as the 'Revised Restricted Fleet' of 1949, the 'Radical Review' of 1953 and the 'Outline of Future Policy' of 1957–8. Each one spelled out a smaller fleet, and one that was less able to cover all the commitments. After demobilisation the navy had an authorised strength of 144,500 men in 1949, declining to less than 100,000 by 1960.

At home, the public had great respect for the navy's achievements during the war, and the sea still held a certain romance for the British, but that was not enough to make them want to join the service or send their sons into it in great numbers. The nation was tired of war, and millions of men and women just wanted to go home and stay there. There was almost full employment. Between the wars there had never been less than a million unemployed, rising to 2.75 million in 1932. After the war the highest number was less than half a million in 1947, exaggerated by the fuel crisis of that year, and in some years it was as little as a quarter of a million.[7] Even those out of a job could rely on far better welfare benefits than before the war. The navy would have to work hard to get recruits of an adequate standard.

DISCIPLINE AND MORALE

In 1946, as hostilities-only men waited for their release, there were some problems with discipline. About to make what turned out to be an extremely dangerous passage through the Corfu Channel, the destroyer *Saumarez* came to action stations, but her torpedo instructor got no reply from the forward switchboard when he tested the line.

> I went along to check, but the two ratings who should have been on duty there were missing. They had gone to the forward mess deck with the forward damage control party and someone had brewed up some tea. There was a lot of leg-pulling when I told these two ratings to get to their Action stations position. They had served during the war and had seen action of one sort or another. 'What the hell was there to worry about?' was the attitude they were adopting.[8]

Meanwhile some senior officers wanted to dismiss the war as an unpleasant interruption to the real navy. The Morale Committee of 1949 recommended 'more regular kit inspections of junior rates, the regular observance of musters such as Divisions and Evening Quarters and the very careful inspection of libertymen'. In addition, 'The use of Christian or nicknames including "Chief", "Killick", or "Hookie" on duty must be stopped.' The committee also stressed 'the importance, in cultivating pride of ship, of Captain's rounds of all departments and accommodation, and the thorough inspection of a proportion of ratings at weekly divisions.'[9]

Britain was still regarded as a Christian country, and the report of 1949 suggested that religion should be the fundamental basis of discipline, though it did not go so far as to recommend the reintroduction of compulsory church attendance.

> Two world wars within a generation have had a very telling effect on all classes of society. The classes to which leadership and sense of responsibility (noblesse oblige) were to a large extent hereditary, have been decimated. The classes which previously looked, with respect, to others for leadership and authority are becoming more educated and articulate; at the same time, however, they are acquiring a selfish, shallow and unpatriotic outlook which expects something for nothing without accepting responsibility. This is due to a variety of reasons such as mass unemployment in the 1930's, broken up homes and consequent lack of home discipline, interrupted education with its over-emphasis on materialism, and apathy towards Christianity. The immediate result is an individual who has an instinctive dislike of discipline and orthodox standards of decent behaviour – 'the couldn't care less type'.[10]

LONG AND SHORT SERVICE

In 1946 it was decided to recruit on the basis of 50 per cent on 12-year engagements and 50 per cent on short service, of seven years with the fleet and five in the reserve. In the long term this would mean a fleet of 75 per cent continuous service men. But it soon became apparent that the traditional 12-year engagement was no longer popular in the days of full employment. It had originated in Victorian times, when a lifetime of service to a single employer was considered normal, and had survived the inter-war period because 12 years more-or-less-guaranteed employment had seemed attractive in an age of mass unemployment. In 1948–9, short service engagements proved very satisfactory with 10,299 men taken on, but only 3,360 continuous service men could be found. And as it was pointed out, 'The essential point is that Petty Officers cannot be produced on 7 years' engagements.'[11]

The recruitment of boys also came under question in the post-war world. In 1946 a petty officer wrote,

> Is our public aware that its young sailors are kidnapped into its senior service at the tender age of 15, and, to ensure that the sentence is binding, they have to sign or have signed for them a document stating that for 12 years, from the age of 18, their souls belong to the Admiralty. Imagine: 15 years signed away by children unaware of life's meaning. Having procured the body, the service proceeds to divorce the mind from its natural environment, from every aspect of life save that of the naval service (early nineteenth century)'[12]

This led to pressure for reform:

> Parliamentary interest in the Seaman Boys arose as a result of concessions the Admiralty had made since 1944, whereby ratings who had entered the Navy for patriotic reasons during the war on Continuous Service engagements were allowed to transfer to Hostilities Only conditions of service, or later to Special Service conditions. These concessions were never at any time allowed to ratings entered as Seaman Boys. Their case was pressed politically even after the war had ended, until it gradually developed into the argument that it was wrong to engage boys at 15–16 to serve until age 30. This was the emphasis of the discussion in the Adjournment Debate of 7th August 1947 ... as a result of which the admiralty promised to give further consideration ...

As a result, 'In December 1947, the First Lord approved that ratings entered as Seaman Boys should be given the option at age 18 of transferring to Special Service conditions', artificer apprentices and marine band boys being specifically excluded from this. It was soon found that 80 per cent of boys took the option of transfer, which is not surprising – they had nothing to lose by it, and they could always transfer to 12 years when the time came.[13]

There was another crisis around 1950 as men who had signed on for twelve years in the boom years just before the war became due for release. This coincided with the start of the Korean War. Many had to be retained beyond the end of their regular service, and around 8,250 Royal Fleet Reservists were recalled, while a bounty of £100 was introduced for those who extended their service voluntarily to 22 years.

National Service

In theory, conscription might have aided the manning situation, but it rarely did. When peacetime national service was adopted in 1947, it was for a period of a year, which was soon extended to 18 months. This was still too short for the navy: the First Lord told Parliament,

> The decision to continue National Service ensures that expansion of the Royal Navy in a future emergency will be less difficult than hitherto, but manning requirements will not be entirely met from that measure alone. A period of 18 months cannot qualify a man for the higher or more skilled rates. National service men can fill complement billets in the Fleet only after their initial training is finished, and even then only to an extent that is limited. In the short time that is available, it will not be possible normally to draft them to foreign stations.[14]

In 1950, with the beginning of the Korean War, it was extended to two years, which was more acceptable because it allowed the possibility of using its men productively, with perhaps six months' training and 18 months in a commissioned ship. But, although it was comparatively little used by the navy, National Service made the services unpopular generally. As one naval captain put it,

> For ten years since the end of the war elder brothers have been called up, done their time, and come out. A national attitude to this service has developed among the young: for the large majority, it is

that they hate the prospect of it, they would go to great lengths to dodge it – some of the tricks to fail the medical are most ingenious – and, once in, although they like it better than they expected, they long for it to be over.[15]

If conscription into the forces was inevitable, many young men preferred to avoid the army as their predecessors had done in wartime. Peter Cobbold was one of 52 young men in a recruiting station in the London suburbs in 1955. "'Please, dear Lord,' I silently prayed. 'don't let me go into the Army.'" But when he put the navy as his first choice he was told, 'It can't be done, old boy!' In the event, citing a distant cousin who had been a lieutenant-commander in the Fleet Air Arm combined with good health and references was enough to get him into the navy, with one other candidate out of the 52.[16] Once in, he soon began to resent his treatment in the Victoria Barracks in Portsmouth:

> When one bears in mind that we were not volunteers, you may understand our resentment at this enforced authority. It was a resentment which was building up in me. I found my enforced imprisonment in the barracks, the manner in which my superiors gave their orders, coupled with my total inability to protest over some of these matters, very stressful and it was fast leading to me 'doing something about it'.[17]

In fact, he confined his protest to wearing a civilian tie over his uniform when off duty, and dragging his feet over commands.

Many became stores assistants or writers, and graduates like Jack Rosenthal were often trained as Russian interpreters, rated as coders and wore fore-and-aft rig. He was greeted by a petty officer with a traditional attitude to education:

> You may all think you're clever little bastards. With your Higher School Certificates and fancy degrees. In other ways you're chalk and cheese and Chinese wedding cake. Some of you were born with

a set of silver golf clubs in your mouth, others with a hobnail boot up your arse. Here, you're all the same – coder specials. Which means you're not special at all. Which means you're not such clever little bastards either. Because coder specials are the lowest branch in the Navy – and therefore the lowest known form of human life.[18]

He was sent to Coulsdon in Surrey for language training:

We were taught by real-life Russians, mostly sad-faced men who'd escaped to a land that didn't bother with portmanteau verbs, packed with suffixes and prefixes, 37 syllables long – and who quickly realised that I was never going to manage Chekov in the original. Not that we were meant to. We were training to be translators of military Russian only, or (if we were among the best 5 per cent) interpreters and packed off to Cambridge. It was clear from lesson one, I was to be one of the 95 per cent.[19]

Like many of the conscripts, Cobbold had doubts about the value of their service:

The Navy held her national servicemen for too short a period to justify any great investment, and in my opinion she tended to train them to such a standard that they were unlikely to fall overboard and could not be expected to hamper proceedings too much! ... They became, I suspect, a bit of an encumbrance to the Service at the prevailing stage of naval development and the national serviceman was to be the logical dogsbody for the ship and shore establishments. Accordingly he marched up and down, guarding the cook-house coal or picking up leaves from the parade ground as part of the barrack guard, or endured life at sea as a basic seaman until the day came for release.[20]

Yet others eventually agreed that they had gained something in the long term, such as Writer William Nuttall:

It was quick growing-up course and taught me how to look after myself. I learned tact and diplomacy, too, and an ability to mix with others from different social backgrounds. Looking back, one rarely remembers the bad times; it was an experience I feel privileged to have undergone. We just accepted the knocks.[21]

Even Peter Cobbold was won over in the end. When asked by an officer if he had enjoyed his time, he answered, 'To be honest, sir, I will miss the comradeship and I never thought that I would ever admit it, but I think I have enjoyed the last year or so. I have been to places that, ordinarily, I would not have had the chance to visit, but I am glad to be going out.'[22]

THE TAS AND ELECTRICAL BRANCHES

At last, in October 1946, the navy did what had long been recommended and split the electrical branch from the torpedomen. At the same time the torpedo branch was merged with anti-submarine. Leonard Williams was one of those faced with a choice, and the possibility of losing his identity as a seaman:

> Electrical work I had always liked, since it produced some interesting problems which one could get one's teeth into. However, I also liked messing about with torpedoes, but to choose the anti-submarine branch would mean that I would be condemning myself to service in small ships, which was something I did not want.[23]

In fact about 80 per cent of torpedomen made the same choice, as it offered the possibility of trade-union recognition as a skilled electrician after leaving the service.

The merger of torpedo and anti-submarine was natural in that all kinds of underwater warfare, including mines, now came under a single branch. However, it posed difficulties of its own, as it included a wide variety of techniques and skills. Torpedomen had to be assessed for their aural abilities as asdic operators, and if they failed they might transfer to other branches, mostly aircraft handling or the shore-based role of boom defence. Asdic operators had to learn a good deal of electrical theory and how to deal with mines. Men from the separate parts of the branch carried the letter 'D' for detector or 'T' for torpedo after their ratings until they were able to undergo a conversion course to learn the other parts of the trade. Schools were re-established at Portsmouth and Portland, but there were only minimal training facilities at Chatham, which did not have easy access to deep water for anti-submarine training, so the principle of the home port system was under threat. New ratings started off as Torpedoman Detector 3rd class after training in their ship,

> to assume the duties of any rating in a torpedo tube's crew; to carry out the control of any A/S weapon; to assist higher ratings in their maintenance duties; to handle torpedoes and A/S projectiles; to fit and unfit depth charges; to operate asdic sets under supervision; to

The duties of the torpedo and snti-submarine branch.

act as a member of a demolition party; and to carry out under supervision the control and streaming of paravanes, wire and influence sweeps, and countermeasures such as foxer and other noisemakers.[24]

After that, and training in HMS *Osprey* at Portland, he might progress to TD2 and leading seaman rate, to TD1 as petty officer or chief, and finally to Torpedo and Anti-Submarine Instructor. The TD3 wore a single star above a torpedo and harpoon, a combination of the old branch badges, and it was expected that at least 2,000 would be needed. The TD2 had a star above and below, and 1,050 were wanted; the TD1 had a crown above the badge, and 200 of these were needed, while the planned elite of 200 TASIs would also wear a star below.

THE SEAMEN

The separation of the electricians from the seaman branch and the expansion of naval aviation tended to accelerate a growing problem. Who was to carry out the routine domestic duties of the ship? These were normally done by the seaman branch but were of benefit to all – cleaning of common spaces, working parties, messmen duties, heads (toilet) parties and laundries. Various regulations already discouraged or forbade captains from using men of the writer and supply, gunnery and torpedo, submarine detector and signal branches away from their specialities except in emergency, and the problem was likely to increase as new systems such as guided missiles demanded even more technical specialisation. One idea was to design and fit ships with as many labour-saving devices as possible, but that would take time and money to implement. Another idea was to recruit a special short-service branch for 'general duties', but that was rejected out of hand as likely to create a 'depressed class' in the navy. An Admiralty Fleet Order was drafted, ordering that 'all departments of the ship shall share in general duties', and captains were to 'organise the duties so that all bear their share and also so that necessary work out of working hours is borne evenly'.[25]

There were always a few men who did not fit and could not get on in the navy. D. O. Lee started well enough by qualifying as a radio control operator third class, but presumably because of bad conduct he was not employed in that role and never even reached able rate in five and a half years. He wrote, 'Am I to believe that a nicely polished binnacle cover is more important than an efficient TS [transmitting station] crew? or that a rating skilled in the use of a deck-scrubber more desirable than one skilled in the art of tracking an enemy aeroplane on his radar scope?' He got sentenced to detention as a misguided attempt to draw attention to his position and managed to persuade the captain of the DQs to support his case. But at the end of his sentence, 'I found myself a civilian with a new suit and a ticket to London.'[26]

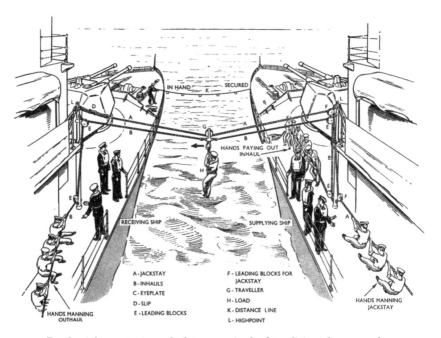

Replenishment at sea led to a revival of traditional seaman's skills with ropes.

The pure seaman's art, in decline since the end of sail, was beginning to revive largely due to the introduction of replenishment at sea, which was learned from the United States Navy. Complicated rigs had to be set up, especially for the most common technique, the abeam method. Two ships steaming side-by-side tens of feet apart called for the most accurate steering. Personnel and goods up to 550lb were transferred by means of the light jackstay rig, heavier goods by the heavy jackstay. Liquids were transferred by pipes suspended from the derrick fuelling rig or the jackstay fuelling rig, all of which had to be set up by the seamen. Manpower was also needed to haul an object or person between the two ships, this being regarded as safer than mechanical power in an emergency. In the case of accident or during the threat of enemy attack, it was necessary to complete the transfer of goods or persons as quickly as possible, to allow for rapidly disengaging and separating the ships, giving them freedom of manoeuvre.[27]

PALESTINE

Most of the navy's operational tasks in the post-war period were remote, unpopular, or essentially thankless. One was to stop Jewish refugees, often victims of the concentration camps, from reaching a new home in Palestine. Petty Officer Jack Powrie was in a sloop in Malta:

> Mermaid also took on planks of wood, chicken wire by the roll and other items of use for building a coop. It turned out that these items kept Chippy and the AB's quite busy during our next few days at sea, building boarding ramps and protection for the boarding parties when encountering illegal vessels. It seems that after the 'Exodus' was chased to Palestine and had grounded herself just south of Haifa, word was that other illegal ships' passengers were hurling anything loose down onto RN ships trying to apprehend them within the three mile shore limit as laid down at the Geneva Convention. Hence the chicken wire protection. ... The only protection the small boarding

parties had was a three foot stick with a tear gas canister at the end to keep people back from injury by flying bottles, nuts and bolts and sometimes bare fists. A lot of RN ratings were badly injured during boarding illegal boats. The boarding and taking of these ships had to be done within a three mile limit of Palestine as laid down in Geneva and so it had to be quick. We had weapons, but again, couldn't use them at any time.

However, they only caught up with one illegal vessel while Powrie was with the ship. Nineteen-year old Peter Cain had an unpleasant experience with the destroyer *Chieftain*:

> We came alongside at 5 a.m. and the Captain called 'Stand by to board'.
>
> I along with others stood outboard of the upper deck safety rails and leaned away from the protection of the Chieftain ready to leap across to the other vessel. 'Boarding parties go, go!' came the final command from the bridge and I leapt across the void. I was fully expecting to land safely on the other side to take up my station on the fo'c'sle – instead I found myself temporarily blinded by a thunderflash.
>
> There followed a sense of falling and within seconds I found myself engulfed in a seething mass of turbulent water ... I recall getting rid of my Sten gun and safely helmet and shouting at the top of my voice as I heard the thrashing of the propellers drawing ever closer ... The Captain immediately ordered 'Stop both engines' ....

He and another man drifted away from the ship but were eventually rescued by boat.

The Cold War

The reality of the coming conflict with the communist states of Europe and Asia was brought home to the navy on 22 October 1946 when the destroyers *Saumarez* and *Volage* passed through the Corfu Channel to establish the freedom of the seas against attempts by the new communist regime in Albania to close the strait. *Saumarez* struck a mine, and her bows were blown off; *Volage* went to her rescue, only to hit another mine, as described by Stoker Stanley Goodwin:

> My mates were blown to bits almost before my eyes. It isn't a nice thing to think about. There was Joss and Mick and Burney and Taffy – you forget their real names but you remember their nicknames. When Sub-Lieutenant Price told me to go aft I turned and went through the doorway in a bulkhead, when there was this almighty explosion, and that was that. There was nothing left of the bow section where I had been; just a gaping hole. I missed death by half a minute or so.
>
> As it was I was blown head first against a bulkhead and I had head injuries and a broken nose.[28]

Both ships survived, but one officer and 43 ratings were killed. As the wounded were brought back to the carrier *Ocean* off Corfu, Naval Airman V. Lane had an unpleasant task:

> I was on duty by the crane helping to get the stretchers on to the flight deck. Each stretcher was then placed on a trolley normally used for carrying bombs to be loaded on our aircraft. They were pushed to the forward aircraft lift on the flight deck and then lowered to the hangar below. Other parties of men then pushed the trolleys through the parked aircraft – Fireflies and Seafires – to the sick bay or the quarter deck ... I still remember the feeling of distress – and anger – as I stood alongside the crane and heard the men in the boats shouting out the injuries of the wounded. 'This one has a broken back,' 'this one is badly burned,' and so on.[29]

In the Far East, the sloop *Amethyst* was on the River Yangtse going from Shanghai to Nanking when on 19 April 1949 she was caught up in the Chinese Revolution and fired upon by communist forces on the shore. Leading Seaman Leslie Frank, a quartermaster with 24 years' service, describes what happened (in the third person):

Several direct hits were registered, the first killing one rating and seriously wounding the coxswain who was on the wheel, in the wheelhouse, leaving one Leading Seaman (L/Sea L FRANK) in the wheelhouse. This rating was also hit on the back and was out for a few seconds, when he came round, he immediately took over the wheel and reported to the bridge. Full speed ahead was ordered from the bridge and rung on from the wheelhouse. Whilst the ship was going at full speed the Gyro warning light came on and then the gyro repeat light went off. FRANK reported to the bridge that the Gyro had gone off, also his magnetic course which he continued to steer, although getting no reply from the bridge, the reason for no reply apparently was that another shell had hit the bridge, wounding the Captain, Navigator, 1st Lieut, Action Officer of the Watch, Asdic Operator and killing the communication number.

The ship went aground and was trapped. The destroyer *Consort* arrived to try to tow her off while Frank and the Gunnery Instructor laid out a line, but she was unable to get close enough. Lieutenant Commander Simon Kerans arrived to take command, while 20 wounded were evacuated by flying boat and 17 dead were buried with full ceremony except for the gun salute. The *Amethyst* managed to get free but was still unable to proceed against communist gunfire. Kerens refused to apologise for firing first and attempting to invade communist territory, and was backed up by Frank (now acting coxswain) and the rest of the crew.

Frank counted the days as the ship was cut off, while the remaining four officers and 69 ratings on board repaired damage, kept the ship running and tried to maintain their morale. According to Frank, after 50 days, 'Everyone seems to be taking this grim situation in their stride and showing all the usual attitudes of indifference, which in fact is the attitude of the British sailor everywhere.' They cheered up when BBC Radio played a record programme in their honour, and when supplies of oil arrived in drums they worked hard to get it on board. By the middle of July they had to go on half rations to conserve food, but 'after the first 24 hours we don't seem to be doing so bad' – for the sailor's normal diet was more than adequate in any case. The admiral informed them they were 'in the forefront of what is called the "cold war"'. After 95 days the men were 'still smiling, cheerful and 100% behind the Captain.'

Eventually on 29 July Kerans called Frank and others to his cabin and announced, 'I have decided to make a break for it tonight.' According to Frank, 'I don't think there was one of us whose heart did not give an extra beat.' He was in the wheelhouse again when the ship sailed that night, as he had been at the beginning of the incident, but he had only a limited understanding of what was going on:

> From the time I went into the wheelhouse at about 2130, I do not seem to have a very clear recollection of what took place, lots of orders from the Captain & a hell of a lot of gun fire, we received a hit in the first encounter with the [Chinese People's Liberation Army], but they would have had to blow us right out of the water to stop us, 22 knots was the speed we were making, and everything was running fine, more orders more gun fire all the way down, until suddenly, after having just been told to steer as perfect as possible, I got the order 'Hard a Star', I had got this on when I got 'Hard a Port', I found out later that we had carved a junk which got in our way ... Later, as dawn was beginning to break, I heard down the voice pipe from the bridge, the most welcome message of all, 'The Concord is in sight,' so then we knew that whatever happened passing the forts assistance was there waiting.

The crew returned to heroes' welcomes from Hong Kong all the way to London, where they were presented to the Royal Family. Frank was belatedly promoted to petty officer and awarded the Distinguished Service Medal along with ERA Leonard Williams, who had kept the engines running in the absence of an engineer officer.[30] In 1957 a film was made, called *Yangtse Incident* using the real ship, but in the River Orwell rather than the Yangtse. Frank was played by William Hartnell (better known for portraying army sergeants before he became the first *Doctor Who* in 1963). Lord Mountbatten ordered a copy of the film to be sent to every training base, as it showed 'without frills how an ordinary seaman behaves under stress and adversity'.[31]

A report of 1949 had much to say on the spread of communist influence in the navy. It recognised that it was not a problem at that moment but recommended a reading list for officers, including Invergordon mutineer Fred Copeman's *Reason in Revolt*, which renounced the creed of communism. It considered the idea of discussion groups, but concluded that 'badly handled, it might do more harm than good' and that 'discussion of this subject is bound to contravene [Kings Regulations and Admiralty Instructions] Article 18'.[32] Instruction by the chaplain was recommended, but it was hardly necessary. The well-publicised Corfu and *Amethyst* incidents had hardened lower deck opinion, and the appeal of communism was far less than it had been during the war years when the country was in alliance with the Soviet Union. In fact, the post-war naval rating was nearly always non-political and 'conservative' with a small 'c'.

The Korean War

The nearest that the Cold War came to a direct conflict between the major powers was when the North Koreans, backed by China and less directly by Russia, invaded South Korea in 1950. When AB Walter Hughes of the cruiser *Jamaica* first heard of this on the radio, his immediate reaction was, 'Where the hell is Korea?' The ship was carrying a group of the Seaforth Highlanders from Singapore to Australia but was diverted. According to Boy First Class Michael Stephens, 'We were so under-manned, these lads finished up by (very capably) manning H1 and H2 4" guns when we were rerouted to Korea at the immediate outbreak of hostilities.' The ship was patrolling off the east of Korea when it encountered and shelled some coastal warships moving along the coast. Three of them were sunk or grounded, and Hughes helped with a rescue:

There were two survivors, from one of the gun boats that we sank, and as we reached them, I reached out to grab one, first off, I pulled his life jacket from him, (he was just clinging to it, and at once, he went under the water, and I had to reach down, and grab him by the hair, and pull him into the whaler, it was almost the same scene, as we went after the second survivor, as he also, was just clinging to his life jacket. (I don't think they had time to put them on).

Next *Jamaica* took part in the Inchon landings, the large-scale amphibious operation that changed the course of the war, and Boy Stephens had a 'grandstand view' from the 4-inch gun director:

It was almost constant bombardment with our 6 inches – first to Wolmi ... Then we turned our fond attention to Inchon itself. We were pretty good, too – hit the main ammo dump in there. The explosion, far away though it was, served to even roll us – and I'm told our American friends were jubilant! We weren't all that dismayed ourselves!

Then they were attacked by

a Russian built Yak who, after missing the USS *Mount McKinnley* [sic], turned his nasty attention to the two British cruisers. My thoughts since, is that the pilot must have been suicidal to have attacked such a formidable target.

As it was, he came in on our port quarter at about 100ft altitude and about 50ft off our side and proceeded to strafe our port side from stern to stem. Big mistake!! Our 4 inches were unable to engage but our pom-poms and bofors opened up almost instantly. Sitting in my tractor style seat in the director, I could plainly see him as he flashed down the opposite side, white/blue flames squirting from his wings – then he was out of my line of vision behind the superstructure. The next I saw, he was tumbling into a flaming dive with bits spraying from him. He hit the water just forward of our bow and the only recognizable part remaining bobbing down our starboard side was his right landing wheel and leg.

Unfortunately his messmate Boy Ron Godsall was fatally wounded in the attack.

SHIPS

In the developed post-war navy the traditional surface fleet was a smaller proportion of the whole than in the past, comprising about half the personnel, while submarines and aviation each made up about a quarter of the number. Apart from aircraft carriers it was an age of much smaller ships. The older battleships were scrapped soon after the war while the newer ones, of the *King George V* class, were laid up until they too were scrapped in 1957. The only battleship in commission during the 1950s was *Vanguard*, designed during the war and completed in 1946. She did not take part in any of the peacetime campaigns, and apart from a Royal Tour in 1947, spent most of her time as a flagship at Portsmouth. It was truly the end of an era when she was scrapped in 1960.

The cruiser, once a symbol of imperialism, was also in decline. It had no anti-submarine function and no role in sea control in those days, and it was too large and expensive for most of the navy's new tasks. Its most useful role, as in the later years of the Second World War, was in gunfire support, and in the Korean War *Belfast* fired several thousand rounds at land targets over ranges of up to 12 miles, more than she had fired in the whole of the Second World War. The destroyer came out of the war with greatly enhanced prestige, as the most versatile of all ships. Post-war, the Battle class had the long range necessary for Pacific operations and a powerful short-range anti-aircraft armament. The Weapons class ships retained a torpedo armament but were mainly for anti-submarine and anti-aircraft duties while escorting the fleet; some of them were later converted to radar pickets. The classic post-war destroyer was the *Daring* class, designed during the war and launched in the early fifties, large and glamorous ships that were popular with the lower deck. They were the last 'true' destroyers before the large, missile-armed County class took over.

The frigate, now recognised as the main anti-submarine vessel, was at the centre of the post-war surface fleet. Around 30 of them were in service for most of the fifties, with more than a hundred in reserve until 1958. The navy tried a cheap version, the *Blackwood* class, with no main gun armament, known officially as utility frigates – and 'futility' to the lower deck. But nuclear submarines demanded much faster ships to chase them, and as a result many destroyers were fully or partly converted by fitting new superstructures, or partly converted by adding new weapons and sensors to frigates. Meanwhile the highly successful Type 12 design was developed through the *Rothesay and Whitby* classes. Their characteristic bow was designed to let them chase submerged submarines into rough seas. The four ships each of the 'big cat' and 'cathedral' classes were even more specialised, all on similar hulls and for the anti-aircraft and aircraft-direction roles respectively. They were among the first large surface ships to use diesel engines.

The navy saw no role for coastal forces of the type deployed during the Second World War apart from a few experimental vessels, but a new small-ship navy began to develop. Mines were a serious threat, and it was believed that the Soviet Union might seal off British harbours by delivering mines by air or submarine. This was the main motivation for building more than a hundred coastal minesweepers of the 'ton' class throughout the fifties. In fact, they soon found other roles as general-purpose small warships. They were the mainstay of the Royal Naval Reserve, whose local units were expected to gain good knowledge of their own area and clear them of mines in the event of war. They were used in the Borneo campaign of the mid-1960s, as well as for less dangerous tasks such as enforcing the traffic separation scheme in the English Channel. One of them, *Iveston,* would gain a particular notoriety in 1970.

THE RESERVE FLEET

Fearing a new Battle of the Atlantic against 200 Soviet submarines, the navy kept a large number of ships in 'mothballs' in ports round the country – there were 387 ships and 58 submarines in this state in August 1947. By 1950 this had been reduced to 285 ships and 50 submarines, but it was still a huge force needing 10,000 men to maintain it.[33] Positions with the reserve fleet in the home ports were considered desirable by the 'barrack stanchions' who had seen enough of the sea and simply wanted a 'cushy' life near home. It was very different for ships that were laid up in remote creeks and lochs around the country: Gareloch, for example, was home to three battleships, two aircraft carriers and a number of cruisers. Facilities for their crews ashore were very limited, and buses to the nearby town of Helensburgh became grossly overcrowded.

The Reserve Fleet reached a crisis in 1953 as the Korean War ended and 56 more ships were to be paid off while many reservists and retained men were released. Though the admiral in charge claimed that the Reserve Fleet was 'the Royal Navy's biggest asset', and a 'fleet in being', it required 12 working weeks and up to a hundred men to preserve a destroyer and ensure that its complex systems would not deteriorate. Ideally it should be done by the old crew, who had an interest in the ship, but many of the crews were anxious to get home. The Royal Dockyards were not interested in the work, and newly trained regulars, it was agreed, needed 'an inspiring start to service life',[34] so national service men were often sent to do the menial jobs. Peter Cobbold was posted to the Reserve Fleet at Chatham to see out his time as a national serviceman in 1957 and found himself as part of a pool of cheap but rather inefficient labour:

> The routine was always the same. We lined up on the upper deck and a Leading hand or a Petty Officer came along with a clipboard. Some ratings were sent into the dockyard to work; others were given the name of a ship to report to. Usually we were sent in a group and

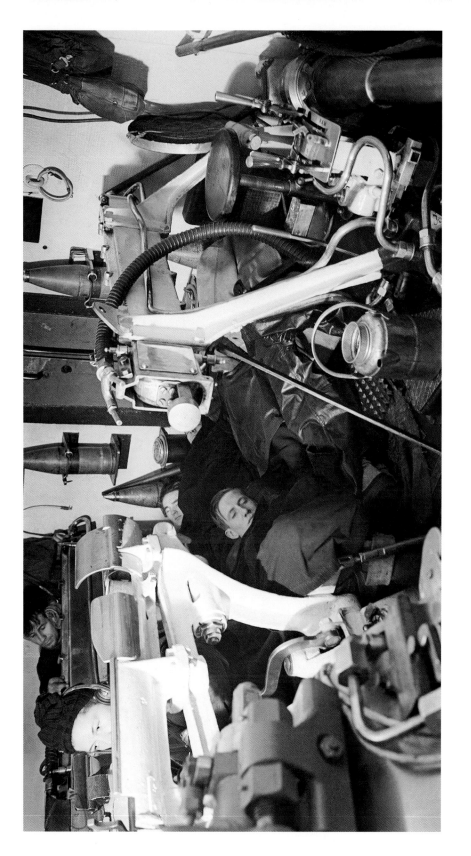

Men resting in a 6-inch turret in HMS *Rodney* in 1940. (IWM A2134)

The depth charge crew of HMS *Viscount* brings up new charges in a rough sea after an attack in 1942. (IWM A13370)

The telegraphist air gunner of a Swordfish with his Lewis gun on the famous carrier HMS *Ark Royal*. (IWM A3843)

Above: A Walrus flying boat ready for a catapult launch, as seen from the hangar of the battleship HMS *Prince of Wales*. (IWM A3881)

Below: A Swordfish being prepared for flight on the deck of HMS *Battler* in 1943. (IWM A16649)

The crew of Tank Landing Craft 2130 in 1944. Neither the petty officer (probably a motor mechanic) nor the leading seaman has a good-conduct stripe, which would be unusual in general service. (Conway Archive)

The crew of a motor torpedo boat prepare to go to sea from Felixstowe. (IWM A4251)

Naval pensioners recalled from the reserve had high priority for demobilisation in 1945.

(IWM A29287)

Left: Jack Rosenthal as a leading coder. (Anova Books)
Below: The destroyer HMS *Volage* damaged by an Albanian mine in the Corfu Channel in 1946. (IWM A31208)

The crew of the *Amethyst* after their escape. (Getty)

Ships of the reserve fleet, including destroyers and frigates, are laid up at Penarth in Wales, one of many ports where such sights could be seen. (From Eric Grove, *Vanguard to Trident*)

Tank Landing Ships approaching Suez in 1956. (IWM MH23499)

this meant that we marched through the dockyard until we reached our appointed destinations. A lot of the time was spent hanging about waiting to begin work and usually, nothing much was accomplished before 'Stand Easy'. Eventually we would get going after this small quarter of a hour break. Sometimes we waited to receive the mooring lines of an incoming ship and would stand in a small hut, out of the wind and rain, or stand 'sunbathing' if it were fine, swapping yarns and smoking out of sight of the stream of officers and other personnel going about their daily business. I felt like the great forgotten. I felt like the Navy no longer needed my services.[35]

A large backlog [of?] was developing, and there was no sign of extra men or money to reduce it. With the defence cuts in 1957 and the growing realisation that it would be irrelevant in a thermonuclear war, the Reserve Fleet was drastically reduced. The merchant seamen of the Royal Naval Reserve and the amateurs of the Royal Naval Volunteer Reserve had been kept up to strength after the war partly to man the ships of the Reserve Fleet if they came into service, and after the reduction they took on the role of minesweeping in their local areas, while the professionals and amateurs were merged into the new RNR in 1958.

THE BOYS TRAINING ESTABLISHMENTS

With full employment and less deferential social attitudes, a long-term career in the navy was becoming less attractive to youth. In 1950 it was reported,

It would be a mistake to suppose that we are getting the pick of the youth of the nation into the Navy. I consider the boy entries are on the whole good, but they tend to deteriorate if they are relegated to shore service for any length of time. Many of the Special Service entries are of a poor type, not to be compared with the general run of National Service men which for the most part are very good material.[36]

David Phillipson joined in 1947 and spent the first five weeks under 'strict quarantine' in the annexe of *Ganges* whose 'extreme and depressing ugliness' had been described by John Davies. After that he and his colleagues transferred to the main barracks where, 'Our waking lives ... were ordered and fenced about with regulation and a prescribed punishment, individual or collective, for every infringement, great or small, so that punishment was all but impossible to avoid, after *Ganges* nothing one later experienced was too bad.' Training consisted of three parts, seamanship, gunnery and schooling, the last being considered the least important. Seamanship training involved the use of some ingenious equipment: 'In the boatwork room for instance, were beautifully made and detailed scale models of service boats: whalers, cutters, pinnaces, gigs. There were more models in the anchors and cables room, again wonderfully detailed and exact, of battleships' forecastles, complete with miniature working capstans, tiny anchors and fathoms of Lilliputian anchor cable.'[37] Gunnery was altogether harsher and consisted, in traditional fashion, of a good deal of foot drill. 'We had learned the rudiments of drill in the annexe; now we drew battered old Lee Enfield rifles and First World War sword bayonets from the armoury and took to the vast, empty parade ground at the tender mercy of Chief Gunner's Mate Blenkinsop.'[38]

Some could not stand the routine. In 1947, 'desperate boys still sometimes "ran"; rarely got as far as Ipswich before recapture (the location of Shotley Barracks had been chosen with care); were returned to be placed in cells and to receive six cuts in the morning; twelve for a second offence.'[39] By the early 1950s, the authorities were becoming seriously worried about the numbers of boys who broke out – 32 during the last quarter of 1954 alone, not counting four who ran away twice, making a total of 36 escapes. The figure was far lower at the other training ship, *St Vincent*, near Portsmouth, where the regime was much less strict and getting out was in fact far easier. Deserters from *Ganges* were invariably recovered, usually within a few hours and severely caned when they got back. According to one officer, 'it seems necessary to regard these incidents not as being, in essence, calculated attempts to escape service in the Navy – which a moment's reflection would show to be an unprofitable undertaking – but ill considered enterprises taken in moments of acute depression or irresponsible escapades.' It was agreed that at *Ganges* 'discipline is severe and is fairly rigidly applied'. The Senior Psychologist of the Navy wrote that *Ganges* had 'a Procrustean system, oppressed by size, bleakness and isolation from naval purpose and seagoing activities.' An analysis of the figures for late 1954 showed that 14 boys, nearly half the total, had broken out because they were 'fed up with *Ganges*'. Five more were tired of the navy in general, or wanted to get out. Half a dozen were homesick or worried about affairs at home; one admitted to being unpopular, with no friends; another 'couldn't understand gunnery'; and only three admitted to doing it 'for a skylark'.

Several individual cases came to the attention of the authorities. John C. Wilson did well to start with and was one of the boys chosen to attend the Coronation Naval Review, until he was given the 'terrible punishment' of No. 10, frog-jumping for an hour under a petty officer. According to his father, an ex-naval man, 'this treatment broke the boy's spirit and the pride he had for the Royal Navy.' James Beaumont disobeyed orders, escaped, was caned and was found to be 'a miserable, lifeless boy'; at an interview with his divisional officer he 'stated that he would go to any lengths to obtain his release from the Service mentioning *inter alia*, suicide.' Despite official fears that he was trying to 'work his ticket', he was eventually discharged as 'unsuitable'. And in September 1953 the Admiralty received a letter from 15-year-old Boy Second Class A. K. Blair 'on behalf of myself and many others, who, for naval regulations, have to remain anonymous'. He complained that he would still have to serve at least ten years in the navy despite his young age at recruitment, but also that life at *Ganges* was intolerable. 'I joined with the view of making a good thing of it, getting on, and being happy in it. All that was squashed in the first six weeks. Now I hate the service like poison and would do anything in my power to get out of it. The place is like a prison. The officers are pure tyrants and the food is better not talked about.' Blair's identity was soon discovered. He had made a vague threat at the end of his letter – 'if someone doesn't do something about conditions here, we, ourselves, will, and I don't think anyone would like that.' Despite that, the authorities decided to take no action against him, possibly because they feared public exposure.[40]

An inspection of *St Vincent* by the Department of Education produced a far more positive picture. Sixty-nine boys were entered at five-week intervals, mostly from London, the south coast and south Wales, with 573 in the establishment in October 1952. The education was generally good, though by normal educational standards it suffered from a rapid change of personnel and an over-restrictive syllabus. A third of the boys were in the advanced class, having much more time in school and less in technical instruction than general-course boys. The purpose of the advanced class was 'to give intelligent boys of good character and personality a more advanced education in order to provide men suitable for higher rating, branch rank and commissioned rank'. Seamanship classes were 'designed to teach boys the language of the sea and the elementary principles of seamanship'. There were plenty of teaching aids, almost too many in that the area was overcrowded, but instruction afloat was only done in a single sea boat. It was suggested that 'visits to fighting ships early in the course would be most helpful. A destroyer or similar vessel, moored to buoys ... would be useful for forecastle work, damage control, boat work and additional hoisting and lowering of sea boats. It might also be used for instruction on mess deck routine, cleaning, painting and scrubbing, hoisting and lowering a gangway etc.'

The boys' day started at 0545 and went on until 2045, which, the inspectors commented, did not allow 'a great deal of time for deploying general interests'. There was much instruction in electricity, English, mathematics, mechanics and chart-work, but general subjects such as history, geography and citizenship were 'seriously neglected'. The inspectors did not look at the most purely naval aspect of the course, gunnery, which was intended 'to develop the smartness, alertness and bearing of boys by instilling discipline by drill', as well as giving them 'an elementary knowledge of gunnery duties'.

Officers continued to worry about what happened to the boys when they left the training establishments. Often there was a gap before they could be appointed to a ship and even after that happened, the picture was not good: 'It is an undoubted fact that after only a short time at sea, boys have often been allowed to fall back to such an extent that they would hardly be recognised if they returned to their Training Establishment either individually or as a corporate body.'[41] It was claimed that 'after their initial intensive training, these young recruits of first class material ... [but] on first coming to sea, are easily led astray by the bad type of rating or the discontented National Serviceman ...'[42] It did not seem to occur to the authorities that boys in a highly restricted environment, under numerous and carefully selected petty officers, would naturally exploit their relative freedom once they got to a ship.

STOKERS AND MECHANICS

By 1944, as the navy looked forward to peacetime, there had been concerns about future recruitment to the stoker branch.

> It is apparent that in times of peace the best type of man is not being attracted into the Stoker Branch and the idea still persists that a Stoker shovels coal all day and any day into a furnace and that he works under appalling conditions of heat and dirt. Undoubtedly this is due to, and fostered by, the continued use of the obsolete title 'Stoker'.

Ideally the title could have been changed to 'engine-room mechanic', but that was already in use for 'dilutee' ERAs who were almost all hostilities only and were not held in high regard at the Admiralty. It might have been possible to adopt it for the stokers after the HO men had left the navy, but instead the compromise term 'stoker mechanic' was adopted in 1947. The term 'boy stoker' was adopted for the first time in 1956, and the 'stoker second class' simply became 'stoker', while the 'stoker first class' was now a 'stoker mechanic', led by leading stoker mechanics, petty officer stoker mechanics and so on.[43]

During the Korean War the engine rooms were manned by 'retention of expired men and calling up of R.F.R.s [Royal Fleet Reserve, made up of men who had served their time in the navy] large Special Service entries, reduced manning standards, dilution of higher ratings by lower ratings and enforced advancement of ratings without adequate training'. When the war ended in 1953, a crisis was looming. Moreover, recruitment was falling – entries of CS and SS men were almost adequate in 1950–2, but 16 per cent short of requirements in 1952–3 and 23 per cent short for the first three quarters of 1953–4. Most of them were recruited for Special Service, but only about five per cent of these signed on for the full 12 years. Captain N. E. Dalton was appointed to enquire into the matter and concluded that one of the greatest problems was that, at its lowest level, the stoker mechanic's job was still a very dirty one. He no longer had to shovel coal but,

> There still remains a considerable amount of dirty and unpleasant work which is today performed by Stoker Mechanics, the cleaning of boilers, both internally and externally, the cleaning of funnels and uptakes, cleaning of oil fuel tanks, scraping and painting the double bottom and wing compartments and other confined spaces and the cleaning, scraping and painting of bilges, in addition to the normal domestic duties performed by all branches. This is mainly menial and unskilled work of the lowest order, requiring little or no intelligence, except on the part of the supervisory ratings, but a tough constitution and an almost unhealthy disregard for diet.[44]

But at its highest level the work was very different:

For the other and more important duties of the branch, mechanics are required capable of operating and servicing highly complicated and extremely expensive machinery. For the higher ratings a very high degree of intelligence with the capability to think and act quickly and correctly, coupled with the ability to lead and take charge of other men, are required.

It might have been possible to share the dirtier tasks with the other branches, but that would not have been popular and would not have helped recruiting generally. A new branch of unskilled labourers could be created mostly on short engagements, but that would be 'an administrative and probably a disciplinary nightmare'. Dalton favoured the use of civilian labour for the dirty work, which was usually done when the ships were in port in any case.

The Admiralty enquired into this very seriously, but soon found that, with almost full employment, it would be difficult to recruit the men needed. There were already problems with retaining unskilled civilians for dirty work in the home dockyards, and even more unpleasant duties would not be attractive. The recent wave of Caribbean immigrants would not help, as 'limited experience at Portsmouth had shown that they were no more prepared to undertake dirty work at labourers' rates of pay than their English colleagues ...' It might be slightly easier in Northern Ireland, where there was high unemployment, and in overseas bases such as Malta, Singapore and Hong Kong, but employment would be casual and intermittent. Gibraltar had no civilian labour force, and at Simonstown in South Africa it was considered 'undesirable to attempt to recruit labour, which would inevitably be coloured labour ...'[45] The stoker mechanic was stuck with the tasks as long as steam power lasted, which seemed indefinite in 1954; only about 15 per cent of stoker mechanics had to be trained in the alternatives of diesel and gas turbines.

This created difficulties for Dalton's other solution, to upgrade the status of the stoker mechanic at the higher end. He did succeed in having the stoker belatedly renamed the engineering mechanic in 1956, almost a decade after the last of his hostilities-only namesakes had been demobbed. But he could do little about another grievance, that they spent far less time in shore billets in the home ports than other branches, mainly because there were fewer training courses available to them.

The two aspects of naval engineering work, operation and maintenance, had to be distinguished. The ERA and mechanician should be almost solely concerned with maintenance, while the stoker mechanic, or his successor, should do most of the operating and carry out simple maintenance. Dalton foresaw a decline in the work of the ERA with the rise of 'repair by replacement'. The operator 'cannot do anything about the inside of the machine and even the maintainer can do very little except replace a worn or defective part with a new or overhauled part from store. Efforts on the part of designers and manufacturers to ensure reliability also tend to simplify operation but perfect reliability can never be attained.' Therefore ERAs would be concentrated more in shore bases in the future, leaving the stoker mechanics to do most of the work at sea. Large numbers of inshore craft such as minesweepers would be 'non self-maintaining' in that they would be 'fitted and manned for operational use only, all maintenance being undertaken by base staff and maintenance ship staff'.

ERAs did not do well at petty officer school:

> They feel they have a right to Petty Officer status without having to be bothered with the disciplinary responsibilities which that rate carries. Their superior intelligence is often superficial and wrongly applied to the wider issues and they are susceptible to the views of the less reputable press. They lack both personality and the will to lead men either by precept or example outside their immediate sphere.[46]

If the stoker was upgraded then there would be less need for the mechanician, and Dalton was sceptical about his value in any case. 'Mechanicians by reason of their early station and somewhat limited training and instruction cannot compete on anything like equal terms with E.R.A.s in either the educational or professional subjects of the competitive examinations and it is rarely that they secure any promotion at all.' This, however, differed from the opinion of the CO of the Petty Officers' school at Cosham: they were 'quite different' from the stoker petty officers and 'of a high standard'.[47]

But Dalton's plans, inasmuch as they could be executed, would be interrupted by the development of new kinds of power – diesel, gas turbine and nuclear.

THE ADMINISTRATIVE BRANCHES

Like many twentieth-century organisations, the navy became concerned about the amount of paperwork that had to be done, and its effect on the writer branch of the service. It was involved in much shore work, for example, in admirals' headquarters. The C-in-C's office at Portsmouth employed five chiefs, three petty officers plus one part-timer, ten leading writers and four writers, including three Wrens. The branch was also responsible for administering the Royal Fleet Reserve, including 30,000 men, and the Portsmouth office alone needed eight chief and petty officer writers and 20 junior ratings. In addition to that, each seagoing ship had to have its own administrative staff.[48]

In 1951 it was found that large numbers were failing the initial training course at HMS *Ceres* near Wetherby. It was suggested that the pre-war competitive examination might be revived, but instead writers were to be selected from those who scored a minimum of 55 in intelligence tests at the recruiting centre, compared with 50 for a stores assistant, SBA or signalman and 45 for a seaman. After that they were interviewed at the Admiralty and asked if they were willing to become stores assistants if they failed.[49] Denis Sherringham joined *Ceres* as a trainee stores assistant in 1947:

> We had daily classes in which we were taught the four principal disciplines of store-keeping. These were, namely, Naval Stores, otherwise known as 'nuts and bolts'; Victualling, which dealt with our responsibility to feed the ship's company, including supplying its rum ration; Messtraps, or in other words, crockery and cutlery etc.; and, finally Clothing, which included 'Slops' ... and loan clothing.

Aboard a destroyer the administrative staff was quite small:

> On a ship the size of HMS *Aisne*, the entire feeding of the ship's company, other than the officers, is on the shoulders of four people. There is the Petty Officer and his assistant. To them are allocated a Tanky, who is an able seaman, usually older and naturally more cunning than most on board. He is also the man that the Boatswain is most willing to release from his work force. His job is to assist the stores staff generally. Then there is the Butcher who is his counterpart released by the Chief Stoker. A young and green stores assistant has many lessons to learn from these colleagues, and some of these lessons could be painful, especially if he should forget himself and speak out of turn.[50]

SBAs

A sick berth attendant had high prestige on board ship, especially in a small one where he was often the doctor's only assistant, but it was very different ashore where he was one of many at the lower end of a large naval hospital. Sea time was scarce for junior ratings, which was a cause of complaint. The occupation of 'male nurse' was still considered quite unusual in those days, and it was found that the SBA's duties were 'such as to appeal to only a limited number of young men'. In order to fill up vacancies in the later 1940s the necessary test score for entry was lowered from 50 to 35, but this only filled up the courses with young men who could not cope: it was pointed out that, 'Nothing saps one's interest in a training course more than finding the course miles over one's head.' On the other hand, seamen were able to transfer to the branch, which some did after seeing their prestige at sea. It was also suggested that the name might be changed to something like Royal Naval Medical Assistant, but major reform had to wait until 1965, when the title was indeed changed and those in the more skilled branches were known as medical technicians.[51]

5

THE NAVY IN THE
AFFLUENT SOCIETY

Men retained during the Korean War were released by April 1954, nine months after the end of the war, having served between four and 18 extra months. This in itself did not aid the manning position, and another factor was that men who had signed on for seven years in the late forties were now approaching the end of their terms. Everything depended on persuading them to sign on for a further five years, with good prospects of promotion. However, this was not very successful, and numbers were consistently described as 'disappointing' and 'very low' in the First Lord's statements to Parliament. Re-engagements of 12-year men were far more successful, at 40 per cent (though that was well below pre-war figures of 60 per cent). But less than 2,000 men came to the end of such engagements in 1956, compared with 8,000 who were completing their seven years. It seems clear that men on seven-year engagements did not envisage a full naval career, always had an eye on 'demob' and did not seek promotion as hard as they might. A large proportion of those on 12 years, on the other hand, had already gone a considerable way towards a pension, had become accustomed to naval life and were prepared to stay on. Meanwhile the recruitment of regulars continued to disappoint, dropping from 11,000 in 1951–2, to 7,500 in 1955–6. The Suez Crisis of 1956 caused another extension of engagements and recall of reservists, with 1,200 seven-year men being kept on for up to four months. But the long-term manning problem remained, and reform was needed.

The Admiralty settled on a compromise period of nine years as the standard engagement. By an Admiralty Fleet Order of March 1956, the initial nine-year engagement (LS1) might be followed by LS2 to take it up to 14 years, and a further one, LS3, to complete time for a pension. The main exception to this was the artificer apprentice, who was to remain on 12 adult years because of his long and expensive training.[1] It is significant that, despite the great privileges granted to artificers, recruitment of apprentices remained low under the new scheme – only about 400 were recruited per year instead of 525 needed. But for other branches it proved far more satisfactory, and in 1958-8 around 8,200 were recruited compared with 6,800 at the low-point the year before. This was enough to cover the needs of a fleet that had been reduced to less than 100,000 men and was indeed planning the early retirement of up to 950 older ratings.

BOYS INTO JUNIORS

Captain Michael Le Fanu was one of the most progressive officers, and he had seen a good deal of American ways. Things began to change rapidly when he was appointed to the command of *Ganges* in 1954:

> Arguably the most feudal of all the Navy's institutions was HMS 'Ganges', the training establishment for new entrants situated on the Suffolk coast at the junction of the Rivers Stour and Orwell. Generations of young lads, separated for the first time from home and parents, made their first acquaintance with the Navy in this place. Many of them hated it, and most found it hard at first to come to terms with Naval routine ... the treatment the boys received ... would probably have been little different had the year been 1914.[2]

Meanwhile, the Admiralty was planning an extension of the boys' training scheme into other branches – stokers, for example, no longer had to be fully grown to shovel coal. By an order of March 1956, it was planned to recruit boys in the proportion of seven seamen to two engineers, one electrician and one air mechanic. They were to be renamed 'juniors' and the designation 'Boy' was to be eliminated. Electricians and some of the seamen would go to *St Vincent* for their basic training, while the rest of the seamen would go to *Ganges* with the engineers and naval air mechanics. There would be a common course for all for the first half, and in the second half there would be 'an increasing bias towards the technical requirements of the branch to which the rating belongs'. Juniors would then go to more specialised schools because, 'The more expensive technical equipment needed in the later stages of technical training can be supplied only at the Technical schools.'[3]

THE BRANCH OFFICER AND THE SD

The naval warrant officer had not come well out of the war. As well as being dismissed as 'those forlorn and most pathetic of creatures' by John Whelan and 'Martinets, sticklers for the letter of the law' by George Melly, increased contact with other services exposed the anomalies of their position, for they tended to be treated as glorified NCOs like their army and air force namesakes. When captured during hostilities, they often struggled to establish their officer status, otherwise they were sent to a camp for NCOs. The Admiralty still had a good deal of regard for the warrant officer and tried to improve his position. It found that only a third of them were serving in seagoing ships, mostly larger ones where they tended to live in separate messes. But in shore bases, separate warrant officers' messes were quite rare, and there were none in air stations, so the social segregation of the warrant officer was becoming obsolete. New titles for the rank were suggested, including 'mate', but this would have been awkward as it traditionally meant an assistant to a warrant officer, such as gunner's mate. It was decided to use the title of 'commissioned boatswain', 'gunner', etc., for the basic warrant officer and upgrade the former commissioned warrant officers to 'senior commissioned officers'. The group as a whole were now to be known as 'branch officers' and the term 'warrant officer' disappeared from the navy.[4]

This situation lasted until the mid 1950s, when it was decided to upgrade the branch officers to become true commissioned officers.

They were to be known as 'special duties officers' and wore the same uniform as other officers – an attempt to give them different buttons was excoriated in the press and withdrawn. They were naturally considerably older than other officers on being commissioned, and promotion tended to be much slower after that. The path only took them up to commander, but posts at that rank were rare and most would expect to retire as lieutenant commanders.[5] Though a few had the chance to transfer to the general list for greater opportunities, the majority were expected to accept that they had done very well in reaching commissioned rank at all.

The officer corps itself had changed during the years after the war. An attempt to recruit cadets for Dartmouth at 16 rather than 13 had failed, and now they began at 18. The entry to Dartmouth was broadened, the navy relying less on traditional naval families. The seagoing midshipman was abolished, and instead cadets spent some time in a training ship doing menial jobs and learning some, at least, of the work of the lower deck, so the gap between the lower deck and the quarterdeck was narrowed considerably. A supplementary list was set up, initially for aviators, of officers who did not expect a full career in the navy. These, along with the new SD officers, would fill out the lower ranks, which were needed in large numbers because of the demands of naval aviation, greater technical skill and an increase in the number of small ships such as minesweepers. An ex-Dartmouth officer now had a 75 per cent chance of reaching commander as against 50 per cent in the past.

Suez

In 1956 President Nasser of Egypt nationalised the Suez Canal, which was still regarded as essential to British interests. The British and French governments colluded with Israel, who launched an attack on Egypt across the Sinai, whereupon the two Western powers embarked upon a spurious peacekeeping mission to keep the two sides apart by landing near the Canal. David Grantham was given a sudden draft chit, a 'pier head jump', to join an old landing craft at Llanelli in Wales:

> We didn't know why we were bringing this ship back into commission, but we had an idea that the crisis in the Canal Zone might have something to do with it. Cleaning her up was probably the dirtiest job I have ever been involved in. Once we had cut our way into the ship we found that everything had been covered with a thick coat of black grease, to stop everything rusting. We had been given a week to bring her back into commission. How the Engineers and Electrical departments got all the machinery working, I don't know. But a week later we sailed her out of Llanelli and took her to Devonport to store ship. Once we had taken on board all the materials needed to fight a ship we sailed for the Med ...

Eventually he went into action:

> We went to Action Stations a couple of hours before dawn. We had had something to eat a bit earlier, not that we felt much like eating. I was up on the Fo'c'sle, strapped into my gun, the ammunition drum was in place, and the loading number was ready with the next full one. All set to create mayhem!! Then the Bombardment began. The British and French ships opened fire on Port Said ... We could see fires breaking out all around the Port, the Oil tanks just at the start of the canal went up. What a sight that was ... The significance of our being loaded with Communications Wagons became obvious to us. As dawn broke we sailed into Port Said Harbour behind some Minesweepers ... We were the first Landing Craft in. The first thing that we saw was the masts and funnels of ships that had been sunk in the Harbour and the entrance to the Canal ... They precluded any normal ship from passing through the harbour to the Canal. Of course as we had a flat bottom we were able to negotiate the 'block ships' without endangering ourselves with collisions ... The bombardment must have been very successful for not a single shot was fired at us. So I didn't have the opportunity to show my undoubted skill at firing my gun!!

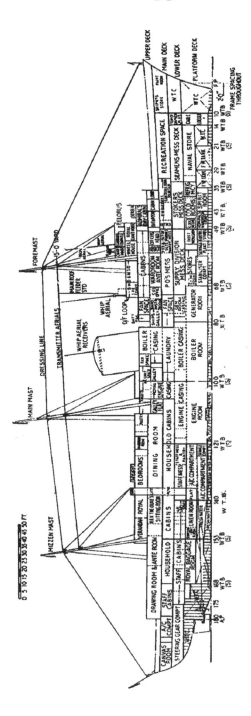

A section of the Royal Yacht *Britannia*, showing the crew's quarters forward.

The Americans were outraged by the attack and exercised economic pressure, which caused the British and French to withdraw. Grantham believed that 'the Americans had let us down badly', but a more common view was that the whole affair, though well handled militarily, had been a reckless political gamble, and it soon led to the resignation of the Prime Minister, Sir Anthony Eden.

One result of the Suez Campaign was a renewed emphasis on amphibious warfare, which had languished since the war but now became one of the navy's main priorities. 'Minor' landing craft operating from ship to shore were mostly manned by Royal Marines, while the army had its own fleet of tank landing ships and craft, and the six landing ships (logistic) of the *Sir Lancelot* class were manned by the Merchant Navy. This left the Royal Navy to man the landing ships that would transport the smaller landing craft to the operational area and launch them. The most notable were the assault ships *Fearless* and *Intrepid*, which were built in the mid-sixties. The success of 'vertical envelopment' at Suez also meant that aircraft carriers *Albion* and *Bulwark* were converted to commando carriers, with a complement of up to 900 troops and 16 helicopters.

THE NAVY AND THE MONARCHY

The navy had been closely connected with the Royal family for more than a century. Since the funeral of Queen Victoria it had been customary for the seamen of HMS *Excellent* to pull the gun carriage bearing the coffin, and this was maintained at the funeral of George VI in 1952, seen by millions on cinema newsreel. The new queen was married to a naval officer, Prince Philip, and two of her sons would in due course go into the navy. The Coronation Naval Review of 1953 provided an impressive display of British sea power – but some of the carriers had come straight from the reserve and had no aircraft allocated to them.[6]

The association with royalty was important in an age when the monarchy was almost unquestioned, and it was reinforced when the new Royal Yacht *Britannia* entered service in 1954. At first the crew members were intended to serve the remainder of their careers in the ship, only being returned to general service on the grounds of unsuitability, but that was relaxed in 1955. They were allowed a shilling a day extra, partly in compensation for the lack of promotion opportunities, for seaman would not be able to get essential specialist qualifications. They did long periods at sea and often at short notice, but according to the Rear Admiral Royal Yachts, the privileges included serving the Royal Family, freedom from normal drafting, good shipmates, prospects of employment to the age of fifty, and periods off duty in Portsmouth when the ship was refitting.[7]

They had to conform to a very strict dress code – 'Royal Yachtsmen should be the best dressed men in the Navy. It is inexcusable for Royal Yachtsmen to wear dirty or torn uniforms, faded badges or dirty gym shoes.' They wore a special badge, the Royal Yacht flash, on the right arm, and gym shoes were normal wear so as not to disturb the royals. Going ashore they were not allowed to wear zip-fronted jackets, except in Portsmouth; however, overdressing could also lead to trouble: 'Once ashore, if you feel conspicuous against potentially abusive or hostile people, and there is nowhere else you would be less threatened, jackets and/or ties may be discreetly removed (senior man present to decide).' And off duty on board, rules had to be obeyed. 'In Harbour sunbathing may take place on the FX [forecastle] out of working hours provided that semi-naked bodies are not visible from outboard.'

Among the first engine room staff was Leonard Willlams, who had kept the engines of the frigate *Amethyst* running in the Yangtse: 'Then followed 12 wonderful years, with three round-the-world trips and visiting so many countries with wonderful welcomes.'[8] Dave Rushforth also worked in the engine room, 'remembering that 30ft above your head was Her Majesty'. He took part in the Silver Jubilee tour of 1977, doing 44,000 nautical miles and visiting New Zealand and Australia, the West Indies, the United States and the Pacific Islands. 'We saw every beautiful country. When you are on this ship, you get the best parking spot in town. In New York, we went to Manhattan. It was a fabulous year, though we were all very busy.' On a more homely note, the yacht made an annual trip to the Western Isles of Scotland as recounted by Colin Manson: 'It was very informal and we went to private places, such as beaches which weren't accessible by road, where they would have barbecues. You'd get an eclectic crowd. The Royal Family would go to church on Sunday with you.'[9]

THE IMAGE OF THE NAVY

The navy, like the other services, enjoyed a certain post-war glow that was reflected in the wave of war films during the 1950s. *The Cruel Sea* and *Above us the Waves* both had elements of the 'stiff upper lip' film of the time, though the lip wavered considerably in a scene where Jack Hawkins as a corvette captain comes close to a breakdown. However, by the time *The Battle of the River Plate* was released in 1956, there were signs that the critics, if not the public, were becoming tired of war films. *Dunkirk* was vague about the navy's efforts to rescue the troops, concentrating on an army section and civilian boat owners. *Sink the Bismarck* of 1960 was almost purely naval, but it could not avoid the ambiguity of the victory of 1941 – *Hood* was lost through neglect and *Bismarck* was only sunk by a lucky torpedo hit and the use of vastly superior forces. After that, war films tended to move into fantasy and American domination. Another side began to appear in the film industry in the mid-1950s. Young men doing national service began to feel that their time thus spent was futile, and a wave of army comedies, starting with *Private's Progress*, showed soldiers as essentially lazy and corrupt. The navy largely escaped from this, except for *Up the Creek*, with an early film performance by Peter Sellers as a chief petty officer running a ship in the reserve fleet and fuelling the local economy with pilfered naval stores.

Society was changing fast by the late 1950s. The defeated powers of Germany and Japan had revived and threatened Britain's industrial strength. The Suez episode ended any hope of a truly independent foreign policy, while the final wave of decolonisation began with the independence of Ghana in 1957. There were full employment and high wages ashore, and the standard of living improved visibly year by year, with families buying cars, washing machines and television sets in increasing numbers – Harold Macmillan never quite said 'You've never had it so good', but the slogan did contain a great deal of truth. It was the first age of youth culture, as rock'n roll was imported from America with the music of Bill Haley and Elvis Presley and the home-grown Teddy boy. The growth of international air travel really began in 1958 with big jets like the Boeing 707, and this had profound effects on people's relationship with the sea. Ocean liners were no longer the best way to travel, while cheap flights and business travel meant that becoming a seaman was no longer the only way to see the world. Strikes were on the increase, and industrial relations within maritime industries such as docks and shipyards were notoriously bad. At sea British shipowners were innovative in developing the roll-on roll-off ferry and the gas tanker, but were left behind in the ever-increasing size of oil tankers. And the British merchant navy was no longer supreme in the world, as more shipowners moved to flags of convenience such as Panama and Honduras, while smaller countries like Norway and Greece produced some of the most active entrepreneurs.

Economic changes made the old-style naval career less attractive, as noted by the Director of Naval Recruiting in 1955:

In the days before the war we had something of real value to offer; we relieved the parent of the cost of maintenance of the boy, continued his education, gave him a training, ensured him a place in the Navy when entry was strongly competitive, and gave him the benefit which was then substantial of a guarantee of continuous employment up to age 40. The situation is now much altered. The parent of the normal family tends to suffer financial loss rather than gain by sending the boy to GANGES as it is not difficult for boys of that age to obtain wages which enable them to contribute substantially to the family budget.[10]

The educational climate was not particularly favourable to recruitment:

> Parents and schoolmasters are coming more and more to rely on the
> Youth Employment Service to find jobs for their boys at the cost of
> no effort to themselves or the boys, which can be bad for character.
> In inland towns, particularly, the Employment Service is subject to
> considerable and growing pressure from local industry which the
> Forces are in no position to counter ... In my opinion a woman, and
> most Employment Officers are women, is not the right individual to
> advise a boy about careers in the Forces. Several women to whom I
> have spoken baulk at the idea that a boy who joins the Forces may
> one day have to fight ... Some education authorities take the view
> that the Seaman Boy entry is unworthy of the standard expected of
> a boy selected for extended secondary education and that these boys
> should aim at entry as Artificer Apprentices or Cadets if they want a
> Service career.[11]

But relations with the press and media were excellent, according to
the Chief of Naval Information in 1954:

> The Navy still gets better free publicity than the other two services
> ... particularly so in the case of the BBC, both Sound and Television,
> where rarely a day passes but there is some mention of the Navy,
> either in the news, newsreel, feature programme, quiz or general
> knowledge programme. In fact the C.N.I. is credibly informed by his
> BBC contacts that their predilection towards the navy frequently
> gets them into hot water with the other two services ...[12]

ACCOMMODATION

Operating with the United States Navy in the Pacific near the end of
the war, naval ratings began to notice many anomalies in their
conditions. The authorities were shaken by an essay on 'Why I prefer
Civvy Street' by a rating in the cruiser *Black Prince* in 1945. There
were several reports on conditions in the US Navy all emphasising that

sailors on American ships slept in bunks, messed in separate cafeterias and had such amenities as recreation rooms, laundries, barbers' shops and even soda fountains. Michael Le Fanu recommended modernised washrooms with more showers, greater distilling capacity for water, laundries, barbers' and tailors' shops, more recreation facilities and films three times a week – though he emphasised that this was a personal view. Early in 1946, in an unaccustomed attempt at democracy, the Admiralty asked the admirals to report on ratings' preferences for folding bunks, tiered bunks and hammocks in different climates. The replies were overwhelmingly in favour of the folding bunk. This came before the Admiralty in July, where it was pointed out that the results were mainly from HO men rather than from regulars; furthermore, the adoption of an American system would mean the elimination of mess life, which had been the basis of the navy's morale for many years. It was decided not to proceed with the fitting of bunks, especially in view of the financial stringency of the period.

The issue was revived two years later as the new aircraft carrier *Hermes* was fitted out. She already had centralised messing, in which the canteen took up a good deal of space, and it was impossible to find enough room to sling hammocks without using corridors and other communal spaces. A trial was carried out on the converted aircraft carrier *Perseus* using portable three-tier bunks, which could be folded up during the day. Figures showed that a hammock needed ten feet of space to sling it, while a bunk only needed six feet and could be fitted in three or four tiers. The bunk was heavier and more expensive at £78 for a three-tier arrangement, but the practice of lashing up hammocks in netting was now regarded as insanitary. It was decided to adopt bunks for large ships, but the doubts about small ships continued well into the 1950s. Though a report from the Far East at the time of the Korean War showed the advantages of bunks, the debate was not allowed to re-open until a working party was set up in 1955. This recommended centralised messing and bunk sleeping throughout the fleet, with 17 square feet per man for sleeping and 4 square feet in the dining hall. This was to be carried out in new ships, including the *Hermes* class carriers, *Tiger* class cruisers, County class destroyers and the Tribal and *Leander* Class frigates; it was too late to make changes to the aircraft direction and anti-aircraft frigates of the 'big cat' and Cathedral classes. This was approved and became official policy in March 1956.[13] It took some time to work through, and it is not clear when the last hammock disappeared from the navy, but when the frigate *Jaguar* (one of the 'big cats') was taken out of the reserve in 1975 for use in the third Cod War, she still had a large proportion of men sleeping in them.[14] In 1985 the Royal Naval Presentation Team was asked, 'Do Wrens sleep in hammocks?' 'This took the team unawares, partly because most of them could hardly remember what a hammock looked like.'[15]

THE FAMILY

Though the navy had quite sophisticated welfare systems on board ship, it was a long way behind the RAF in recognising the serviceman's life off duty. Since recruiting could no longer be taken for granted, the navy at last had to recognise the existence of the sailor's family. Rear Admiral (later Admiral of the Fleet Lord) Lewin observed in 1968, 'The greatest single factor is no longer the man but the man and his family, and the wife has the greatest effect on the re-engagement rate.'[16] But to start with it was outside pressure that obliged the navy to build its first married quarters, just after the war, as government moved towards equal conditions for all three services. Post-war housing problems were also a factor, particularly in heavily bombed cities such as Portsmouth and Plymouth, and in 1949 it was reported, 'Largely due to acute housing difficulties, the wife of today is much more dependent on her husband; the incidence of wives suffering from neurosis and nervous debility requiring the presence of a husband is on the increase.'[17]

Initially married quarters were only planned for personnel serving abroad and for remote stations at home, especially the numerous and often isolated Royal Naval Air Stations that had been built during the war, where private rented accommodation was almost impossible to find. The navy had no existing stock of such accommodation, and only 2,378 units had been built by 1955, but it was decided to extend the policy to the home ports, where it had always been assumed that married ratings could find their own lodgings. There were plans to complete 4,500 more dwellings by 1960. As the Admiralty Fleet Order (AFO) commented, 'This extension presents its own problems: how to allocate the quarters which will become available so that all married personnel wishing to occupy a quarter shall have a fair chance of doing so.' All married ratings over 21 were entitled to apply, but priority was to be given to those who were definitely living together, 'to ensure a maximum of home life during the occupancy'. In addition, 'The first claim ... should be with those who have been separated from their families for fifteen months or more without being joined by them or to visit them during seasonal leave periods.' No one was to occupy the same quarters for more than three years. There were separate waiting lists for CPOs, who would have 30 per cent of the accommodation; petty officers who would have another 30 per cent, and junior ratings who would have the remaining 40 per cent.[18] In 1958 it was decided to extend the scheme further to aid recruiting; by 1960, 7,000 quarters had been built, with 1,300 more under construction.[19]

Another post-war privilege for families was the right to paid travel to join a man on foreign service. The journey out was done by sea, and meeting up could be a chancy business, as Petty Officer Leonard Charles Williams discovered. He found a home in Bermuda, but his cruiser, *Glasgow*, had sailed before his wife could come out: 'My wife and son's passage had been booked in M.V. *Reina del Pacifico* due to sail from Liverpool in January, which meant that they would be arriving whilst we were away on our cruise. However the Commander-in-Chief's wife, Lady Tennant, and her navy wives committee, always received new arrivals from home, so I had no worries on that score.' But he did have a scare during the cruise when he heard that he was to be drafted to the China Station, without a chance to rejoin his family – he quickly had it cancelled on the grounds that seasickness made him unfit for the small ship he was to join. Finally back in Bermuda, he was delighted when Lady Tennant brought his wife and son out with her in the admiral's barge. 'After our meeting, I went ashore for the rest of the day, and from then on, until *Glasgow* sailed for the summer cruise, we enjoyed an idyllic family life with me coming home from the ship each day at 4 p.m. Before tea, we could go for a swim in the natural bay at the end of our garden.'[20]

Denis Sherringham was posted to Malta, where Lady Mountbatten was just as active in support of naval families. This was a comfort to his wife, who like most women of the day had never been abroad before. They found a flat and lived on 'ration allowance', which was paid to men and their families living ashore. They employed a 14-year old Maltese maid, 'a hard-working young lady who would arrive at dawn and stay all day for just a few shillings a week'. Again there was confusion as his ship, *Armada*, was sent home. His wife was due to fly out, but fog in England led to a great backlog of naval personnel waiting to fly home, and there were many delays. And there was a scare when an RAF plane (not the one she was on) was lost in a collision.[21]

In 1954 the Admiralty introduced the general service commission, in which a ship's company was kept intact as far as possible for eighteen months:

The primary need for personnel in a ship is to enable her to fight efficiently in war and to carry out her stated task in peace ... The Peace Complement must be able to maintain, administer, and clean a ship so that she can fulfil her peacetime functions such as showing the Flag, providing small landing parties for simple ceremonials or to aid the civil power, and also to maintain the ship at the high standard which is required at the outbreak of war. The complement, which should include a dilution of trainees to meet the training commitments of the Fleet, must be able to steam her and meet the needs of cold war emergencies and the early days of war, until she can be brought up to war complement.[22]

UNIFORM

As early as 1937, Captain Rory O'Conor had noticed the gap between the seaman's square rig dress and the one-piece overall worn for working:

> Wanted! A practical working rig for the modern seaman: it would solve most of our overall problems. The requirements of cooler climates seem to be some form of washable seaman's suit made of a similar but better material than the overall. It should be a better fit than the present overall, which always tears under the arms. The drawback in making it a two-piece suit is that the two pieces would soon be washed in different colours.[23]

The US Navy already had an answer in the the from of a light blue shirt worn with dark trousers. This was adopted by the Royal Navy in 1948 and reviewed in 1950 after some practical experience. It was known as 'action-working dress' or 'Number 8', and was to be worn 'in temperate, warm and hot climates', but not in exceptionally cold ones. It was used during action stations and in normal working, though not at night. Despite the disapproval of the commander-in-chief at Plymouth, it could be worn by crews formed up for leaving harbour, but not outside the ship or dockyard except for men 'moving in formed bodies or travelling in motor transport'. In cooler weather the uniform could be worn under the seaman's jumper, or the jacket of Class I or Class III uniform. Ratings were to wear blue substantive badges on the left arm, on a white background, and similar non-substantive badges on the right.[24] In the past, naval manuals had invariably shown men dressed in full Class II uniform, even in the most inappropriate circumstances, such as swathed in bandages; now manuals tended to show men in the new Number 8 working dress.[25]

Meanwhile the Admiralty was considering improvements to the traditional uniform. After a proposal to make them in diagonal serge was turned down by the Treasury as too expensive, they had to compromise on quality. Changes finally came in 1955. Jumpers were fitted with zip fronts, while the collar was now to be fitted to a kind of waistcoat so that it did not have to be passed over the head, and trousers were fitted with conventional side pockets and a fly front with a zip fastener. Caps were now to be worn with white tops rather than changing to blue for winter, and a plastic white top was designed so that it could be cleaned more easily. Peter Cobbold wrote:

> At about this time officially a long zip could be inserted down the front of the jacket making it much easier to struggle in and out of it, but you had to alter your uniform yourself or have this labour-saving device incorporated in any new uniform that you bought from a naval tailor. However the old tube-style ones were still being issued as uniform in 1961.[26]

A more obvious change was the adoption of Class II uniform by all ratings below petty officer, so that writers, cooks, sick-berth attendants and so on now looked exactly like seamen. The Admiralty was keen to apply this, though it was agreed that the junior ratings in the branches concerned would not like it, so it was accepted that those already in the supply and secretariat and medical branches could continue to wear fore-and-aft rig. Any effect on recruiting would have to be accepted, and for the moment it was quite satisfactory for the branches concerned, except for stewards. The chiefs and petty officers of the branches were naturally in favour of the change as it tended to enhance their status, but the strongest objections came from the medical branch. In the first place, square rig was unsuitable for medical personnel, who might have to slip off their jacket and go into operating-theatre clothes quickly in an emergency, whereas taking off a jumper was 'almost a major operation'. A sick-berth attendant also needed pockets, which were sparse in square rig. He was often the only medical staff in a small vessel, and his status needed to be protected – in fact it might be better to distinguish him even more from the common herd, in the manner of a 'redcap', or military policeman, in the army. Moreover, the square-rig uniform then issued was too tight around the waist and arms, which could contribute to skin disease, while the woollen jumper was worn next to the skin and was difficult to wash, so it was often worn dirty. The dress offered no protection round the neck and shoulders, which were vulnerable to the flash of an explosion. The peaked cap offered better cover than the seaman's cap, and the bell-bottomed trousers would give no protection in a nuclear blast.

The Admiralty was 'not disposed to attach too much importance to these criticisms'. The new-style zip-fastened uniform, when adopted, would be easier to remove and would have more pockets. In battle or in danger of attack, seamen would almost certainly be wearing the new Number 8 uniform rather than square rig, which was to be reserved for ceremonial occasions and 'walking out'. There was only the remote possibility that men getting ready for a night ashore might be subjected to a sudden air attack. It was decided to apply the changes.[27] All petty officers, including those with less than one year's seniority, now wore fore-and-aft rig. Once the division between the two uniforms had been completely vertical, with all seaman ratings from boy to chief petty officer wearing the bell bottoms and square collar, and the miscellaneous 'men not dressed as seamen' in peaked cap and collar and tie. Now, after a series of stages, it was completely horizontal – all petty officers and above wore fore-and-aft rig, and all junior rates wore square rig.

It was gradually becoming accepted that sailors could wear civilian clothes when going ashore, though there were still restrictions on those below petty officer. Wartime rationing had ended, and clothes were relatively cheap, so that even the lowest-paid rating, such as a national service ordinary seaman, could afford to buy some. In 1956,

We were not allowed civilian clothes when going ashore from either ships or barracks in those days. We were sailors and had to dress accordingly when ashore, but many chaps would slip into the toilets at the top of the Khyber Pass [near Chatham naval barracks] and change into their civvies there. A wander about the town seemed all the sweeter when dressed as a free civilian ...[28]

By 1958, however, ratings were allowed to wear plain clothes when going on leave:

Although additional stowage space is not provided, it is evident that nearly all ratings contrive to keep some plain clothes on board and it is common practice for ratings below Petty Officer serving in ships to take plain clothes ashore with them in the U.K. and certain places abroad (e.g., Malta) and change in some convenient place – Service clubs, pubs, lodging houses etc.

To the junior ratings themselves this was 'irksome'. 'They found it difficult to understand why it should be necessary for them to wear uniform solely for the boat journey to and from shore or for the walk down the gangway and out of the Dockyard.' Nevertheless, the Director of Welfare and Service Conditions wanted to maintain the rules:

If the privilege of leaving and returning to ships at Home and at bases overseas in plain clothes is extended to all ratings, there would certainly be a marked reduction in the incidence of naval uniform being seen ashore since under the present arrangements not all ratings take the trouble to change on shore. Uniform will thus become more and more something to be worn only on ceremonial occasions and in foreign ports, particularly since No. 8's (working dress) is the normal dress of the day on board. Thus the beneficial effect of re-introducing gold badges, for example, will be partially nullified and recruiting might suffer more than it would benefit from the added privilege of extending the plain clothes rules.

The Director of Naval Recruiting agreed – 'The more that Naval uniform can be seen ashore the more it helps to keep the Navy in the public eye and the better it is for recruiting.' But they were swimming against the tide.

Caps remained a problem as it became increasingly common for civilians to do without headgear. The naval cap in particular was round and did not conform to the shape of the head, which aggravated the custom of wearing it 'flat aback'. In 1944 it was recommended that it should be given 'a degree of ovality' to reduce the problem, but that did not happen.

Badges were another bone of contention, though the authorities made a habit of consulting the men concerned before making any changes. In 1945 a new design for radar-control ratings was rejected on the grounds that 'it lacked decorative value and would be unpopular'. But the whole issue of badges was out of control, and there were 'many anomalies'.[29] In some branches, 'stars and crowns had been added to basic designs to indicate higher substantive rating even although this was already apparent from the rating's substantive badge'.[30] Badges had been red during the war, but increasingly gold ones came back into use. By 1955 they were part of the compulsory kit for all petty officers and leading rates on their 'best blue' suits.

ADMINISTRATIVE REFORM

The mid-1950s saw a series of reforms in the structure of the navy, which often swept away ancient practices, or changed more recent ones dating from the late nineteenth century. For the rating the most important was the ending of the old home port divisions, which no longer reflected the needs of the navy. With a smaller fleet and an increasing number of specialisations, it was not economical to keep up training schools for every branch in three different sites. In 1947 the C-in-C at the Nore objected to the running down of some of the training schools in the Chatham area:

One of the major objects in having three Home Ports is to enable those who have made the Navy their career to install their families close to it. It is necessary for a senior and highly trained rating to have access to his technical school during his home service ... The effect of closing the schools will be that the drafting of senior ratings to jobs near their homes, during their home service, will be eliminated ... Thus the closing of schools will seriously affect the morale and contentment of the officers and senior ratings.[31]

But this was a cry in the wilderness. By the mid-1950s two-fifths of the navy – officers, submariners, Fleet Air Arm, Royal Marines and WRNS, were already outside the home port system. As for the rest, the Admiralty recognised the advantages 'for men who have their homes in the south of England and near to the Home Ports', but it also had grave disadvantages. In particular,

The small size of the rosters in the three Port Divisions results in frequent disturbance to ratings. When a large ship commissions, for example, the Drafting Officers have to dip a long way down the many rosters to man her, and this means that some men of the Port Division concerned may find themselves drafted from their shore billets earlier than their opposite numbers from other Depots.

A man did not always have a choice in allocation to a division and could not exchange it without finding a man of the same branch and rating. He could only be sent to a shore base within his own command, and his prospects of promotion might vary from one division to another. In any case, large numbers of shore billets were some way away from the home ports. Instead a new system of 'centralised drafting' was introduced in 1955, which would even out the promotion prospects within each branch and give a fairer allocation of sea/shore time. Men could still state their preferences for the area in which they wanted to serve, and the Admiralty had no intention of disrupting family life, but this and the increased provision of married quarters meant that the adjustment could be made.

A new Naval Discipline Act came into effect in 1957. In the interests of service cooperation it abandoned the old claim that the navy was what the 'wealth, safety and strength' of the kingdom 'chiefly' depended upon and substituted 'so much depends'. It was more ecumenical in that the clause on religious observance deleted all reference to the Church of England. And it no longer applied solely to persons in HM ships and vessels but to all members of the navy – it was no longer legally necessary to keep up the fiction that a shore base, or even a naval air station, was in fact a 'ship'. Until then, for example, hundreds of people in HMS *Heron*, the air station at Yeovilton, were nominally attached to a 72-foot harbour defence launch with an actual crew of 14. But tradition was maintained, and practically all seamen were still attached to one 'HMS' or another, apart from those on the staffs of admirals – at first it was disconcerting to see a seaman with the cap tally 'Commander in Chief'.

Perhaps the most far-reaching reform was the setting up of a unified Ministry of Defence in 1964, sweeping away the Board of Admiralty, which had ruled the navy for centuries. This measure had less immediate effect on the lower deck, except that the Admiralty Fleet Orders were replaced by Defence Council Instructions (Navy).

THE FLEET AIR ARM

The value of naval aviation had been proved decisively during the war, and the possession of adequate aircraft carriers would define the navy's morale down to the present day. After a great deal of post-war scrapping, the navy settled down to use the remaining ships of the *Illustrious* class, of which *Victorious* was the longest lived and was fitted with the new-style angled deck in 1950–8. Many ships of the 'light fleet' classes were sold to allied navies, while *Hermes* was not completed until 1959 and *Centaur*, an improved version, entered service in 1953. *Albion* and *Bulwark*, completed in 1954, spent most of their careers as commando carriers. The greatest prestige ships of the navy were the 44,000-ton carriers *Eagle* and *Ark Royal*, designed during the war and completed in 1951 and 1955. The navy also needed shore bases, the Royal Naval Air Stations, for training, maintenance and to land carrier aircraft so that they could carry on training while their ship was in harbour. In the early 1960s these were at Brawdy in Pembrokeshire, Culdrose in Cornwall, Lee-on-Solent, the main base, near Portsmouth, Lossiemouth in Scotland and Yeovilton in Somerset.

The idea of rating pilots and observers was revived after the war in parallel with a similar RAF scheme, but abandoned by 1949 when it was decided that all aircrew should be officers who might be recruited from civilian life for eight years of service. The old TAG was falling into disuse, for modern radio did not necessitate a specialist operator to the same extent, and post-war aircraft did not carry non-fixed guns. The rating Aircrewman, however, began to revive in the 1950s with the use of Seamen (Underwater Control) who volunteered from the anti-submarine branch and were trained for nine weeks in the anti-submarine equipment used in helicopters, using 'dunking' sonar, which could be lowered from a helicopter to a depth of 60 feet below the surface of the sea. The Naval Airman (Air) was a volunteer from the aircraft handling, safety equipment or photographic branches, also trained for nine weeks in the use of equipment fitted in air-sea rescue helicopters.

The non-flying part of the Fleet Air Arm tends to be rather self-effacing and live in the shadow of the aircrew. It divides naturally into two parts – those directly concerned with the servicing of aircraft and the others of the naval airman branch. In the early 1950s, Fleet Air Arm recruits went to Lee-on-Solent where they had their initial training and were graded in three classes. Class A, up to 75 per cent, went straight on to technical training, usually as air mechanics. Class B spent six to eight weeks on 'general duties' at naval air stations and then went on to train for various roles as 'naval airmen' – aircraft handlers, photographers, safety-equipment ratings and meteorological observers.

The remaining five per cent or so, Class C, contained the misfits and were given three months' more disciplinary training in the hope that they might fit in somewhere. Thereafter, a man who still seemed unsuitable would be reported to the Admiralty, which would decide whether he was trying to 'work his ticket'. If kept on, he was likely to spend the rest of his career in the euphemistically titled 'executive duties' at a naval air station – menial work as a messenger or cleaner.[32]

The Fleet Air Arm used a great variety of aircraft in the 1940s and '50s, though the end of Lend-Lease with the USA in 1945 meant that spares for American types were no longer available and many of them were literally pushed over the sides of carriers. The branch was often technically advanced – a De Havilland Sea Vampire was the first jet aircraft in the world to land on a carrier, late in 1945. But lack of money meant that lead-times were long, and technology often lagged behind that of the Americans. In single-seat fighters alone, the Fleet Air Arm used the Hawker Sea Fury from 1947, the jet-engined De Havilland Sea Vampire of 1945, the Supermarine Attacker in 1951, the Hawker Sea Hawk of 1953, the Sea Venom of 1954 and the Supermarine Scimitar in 1958. The British never developed a supersonic naval fighter, so in 1968 they began to operate the two-seat McDonnell Douglas Phantom from America. In addition there were turbo-prop submarine hunters such as the Fairey Gannet, plus a growing number of helicopters. It is not surprising to learn that in 1952, 'Owing to the diversity of aircraft and equipment in use it is not practicable to teach a rating to maintain ... every kind of aircraft or equipment in service.' Instead he should be given 'a sound knowledge of the basic principles and a more detailed knowledge of the main types in use'.[33]

Air engineering ratings (apart from artificers) were divided into naval air mechanics (airframe), (engines) and (ordnance). After new entry training, naval airman mechanics (airframes) spent 15 weeks learning the trade. They were issued with tool kits and instructed in their use – important for Wrens who had not necessarily learned about such things from their fathers as boys usually did in those days. They were to learn 'to undertake first and second line servicing of Airframes on a single aircraft type' over 215 hours of basic technical training, 150 more hours on a particular type of aircraft, plus 62 hours of general education 'to prepare ratings mentally for the technical training to follow', plus 62 hours on discipline and morale, including rifle drill (not for Wrens) and naval customs. After training they started off in the equivalent of the able rate after training, but had fairly fast promotion to leading rate, for substantive rank was much more closely linked to technical skill than in the seaman branch. In 1961 it was complained that in the branch, 'the half and half proportion of Leading to Junior Rates resulted in a low standard of Leading Hand who, while being technically competent, had little or no opportunity to exercise his authority or powers of leadership'.[34]

The course for leading airman mechanic (airframes) would equip a man or Wren to 'carry out all first and second line servicing operations other than those requiring the use of metal cutting tools or the stripping of complicated components'. It too included some discipline and morale training, 'to inculcate qualities of leadership and ability to take charge'. Another role was the short-lived rating of pilot's mate, a leading naval airman mechanic (or Wren in a shore base) who assisted the pilot with pre-flight checks, on the scale of one per aircraft. On reaching leading-hand level they were eligible for six months of training as petty officer air fitters, which would equip them to deal with 'any maintenance work normally expected of a Naval Manned Unit that does not require the use of a machine tool'.[35] Naval airmen petty officers were reported to have 'a very marked pride in their branch, confident that the future belongs to them, and they take an obtuse pleasure in the belief that the rest of the Navy does not realise it'.[36]

Wrens were employed in some numbers on Royal Naval Air Stations, where they provided a certain amount of stability because they could not be drafted to sea. This caused mixed feelings among the male ratings who worked with them. On the petty officers' course in 1951, it was reported that the participants 'intensely dislike having to work with Wrens', but the air branch commented, 'This is largely a matter of taste. In remote stations most ratings are only too pleased to have Wrens included in the complement. Quite often the presence of Wrens makes ratings dress and behave better.'[37] But Wrens in the kitchens or offices were a different matter from those doing manual work in very close contact with male ratings, an issue that would come to prominence much later.

The less technical branches were becoming increasingly important. Wartime experience, and working with the Americans, had shown that effective use of an aircraft carrier demanded swift handling of the aircraft on deck and in the hangar, for example striking them down below to clear the decks for others to land, and launching as quickly as possible so that a large strike could be mounted without having to turn the ship into the wind for too long. All this demanded far more training than the casual use of seamen and stokers early in the war, and the aircraft handler, though usually inferior to the air mechanic in terms of examinations passed, was an important member of the team. A team of a leading hand and nine able rates was used for each hangar for aircraft weighing 20,000lb or more, down to a leading hand and five able rates for a smaller plane. In addition there was a flight-deck party of three men for each aircraft in the complement, plus a damage-control party of a petty officer and nine men per hangar deck.[38] Aircraft handlers were trained ashore in parking and ranging aircraft on a flight deck, on picketing them to keep them down in strong winds or bad weather, in the use of chocks and the deck hook, in rigging catapults and acting as the 'talker' to the deck landing control officer, or 'batman', who guided aircraft in when the mirror landing sight was not in use.

In time, aircraft became even larger – the supersonic Phantom weighed 58,000lb when fully loaded, compared with 12,660 for a Sea Vampire. This meant that mechanical power was increasingly needed to move them on deck and in hangars, and by 1952 the rating of aircraft handler (motor transport driver) was being recognised. Most of his work was in naval air stations, but he was also expected to know how to drive flight-deck vehicles.

Despite a general lack of resources, or perhaps because of it, the Fleet Air Arm was highly inventive in the 1950s and developed the steam catapult, the mirror landing aid and the angled deck. All these meant that much more could be done simultaneously on a flight deck, perhaps with landing and taking off going on at the same time. But it was a confined and highly dangerous environment, with fast-moving aircraft and vehicles, intense heat from jet exhausts, helicopter rotor blades and the constant danger of falling down a hole or over the side. This increased the skills of the aircraft handlers. By 1960 the informal post of 'captain of the flight deck' had emerged, a chief petty officer under the command of the flight deck officer who was 'responsible to the F.D.O. for organising the removal of the aircraft from the hangars and returning them and ensuring that the flight deck is ready at all times as required by the F.D.O.' He had to have 'a high degree of physical fitness which does not always agree with the age of the Chief Petty Officer; an intimate knowledge of deck work in all its aspects ... [and] a very high degree of power of command'. For,

> The safety margins in these days of high speed aircraft are immeasurably smaller than they were. Accordingly, the rating who is in overall charge of the various rating groups on deck has to be much more efficient and alert than before. He has to be versed in all the flight deck techniques of steam catapults, landing-on mirrors, firefighting, lift operating etc., as well as having the ability to keep an eye on every aircraft on the deck.'

R. G. A. Claridge served in this role in 1963 in HMS *Victorious* with great success, though he was only an acting CPO. When a colleague came to the head of the roster and was advanced to full CPO, it was felt necessary to displace Claridge, though the other man was far less efficient. This eventually led the authorities to establish captain of the flight deck as a formal rating in 1966.[39]

PETTY OFFICERS

The old problem with the supply and 'power to command' of petty officers did not go away completely after the war, though it was never quite so intense as it had been in the past. There was something of a supply crisis around the end of the 1940s as the men who had enlisted just before the war came to the end of their 12 years; according to a report, 'The great reduction in recruiting for C.S. and S.S. ratings during the war has put the whole structure of the Lower Deck out off balance. This, together with the relaxation of standards during the war, has generally lowered the quality of Leading and Petty Officer rates.'[40] As always, there were doubts about whether the increased pay made the petty officer rate worthwhile. In 1949 there was 'a strong feeling among Petty Officers that the extra pay is not worth the extra responsibilities, and that the proportional increase in pay of the Petty Officer has not been so great as that of the Able rate'.[41] And as always the petty officer found himself squeezed – 'Pressed from below and too frequently unsupported from above, many Petty Officers have seen little point in making themselves unpopular on the messdeck by enforcing a strict discipline ...'[42]

A petty officers' school was opened at Cosham in 1946, taking the name *Royal Arthur* after the wartime RNVR training base. Attendance was not compulsory, but there were 300 trainees in the summer of 1951, with a weekly intake of about 45 for a six-week course. In 1951 the CO commented that, 'The general level of Petty officers passing through this school is high. They are good material and if handled properly will, I am convinced, be fully capable of maintaining discipline and upholding the high reputation and traditions of the service.' But they had their faults – lack of pride in the service, a 'lowering of pre-war standards of discipline' and of religious belief. They were also 'allergic to History or Tradition. The mention of the name of Nelson, for instance, produces an immediately hostile reaction' – perhaps a result of Hannen Swaffer's *What would Nelson Do?*, which criticised the living conditions in the navy. The petty officers wanted to get into plain clothes as often as possible, they were highly influenced by wife and family and they felt the material superiority of the United States Navy keenly. They differed from branch to branch, the seaman petty officers were best at 'power of command' and showed 'a very marked superiority over all others in powers of leadership, ability to take charge and initiative'. Supply and secretariat petty officers varied widely, those of the Fleet Air Arm were 'just above average' but showed great pride in their branch.[43] The petty officer stoker mechanic was a special case, according to Captain Dalton in 1954.

> The P.O.S.M. spends almost the whole of his time as a watchkeeper, both at sea and in harbour; even the smallest ships, destroyers and frigates, usually have to keep steam in harbour now because of the inadequacy of shore or depot ship facilities for the supply of fresh water and electrical power. Whether this is good or bad is difficult to determine, some Petty Officers like watchkeeping and some dislike it. Experienced and observant Engineer Officers have noticed that prolonged watchkeeping tends to lower the morale of the watchkeeper – he lives a life apart from other men and gradually loses interest in the ship's activities.[44]

This was largely borne out by the report from the Petty Officers' School in 1951. POSMs tended to be young, often promoted at the age of 22–4, but 'they age quickly and are very parochial and set in their ways' due to their 'troglodyte existence', though the school's CO had no doubt about their professionalism. 'Despite these failings they have a sterling worth and I have the impression that in their own boiler rooms they would never let the side down through lack of guts or initiative.'[45] Later it was reported more sympathetically, 'There will always be an easier relationship between senior and junior rates whilst on watch, as it is almost impossible to adopt the more Olympian air of, say, the G.I. [gunnery instructor] when one has perhaps only two or three juniors in the same compartment for hours on end.'[46]

The year 1960 saw another landmark in the development of the navy. The last battleship, *Vanguard,* was towed away for scrap, and the first nuclear submarine, *Dreadnought,* was launched. In the preceding decade the navy had reformed itself almost as much as in the 1850s, though it kept the old forms. It still sailed mostly in grey ships (though not battleships and rarely cruisers) and wore uniforms and badges that would have been recognisable a generation earlier. But internally much was changed. Uniforms were much better adapted to the modern age. It had given up conscription and relied less on the boy entry, while conditions in the training schools were much improved. Sailors mostly slept in bunks rather than hammocks and ate in cafeterias rather than mess decks. The navy took far greater care of sailors' families. Promotion paths to commissioned rank were as good as they had ever been, and better in many ways. For perhaps the first time in its history, social change moved ahead of technological change. It would be needed in the decades to follow, when the navy had to take on nuclear power and the increasing use of electronics.

6

THE ELECTRONIC NAVY

Life in the Fleet

A recruiting pamphlet of 1963 painted a pleasant picture of naval life, which would have been recognisable thirty years earlier, for example with the Home Fleet:

Christmas finds the Fleet at its base ports, giving a fortnight's leave to each watch and night leave to as many others as can be spared. In mid-January they are off southwards. First to the North African ports; then ten days or a fortnight in the Atlantic, probably the longest sea period of the year, doing large-scale exercises against an 'enemy' conveniently provided by the Mediterranean Fleet; then to Gibraltar for a period when both Fleets are in company, with inter-fleet matches and many a meeting of old friends.

At the end of March, back home for Easter leave, laden with oranges, silk, Moorish leatherwork and all sorts of spoil from North Africa and Spain. For those who don't much care for the English February, the Home Fleet Spring cruise has much to commend it.

By mid-May the Fleet may be at Portland, for a gunnery and torpedo exercise and the pulling regatta. Then, in June, the ships go off in ones and twos, some to the Baltic, others to Norway. The charming handsome people of Scandinavia, living out of doors in the sunshine all summer, have a special welcome for our men everywhere. Then to the British seaside resorts, Portrush perhaps, and Oban, Aberystwyth and Southend. Finally to Torquay for the sailing regatta and so back to the base ports for summer leave.

The Autumn cruise starts in September, when the Fleet may take part in N.A.T.O. exercises. These are often held in Arctic waters and in the Atlantic and visits to ports of other N.A.T.O. countries are usually included in the programme. In early December ships return to their base ports to grant Christmas leave.[1]

There was an increasing tendency for ships to spend more time at sea. In 1949 officers had complained of a lack of sea time, especially for boys who should be drafted to sea as soon as possible, and attributed it to 'the small number of sea going ships caused by the economic crisis'.[2] In 1970, 'Compared with twenty years ago when ships spent 3 days in harbour for 1 day at sea they now spend 3 days in harbour for 4 days at sea. Also the intensity of work at sea and in harbour is much greater today.'[3]

NATO

Britain was a founder member of the North Atlantic Treaty Organisation in 1949, along with the United States and most countries of Western Europe. The Royal Navy had to cooperate with other fleets far more than ever before. The lower deck was particularly influenced by the US Navy, which reflected the glamour and wealth of that country, spoke the same language and had a roughly similar structure. Relations with American sailors, however, were ambiguous:

> That night we first met the USN crews (Elmers as they are scornfully named) they moored where they belonged – astern of us with further to walk. The rumour says that when the yanks meet 'jack', they (the USN) are riot-act-ed – told not to try to outdrink, outsmart, outfight or outanything us under any provocation, as they would fail on all counts singly and collectively. Except some wouldn't listen, and as they came into the DF [duty free] bar at Jufair – we saw it as our birthday and Christmas rolled into one. The USN run 'dry', whereas the RN don't. We had been used, then, to heavy, prolonged drinking bouts. They had been used to their onboard luxury of Coke and ice cream. They would start to drink with us and lose track half way through our normal session, at which time we would leave them to

sleep until we wanted to go elsewhere. We would carry them back, relieve them of their 'Popeye' hats, dump them at the bottom of the gangway and go back ashore ...[4]

Numerous NATO exercises helped fill the naval calendar. In 1961 alone, March saw 'Dawn Breeze', a fleet and anti-submarine exercise with France, West Germany and Portugal in the English Channel. In May in the same area, forces of five countries practised minesweeping. In June 'Fairwind VI' tested fleet and anti-submarine procedures with the Netherlands, Norway and Denmark in the North Sea, and in September there was a submarine-versus-submarine exercise involving the USA, Canada and the Netherlands in the Western Atlantic, followed by an anti-submarine exercise in the Northern Approaches. Finally in October there was a major anti-submarine exercise in the central Mediterranean. The navy still exercised with Commonwealth forces, for example with 'JET 61' in the Indian Ocean, and with the US and other navies in the Indian Ocean.[5] Another role was in helping to patrol the Greenland–Iceland–UK (GIUK) Gap to prevent Soviet submarines from entering the Atlantic. This was not the sort of duty – patrolling the cold and stormy waters close to the Arctic Circle – that featured strongly in recruiting material.

Common vocabulary was adopted by all the NATO armed forces, including the 'Alpha Bravo' phonetic alphabet. It led to a few additions to the seaman's extensive vocabulary, such as 'NATO standard' for a cup of tea with milk and two sugars.[6] Equally close to the navy's heart, the American term 'sonar' replaced 'asdic'.

THE BRANCHES

By the early 1960s, as the navy enjoyed a period of relative stability, it had nine branches for ratings. As always, the seaman branch was the largest, and about 60 per cent of its members were also trained in gunnery. The Torpedo and Anti-submarine Branch was next, and a new category of weapons mechanician had recently been created, open to members of the other branches. There were radar plot ratings and a small number of surveying recorders. The boom defence ratings mostly worked on shore on the booms and nets that protected harbours. Physical and recreational training instructors were still part of the seamen's branch, and selected petty officers might also train as coxswains.

The communications branch included men trained in automatic telegraphy, radio telephony, flashing light and wireless telegraphy, as well as coding, electronic warfare and the use of flags. The engineering branch included artificers and engineering mechanics, the successors of the stokers, a term that was still in use on the lower deck. The Fleet Air Arm had artificers and the less-skilled mechanics who worked directly on aircraft maintenance. Naval airmen included aircraft handlers, safety equipment ratings, photographers and meteorological observers – the last two groups having roles outside the Fleet Air Arm as well. Besides artificers, the electrical branch consisted of four main groups, the electrical and electrical (air) ratings, plus the radio electrical and the radio electrical (air) ratings. The supply and secretariat branch included writers, stores ratings, officers' stewards and cooks, who were still

The new technological image of the navy
as shown by Larry.

divided into Cooks (O) for officers and Cooks (S) for the ship's company. Besides the generalist SBA, the sick-berth branch included specialists such as the radiographer, operating-room assistant, laboratory assistant, physiotherapist and hygiene inspector, most of whom were employed in shore hospitals and bases. The artificers counted as a separate branch, which besides the traditional ERA now included electrical, shipwright and control artificers (weapons). Finally, the regulating branch could only be entered by those already in the navy. It included leading patrolmen, who were usually employed on shore, 'at Naval bases, and in cities, such as London, which are frequented by Naval men'. Masters at arms and regulating petty officers served as the ship's police on cruisers and aircraft carriers, but their role afloat was now restricted because there were few of such ships, and smaller vessels used coxswains instead.[7]

THE WRENS

The Women's Royal Naval Service was not abolished at the end of the Second World War as it had been in 1918, and in 1949 it was established as a regular part of the naval establishment. Wrens numbered between three and five thousand over the next forty years, and as the total numbers in the navy declined, the proportion of Wrens tended to rise slowly from less than four per cent in 1956 to nearly six per cent in 1983. In 1963, Wrens were offered technical jobs mainly in aviation, such as air mechanics. They needed GCE-standard mathematics and 'a bent for mechanical repairs'. Meteorological observers might be required to fly occasionally. The communications branch included switchboard operators as well as radio operators. There were clerical categories including writers and writers (shorthand), for whom certain skills were required before joining. The household categories included cooks for ship's company and officers, as well as stewards for the officers' messes and stewards (general) for household chores in the Wrens' living quarters – they needed to be 'strong and have a liking for domestic work'. Most women applying for medical work were sent to Queen Alexandra's Royal Naval Nursing Service, apart from dental surgery assistants, who mostly had some experience as dental receptionists before entering the service. A small number of regulating ratings were recruited with prospects of fast promotion to petty officer, while quarters assistants would assist in supervision of domestic staff, with fast promotion to leading rate.[8]

There were anomalies in the Wrens' legal status, however. When some male ratings and a Wren were caught smoking cannabis in the early 1970s, the men were sentenced to detention and the Wren to a £200 fine, which in itself was not legal. As a result, the law was changed, and the Wrens became subject to the Naval Discipline Act from 1978. As late as 1985, Wrens were still found to be socially superior to the average male rating. 'The personality difference between officers and ratings does not seem to be as great in the W.R.N.S. as it does among the men of the Royal Navy; many, or even most, of the women could pass socially as either officers or ratings.'[9]

THE SUBMARINE SERVICE

By the 1970s the navy could not rely totally on volunteers for submarines, and 'pressed men' had to be used on occasion. Most were recruited from the training bases with the promise of comradeship and extra money; a few were brought in later in their careers but needed much retraining because the skills required in submarines were considered to be very different from those needed in the surface fleet:

> Once a volunteer service, submarines began to take more and more 'pressed' men, and it certainly wasn't everyone's cup of tea. You could complain bitterly that you wasn't a volunteer, but the fact was that when you signed on the dotted line there was a clause, hidden in the small print, that you agreed to serve on any of Her Majesty's ships or submarines – so there. Once in submarines the majority stayed beyond the four years they were obliged to. This was due in part to the extra pay, which would be hard to give up, but mainly, in

diesel boats at least, there was a great feeling of belonging. And, I suppose, in my case I knew nothing else.[10]

In the submarine training school, some failed the escape tank, in which they had to ascend through 30 metres of water without breathing apparatus. Others did not come up to the medical standard or were 'unable to grasp the relatively high standard of technical knowledge required of them'. Yet more were 'temperamentally unfit for submarines', while a few deliberately tried to fail because they did not want to serve underwater. On board, a submarine was manned 'primarily on their requirement for sufficient specialist qualifications to operate on a three watch cruising system'. Men were taught how to operate steering systems and hydroplanes during their submarine training, and in addition, 'it is the practice for most ratings to learn the necessary skills on board their submarines'. Manual work was far less than in the past: 'Over the past few years the system of weapon handling in submarines had slowly progressed from a purely unskilled handraulic or manual process, with skilled senior ratings and officers in charge, to a mainly power operated system.' Non-substantive rating had far less significance in the submarine service. A man was usually given at least acting substantive rate on the basis of his technical qualification so that one with an underwater control Class 2 rate was promoted to acting leading seaman, and a UC1 to acting petty officer. After completing their service in submarines, men needed further training for the surface fleet, though sonar ratings had some experience of the behaviour of submarines and the effects of water and might be expected to adapt better. [11]

Britain adopted the snorkel from Germany soon after the war, so that submarines could now stay underwater for long periods and were no longer just submersibles. However, it was not necessarily comfortable in a snorkelling boat, as Andy Sugden found in *Opportune*, one of the classic O class of post-war diesel boats:

Despite the myths, not all submariners were volunteers.

Whilst snorting, a submarine is at its most vulnerable. The engine noise can give away the submarine's position and reduces the efficiency of the boat's own sonars, there are a variety of masts and periscopes making plumes on the surface and some aircraft could detect and track the diesel fumes. Therefore, if we were on station seeking Soviet submarines or reconnoitring shore installations, snorting opportunities were limited. A by product of snorting was that the air in the boat was refreshed by the engines drawing it in. The air quality deteriorated if we could not snort, despite artificial means of producing oxygen and removing CO_2. I've experienced atmosphere so bad that a cigarette lighter could barely produce a flame, and that flame a dismal green colour ... When we had crept away to a safer area to snort, the inrush of fresh air could leave you feeling giddy.

Sugden describes his first patrol:

I was, naturally, somewhat excited as my first dive approached. I don't know what I expected but the actual event was something of an anti-climax, other than a bit of a downward angle, a lessening of noise from the waves and a need to clear one's ears, there wasn't much to it. On the other hand surfacing could be quite exciting; we did one emergency surface with the split blow valve (a valve which allows the compressed air to go to both saddle tanks, or to a selected side) inadvertently lined up to port, the panel watchkeeper had been sat upon it apparently. This caused the boat to surface with a severe list to starboard. I was struggling to get out of a bottom bunk in the forward mess at the same time that the mess teapot and assorted crockery was trying to get in.

He soon got to know his companions well in the confined spaces:

Submarines, especially diesel submarines, had always attracted oddballs, eccentrics and grade-one listed loonies; Opportune had its fair share ... The After Mess would not have featured in any Royal Navy recruitment poster. Big and small, many bearded, covered in oil and grease from the Engine Room or carbon dust from the electrical rotating machinery, leering and blowing kisses in my direction — well, I was 'an essence bit of skin' in my youth .... My allotted 'sea daddy' was short of stature with a mop of greasy hair and eyes like a cat in a coal-hole. Despite the permanent grin on his pock-marked face, I doubt even his mother would call him a beauty ...

Undergoing his 'Part III practical training in a submarine', Sugden found himself at the bottom of the heap:

The lot of a Part III was not a happy one, even when off-watch you had to crawl around in bilges tracing ships systems, learning emergency drills, taking in the technicalities of everything from top secret sonar systems to how to blow the sewage tank, it was very intensive and there was an awful lot to take in and memorise. Personally I couldn't quite grasp the need to know the exact specification of the sonar, radio and radar outfits, but, on the other hand, it did give you something useful to let slip during interrogation by the Soviets.

At the end of the patrol the individuality of the crew was even greater:

By the time a boat got back to its home port after a patrol the crew were in a shabby state, long hair and beards abounded, pale sallow skin, disreputable No. 8 working clothes, it drove the Regulating Branch to distraction. There was usually a period of one week's grace before hair had to be returned to naval regulation length, a week that was usually taken advantage of. Once that week was over though the regulators were out in force, I was once picked up for a hair cut in the barber's at Dolphin as I got out of the chair having just had my hair cut ... bastards![12]

Britain's first nuclear submarine was launched in 1960, as the battleship *Vanguard* was scrapped, but its name, *Dreadnought*, was a false echo of the revolutionary battleship of 1906 – the new *Dreadnought* was some way behind the Americans and relied on their experience. Men were sent to the school at New London in Connecticut to learn the new techniques, though it was pointed out that the American ratings on the courses there were highly intelligent and educated – only artificers were likely to compete with that, and then only after some pre-training in the UK. The rating of artificer had been under question in recent years, but it found a new role with nuclear power. A rolling programme was set up from 1958 by which small groups of two or three ERAs and electrical artificers did nine months in the engineering schools at *Sultan* and *Collingwood* followed by a course at New London, after which they went to Barrow-in-Furness to 'stand by' *Dreadnought* as she was built.[13]

She put to sea carrying an unusually high proportion of senior rates. There were only 37 men competing for 24 seats round the table in the junior rates mess, but the senior rates mess had to cater for 47. 'Only 15 seats in Mess with six additional seats for people to sit around. Bunks can be dropped down in bunk spaces to form settees for remainder of ratings off watch.' It was accepted that 'the ratio of senior rates/junior rates is unusual and is unlikely to recur.' The crew slept in 6-, 9- or 24-man bunk spaces but the 6-man space was very cramped and the ventilation was poor.[14]

With the snorkel the crews were already used to spending quite long periods underwater, but the nuclear boat could stay down for months, and that added a new dimension. Routine was unbroken, there were few prospects of visits to foreign ports, and even night and day were almost unmarked. As a result, 'meals were an important focus of interest in a submariner's life. He often ate too much and tended to become too fat.' Even by the standards of naval surface ships, the diet was substantial, and they had 4,500 calories compared with 4,100. It was almost a caricature of the traditional British diet of the day, consisting of meat, butter, cheese, sugar and preserves, with smaller quantities of flour, bread, potatoes and fresh vegetables. 'The menus are no doubt what submariners like, but the menus present the men with unnecessarily calorific and not very imaginative food.' Constipation was common, and even the design of the toilet accommodation was unhelpful here. 'Constipation in submariners must be attributed in part to the present design of the "heads" which are too shallow to enable a man to sit in comfort without risk of soiling or infection.'[15]

ETHNIC MINORITIES

The navy had generally been racially inclusive in its recruitment policies for much of the nineteenth century, but non-whites were absent from the mess decks for the first half of the twentieth, except for locally recruited personnel, who were kept separate. The RAF led the way during the Second World War by recruiting in the West Indies, and in the late 1940s the navy abolished any colour bar, decreeing in 1948 that 'coloured candidates are now eligible to join the Royal Navy ...' despite fears that, 'For men thus brought together in confined living spaces there is an undeniable reaction against the presence of other races.'[16] Recruiting was confined to United Kingdom residents, for citizens living abroad had to be 'of pure European descent', and there were comparatively few non-white residents in Britain at the time, so it was unlikely that large numbers would apply. If they did, recruiting staff were to check that they were 'likely to mix satisfactorily with other entrants and hold their own in the corporate life of the service'.[17]

The large wave of immigration from 1948 to 1961 changed the nature of the British population, and in 1960 it was recognised that 'With the growing number of non-European British subjects living in the United Kingdom it must be expected that young men among them will look increasingly to the Royal Navy and Royal Marines for a career.'[18] The numbers of non-white ratings, however, were never recorded.

A personal description of every rating recruit is noted on his entry documents. This included place of birth, complexion, hair, eyes, etc., from which, taken together, an inference as to his race might be drawn. No notation as to whether or not he is 'coloured' is made anywhere in Admiralty records. It is not possible therefore to say from records how many 'coloured' ratings are in general service in the Royal Navy.

It had to be admitted that there were not many. 'Possible reasons why few "coloured" men are in the Royal Navy are:– that in general the 'coloured' element of the population of the United Kingdom is above the upper age limit for entry, that they are reluctant to undertake the long period of service (nine years) required of recruits, that they find civilian employment in this country more to their liking, that they are below the educational and intelligence standards required ...'[19] It might be added that West Indians traditionally disliked military style discipline, while Asians were often focussed on setting up their own businesses.

A problem arose with visits to South Africa. The navy was determined to keep up its base at Simonstown near Cape Town, particularly during a period when the Suez Canal was sometimes closed by Arab-Israeli wars. This was the moment when the racist 'apartheid' regime in the country was attracting world revulsion, notably with the Sharpeville massacre of 1960. The navy was careful to avoid posting non-whites to the shore base, or to frigates permanently based there, using 'informal knowledge within his organisation of who is coloured and who is not'. It was more difficult for visiting ships. When the carrier

Victorious went there in March 1961, all non-white personnel were taken off beforehand 'in order to protect them from embarrassment or possible incidents arising from apartheid', except for three ratings who had family in Cape Town. This caused great controversy – liberals thought it was 'a concession to apartheid unworthy of Britain', while some elements in South Africa believed that it was an insult to their hospitality, that they could entertain black sailors just was well in their so-called 'separate but equal' facilities.[20]

The passing of the Race Relations Acts of 1965 and 1968 in the UK forced the services to confront these issues. In fact, the acts did not apply to the armed services, but, as one minister put it in 1967, the government 'should set a good example to private industry in the field of race relations'. The army operated a semi-secret 'assimilation level' by which there should not be more than three per cent non-whites in any particular unit, or four per cent for medical personnel. In fact it had 2,400 'coloured' soldiers in 1968, less than the assimilation level figure of 4,700.[21] In general, the forces denied any kind of discrimination. 'Coloured applicants for Forces service are considered in the same way as any other applicants and they are required to reach the same standards for acceptance. They must be able to mix in the closed community of Service life and speak and understand the English language clearly so that they can communicate and understand orders.' [22] Specifically in the navy, 'No distinction whatever is drawn, on grounds of race or colour, in the conditions of service and accommodation of personnel recruited into the Royal Navy in the United Kingdom.'[23] But this was modified for personnel recruited abroad, such as Chinese laundrymen, and conditions were different again on merchant-navy-manned vessels such as Royal Fleet Auxiliaries. As to visits to South Africa, it was decided to give non-white crew the option of staying on, and it was found that, 'those who had gone recently had enjoyed themselves'.[24]

It remained true that ethnic minorities did not join the navy in large numbers. By 1998–9, they made up 6.7 per cent of the British population, but only one per cent of the navy. After a drive involving attendance at the Notting Hill Carnival and the Asian Mega Mela Festival in Birmingham, the intake was doubled in the following year.[25] In 2001–2 it was stated, 'While [equal opportunities] is about ensuring that minorities are not treated less fairly than the majority, Diversity is about recognising that people are different, but that good management can help them to reach their full potential, making them more useful members of their own team.'[26]

BASIC TRAINING

By the early 1960s the 15–16-year-olds, the Junior (U) entry, were sent to *Ganges* or *St Vincent* for a year while youths over 16, the Junior (O) entry, and adults up to 28 went to HMS *Raleigh*, near Plymouth. The course in the Junior Training Establishments was a combination of character-building, schooling and technical subjects. It was now based on a process known as 'hardening off', which was much less harsh than it sounds – 'The aim of this is to encourage the young rating to be self reliant and independent when he reaches his first ship. It takes the form of withdrawing supervision as the young ratings progress through their training, by allowing them spare time in the dog watches when they are encouraged to think for themselves and make profitable use of their time and giving them increased control of their pay and longer leave up to 2300 so they can learn to use both.' These were not concepts that would have been understood by the traditional *Ganges* petty officer. In 1967,

> The first 5 weeks of a Junior's term in GANGES is devoted to new entry routine and kitting up. This is followed by the Main Course of some 45 weeks in which academic, professional and character training take equal precedence. The School room however predominates for all Juniors (U) until ... week 13, or in the case of the less intelligent (about 5% of the average entry) week 17.[27]

The Junior (U) entry would end in the early 1970s as the school-leaving age was raised to 16, leaving much shorter courses for the Junior (O) and the Adult entry – six weeks' basic training and six to 29 weeks of specialised training, according to branch.

It was no longer necessary to maintain three separate new entry establishments in a smaller navy with shorter training periods. *Ganges* had the advantage that it had its own sea front for boat training and, unlike *St Vincent*, was not too close to a town centre where young men might be distracted. Its fatal snag was that it was 'divorced from a Naval atmosphere'. *St Vincent* was on a very restricted site in Gosport and would not be easy to expand. *Raleigh* had old wartime buildings 'of wood and asbestos, well past their normal life and very costly to maintain', but it was the right distance from Plymouth, there was room for expansion, there were boating facilities within a mile and a naval base close by, and Dartmoor was nearby for character-building training. It would cost £4.5 million to rebuild it, but it was considered to be the best option.[28] *St Vincent* was closed in 1969 and *Ganges* in 1976.

Recruits were now allowed to opt out after arrival at the training base, and could buy themselves out after six months at a moderate cost of £20. At *Raleigh* in 1969 (pronounced 'Raaahlly' by the officers), Michael Payne's group was addressed by their petty officer:

> He indicated in Anglo-Saxon that we were here because we had chosen to remain, and that here we were to be for the next sixteen weeks in some cases, and that if we were not prepared for it, we should get back on the bus and go home to mummy now. Or at least that's what it should have come across as. He was rather more graphic and succinct, even to my previously trained ears.[29]

Few left then, but some did soon afterwards. 'Following the crying we had heard coming from the various beds in our messdeck over the preceding days, we were not surprised when several kids got up and left, obviously preferring their mother's warm and tender company to ours.'[30]

SEA TRAINING

After basic training, seaman gunners and engineering mechanics were sent to sea as soon as vacancies occurred and the drafting process allowed. Radar plotters went for ten weeks of further training in HMS *Dryad*, near Portsmouth, potential TAS ratings to *Vernon*, near the centre of the city, electrical ratings to *Collingwood*, across Portsmouth Harbour, supply ratings to *Pembroke* in Chatham, naval airmen to the Royal Naval Air station at Culdrose in Cornwall, and air mechanics went north to HMS *Condor*, near Arbroath in Scotland. There they were trained in the basic non-substantive grade of their speciality.

Ideally they should have been sent to sea as soon as possible after that, but berths were not always available immediately, and boys and men might spend months filling time doing menial work in the barracks. Officers agreed that this was very bad for discipline and morale. In an extreme case, 15 boys spent a year ashore between Plymouth and Portsmouth, including five weeks' training for a rope-climbing act in the Royal Tournament at Olympia. After that they were 'a problem lot, all influenced for the worse by idleness and the lapse of time'. Another group of 15 boys, drafted to sea after only three months ashore were far better when they reached HMS *Caesar* in 1962. It was suggested that 'any sea billet is better than none'.

With the shortage of big ships, such as cruisers, increasing numbers were sent to frigates, where it was difficult to find separate mess spaces and training facilities in such relatively small ships. Aircraft carriers were not often used for this, probably because their flight decks were highly dangerous. However, in 1962 a draft of 60 was sent to the commando carrier *Bulwark*, making up 30 per cent of the total seaman complement, but their ignorance of basic seamanship commands made them 'a menace to themselves and their shipmates'. Captains were often disappointed with the quality of the boys, and in *Bulwark* they were found to 'show little pride in the service and very little in their professional ability. To them the Navy was just another job; they were apathetic and lacked esprit de corps ...' They compared badly with young Royal Marines, who had been 'indoctrinated with the history and traditions of the Corps'. Despite 'hardening off', the transition from the discipline of the schools to the 'freer life of the fleet' was not easy to achieve.

The Admiralty believed that 'how successful a young man will eventually be can depend on his first ship'. It was recommended that the junior seamen arrive as a body. On board they were usually borne 'as part complement', which meant that they had to take full part in the duties of the ship. In *Bulwark* they could be given a separate mess deck but only with 'some other accommodation difficulties'. It was even more difficult in a frigate. A good leading hand was needed to take charge of them, and it was suggested that one should be drafted specially for the task, as it was not always possible to find a suitable man from the complement, even in a large ship like *Bulwark*. It was recommended that they should work no longer hours than the adult ratings, which meant they needed a certain amount of time off watch for schooling, but there was rarely time for a separate 'junior routine'. In some ships they worked a full routine apart from that, but in *Bulwark* they were exempted from night watches, which 'caused some antipathy from the other seamen'. Apart from duties at their specialisation they did 'part of ship' work, which included 'a mixture of cleaning, maintenance and practical instruction, and they should never be treated as "slave labour"'.

Due to the long period on shore, and perhaps a lack of reality in the shore training, most of the youths had 'forgotten much of what they were taught by the time they joined'. The captain of *Bulwark* complained that orders such as '"Roundly", "Handsomely", "walk back" and "Square off" etc. had no message for the Juniors'. Furthermore, they had only learned how to operate sailing and rowing boats, so that putting them in modern, fast power boats was chancy. They did not know how to do the traditional seaman's fill-in work of chipping, scaling and painting. In some ships they were allowed leave until 2300 when in harbour, but the captain of *Bulwark*, with his low opinion of the juniors, insisted they were back by 2100. As he commented, 'they must not be allowed to feel that they are "One of the Lads" before they are fully trained and responsible seamen. It is a pity that they are no longer known as 'Boys'"[31]

THE SHIPS

Warships were still in transition with the decline of old classes, while newer ones such as the destroyers, frigates and submarines were taking on new roles. The last three cruisers, *Lion*, *Tiger* and *Blake*, were uncompleted at the end of the war and were not finished until 1959–61, with a largely anti-aircraft role – though that was already obsolescent as they relied on guns rather than missiles. The last of the older cruisers, *Belfast*, was converted to a museum ship in 1971. They still had a certain value as prestige ships, however, and *Tiger* became famous when she was used as a venue for talks between the prime minister Harold Wilson and the head of the dissident Rhodesian regime, Ian Smith, in 1966. They were converted to the hybrid role of helicopter carriers at the end of the decade, but that did not necessarily make them popular. According to Michael Payne the *Blake* and *Tiger* were 'scare ships' to the lower deck in the mid seventies.[32]

Eight new County class ships, rated as destroyers though at 5,600 tons they were as big as light cruisers, began to take on some of the anti-aircraft role. Completed between 1962 and 1967, they introduced the long-range anti-aircraft missile to the navy. The only immediate follow-up was *Bristol*, sole survivor of a class that was designed to escort aircraft carriers (which were never built). The Type 42 was closer to the old notion of a destroyer in size, but with a mainly anti-aircraft function and fitted with the long-range Sea Dart anti-aircraft missile. It suffered from being literally cut down to size due to defence cuts. Each ship in the first batch was 392 feet long and of 3,500 tons standard displacement, compared with 505 feet and 5,600 tons for the County class. It had a twin Sea Dart launcher and two Type 909 radar weapons directors to control them in round-topped domes, which were the main recognition feature of the ship. It had a helicopter and a 4.5-inch gun, but no room for close-range air defence. The first ship, *Sheffield*, entered service in 1975.

The classic *Leander* class of frigates of the 1960s was developed from the Type 12 *Rothesay* and *Whitby* classes. By the 1970s they were considered too small to carry out all the functions required of a modern frigate and were converted to three different roles; some retained the gun armament, some were fitted with the Exocet anti-ship missile, and some carried the Ikara anti-submarine missile. The Tribal class, seven ships completed in the early 1960s, introduced the concept of the 'general purpose' frigate. They were intended to operate independently in remote areas and carried the imperialist tradition into the post-imperialist age. Each had two funnels and two gun mountings, apparently to impress people in the Middle East where such things were said to be valued. Whatever the intention, they saw widely varied service, and when Michael Payne was sent to HMS *Dryad* after service in *Zulu* he found that 'my fellow course-goers between them had not been to as many places as I had'.[33] In accordance with their 'general purpose' function, the Tribal class introduced the idea of a small Royal Marine detachment of 22 men. This gave the marines sea experience when there were far fewer big ships, but different cultures and standards of discipline caused conflict between them and the naval crew. By 1980, detachments were borne on most frigates but were reduced to ten men under the command of a sergeant.[34]

Frigate design took a different turning with the *Amazon* class (Type 21), which were produced by private enterprise. They were the first to have all-gas turbine propulsion and had a racy, speedboat-like appearance that made them popular with the lower deck; but they had many weaknesses, which showed up in combat, and they could not keep up their speed for long without damage to the hull. The Type 22 was more successful and was the first to carry the Sea Wolf missile for close-range air defence, but in return it abandoned the gun, except for light anti-aircraft weapons. Only three of the class, *Battleaxe*, *Brilliant* and *Broadsword*, were ready for service by 1982.

SEA TRAINING AT PORTLAND

The office of Flag Officer Sea Training was set up at Portland in 1958, giving ships a chance to work in an intense atmosphere in the tradition of the wartime courses at Tobermory. It was all the more necessary because an increasing proportion of small ships meant that few had the resources and personnel to complete the process on their own. For example, the newly converted helicopter cruiser *Blake* arrived at Portland on 4 September 1969, five and a half months after commissioning, for a five-week course. During that time she carried out 34 anti-submarine practices including three live torpedo drops, 45 exercises with her guns, seven blind exits from harbours and four passages through channels supposedly swept of mines; her helicopters flew 150 hours by day and 48 by night, the engineers were tested in a dozen hours of machinery breakdowns and one total steam failure while the whole crew took part in dealing with mock atomic attacks. Detailed reports were compiled on the ship's defects, which were quite numerous and occasionally serious. There were also detailed reports on each of the teams that made up the ship's company. The plotters 'took time to settle down', a process made more difficult by the fact that the surface and underwater teams had to share the same table, which became very crowded during exercises. The local action plot team was very good but not the defence watch; and more use should have been made of the detector, a vital rating in identifying air attack. The sonar controllers were 'satisfactory' and could 'maintain the interest of their team in what could easily become a forgotten corner of the ship'. Seamen organised in two platoons did well in riot control and other land activities in 'Exercise Henry Morgan'. It was noted that the officers and petty officers had 'a strong tendency to become directly involved during evolutions while junior rates stand watching'. Training of petty officers was lacking, which was 'particularly regrettable in a ship the size of HMS BLAKE'. The Fleet Air Arm crews on board, from 820 Squadron, were 'well integrated in the ship.' The messes were rather inadequate, and there was 'considerable dissatisfaction' among junior engineering ratings over their accommodation. A deep fryer had not yet been fitted to the seamen's galley, though otherwise it was adequate. The fact that only six junior ratings had attended the paint course recently did not escape the eagle eye of the examiners.[35]

To Michael Payne,

> Portland meant anchoring out most nights, going alongside rarely, carrying out seamanship evolutions like RASing, towing, mooring, anchoring, coupled with exercise fires, damage control and pretend NCBD attack. And being closed up at Action Stations before the rest of the world was awake, and sailing out of the harbour line astern with all the other ships, knowing quite well it would be you who first saw the tell-tale echo of the Buccaneer [aircraft] from not more than 5 miles away as it came in at sea level to 'bounce' you. By the time you reported it, it was upon you with a roar you could hear below decks.[36]

THE OPERATIONS ROOM

Since the war there had been an increasing tendency to concentrate the operational control of the ship in the action information centre, or operations room, and from about 1960 it was normal for the captain to be there during action stations rather than at his traditional place on the bridge. An aircraft carrier had two operations rooms, one above the other; the upper one included the main command, and it had a perspex screen so that the officers could look down on some of the displays below. In a frigate it was a single room situated close to or just below the bridge so that the captain could alternate between the two. Research showed it was best near the centre of the ship, where the motion of the sea was felt less.

Information was available from various sources, including books of reference and intelligence reports. The availability of other ships and aircraft were posted on notice boards, known as 'totes', round the walls. Signals from other ships, aircraft and shore stations were coming in constantly, reporting their own positions or the movements of the enemy. The sonar picture was displayed on its own plot. But it was radar information that was most crucial and drove the development of the operations room, as ever-faster jet aircraft had to be controlled or countered, so incoming information had to be plotted instantly in a form that would allow the officers to decide what to do. In the older ships this was done manually by radar plotters such as Michael Payne:

> As the contacts were tracked, we used to record their progress on the plotting tables with chinagraph, a greasy pencil really, which shone brightly when exposed to UV light. We also used small widgets, which were colour-coded shapes, green for friendly, red for hostile, orange for 'dunno', which we placed on the contact, so anyone looking at the table would see us, and everything around us, these also glowed under UV, which is what the Ops Room was continuously bathed in. Otherwise the room was in pitch dark, and known as the 'gloom room'. Gloomy or not, we always had an audience – from clanks (stokers) to greenies (electricians) to stewards – they would all come to see the radar.[37]

It was done on an automatic plotting table developed by the Admiralty Research Laboratory just before the war, in which the ship's own movement was plotted automatically so that the true course of an object on the radar screen was shown and its intentions could be worked out. Payne became exceptionally good at this:

> Being i/c of the radar watch at steaming stations was great. I learned how to tell the course and speed of a contact on radar without having to work it out on the old mechanical plotting tables (this was a long

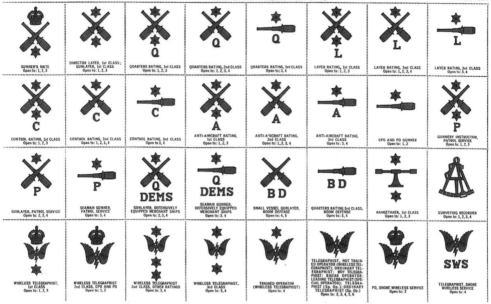

| GUNNER'S MATE Open to: 1, 2, 3 | DIRECTOR LAYER, 1st CLASS; GUNLAYER, 1st CLASS Open to: 1, 2, 3 | QUARTERS RATING, 1st CLASS Open to: 1, 2, 3 | QUARTERS RATING, 2nd CLASS Open to: 1, 2, 3, 4 | QUARTERS RATING, 3rd CLASS Open to: 3, 4 | LAYER RATING, 1st CLASS Open to: 1, 2, 3 | LAYER RATING, 2nd CLASS Open to: 1, 2, 3, 4 | LAYER RATING, 3rd CLASS Open to: 3, 4 |

| CONTROL RATING, 1st CLASS Open to: 1, 2, 3 | CONTROL RATING, 2nd CLASS Open to: 1, 2, 3, 4 | CONTROL RATING, 3rd CLASS Open to: 3, 4 | ANTI-AIRCRAFT RATING, 1st CLASS Open to: 1, 2, 3 | ANTI-AIRCRAFT RATING, 2nd CLASS Open to: 1, 2, 3, 4 | ANTI-AIRCRAFT RATING, 3rd CLASS Open to: 3, 4 | CPO AND PO GUNNER Open to: 1, 2 | GUNNERY INSTRUCTOR, PATROL SERVICE Open to: 1, 2, 3 |

| GUNLAYER, PATROL SERVICE Open to: 2, 3, 4 | SEAMAN GUNNER, PATROL SERVICE Open to: 3, 4 | GUNLAYER, DEFENSIVELY EQUIPPED MERCHANT SHIPS Open to: 2, 3, 4 | SEAMAN GUNNER, DEFENSIVELY EQUIPPED MERCHANT SHIPS Open to: 3, 4 | SMALL VESSEL GUNLAYER, BOOM DEFENSE Open to: 4, 5 | QUARTERS RATING 3rd CLASS, BOOM DEFENSE Open to: 3, 4 | RANGETAKER, 1st CLASS Open to: 1, 2, 3 | SURVEYING RECORDER Open to: 1, 2, 3, 4 |

| WIRELESS TELEGRAPHIST, 1st CLASS Open to: 1, 2, 3 | WIRELESS TELEGRAPHIST, 2nd CLASS, CPO AND PO Open to: 1, 2 | WIRELESS TELEGRAPHIST, 2nd CLASS, OTHER RATINGS Open to: 3, 4 | WIRELESS TELEGRAPHIST, 3rd CLASS Open to: 3, 4 | TRAINED OPERATOR (WIRELESS TELEGRAPHIST) Open to: 4 | TELEGRAPHIST, NOT TRAINED OPERATOR (WIRELESS TELEGRAPHIST); ORDINARY TELEGRAPHIST; BOY TELEGRAPHIST; RADAR OPERATOR; LEADING TELEGRAPHIST (SPECIAL OPERATOR); TELEGRAPHIST (Sp. Op.); ORDINARY TELEGRAPHIST (Sp. Op.) Open to: 2, 3, 4, 5, 6 | PO, SHORE WIRELESS SERVICE Open to: 2 | TELEGRAPHIST, SHORE WIRELESS SERVICE Open to: 4 |

Above: A selection of 'non-substantive' badges, mostly worn by the gunnery branch. This is only one of nearly five pages in an intelligence manual on military uniform, which still did not exhaust all the possibilities.

BRANCH BADGES

Gunnery	Radar Plot	Torpedo and Anti-Submarine	Coxswain
Surveying Recorder	Boom Defence	Tactical Communications	Radio Communications
Engineering Mechanic	Engineering Mechanician	Regulating	Naval Airman and Naval Air Mechanic
Weapon Mechanician	Aircaft Mechanician	Physical Training	Photographer
Electrical	Electrical Mechanician	Supply and Secretariat	Artisan
Sailmaker	Clearance Diver	Sick Berth	

Worn on the right arm except by Chief Petty Officers, who wear the badges in pairs on the collars of blue uniform, or on the right cuff of white uniform. They are not worn on tropical shirts. The device on the badge indicates the branch to which the rating belongs. Artificers do not wear branch badges.

Left: The simplified system of branch badges in 1965.

PERCEVAL.

'Urry up, 'Bert. Is it our's or their's?

Note: Fire on any plane approaching your ship in a hostile manner unless it is recognised as friendly. Learn to recognise, not only planes usually seen at sea, but all types that might be operating in your area.

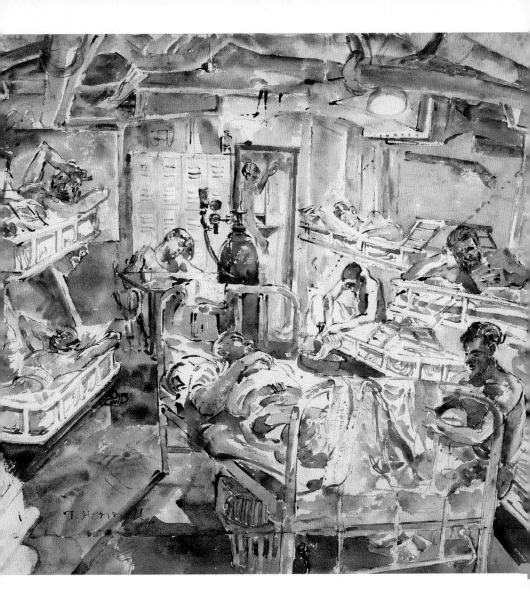

Above: The sick bay of the aircraft carrier HMS *Hunter* in 1945, by Thomas Hennel. (IWM Art LD 5481)

Opposite: Oerlikon gunners have difficulty in identifying an aircraft in this poster. In fact any aircraft on such an approach was assumed to be hostile.
(Fleet Air Arm Museum)

Above: Torpedomen at work in HM Submarine *Tribune*. (IWM TR576)

Left: Old and new style ratings' uniforms – the subtle differences are only notable to experts or those wearing them.
Main image: Sailors on shore in the naval base at Lyness in the Orkneys, with drifters ready to take the men to and from their ships. Painting by Charles Cundall, 1942. (NMM BHC1562)

The *Hermes* returns to an ecstatic welcome after the Falklands War. (Press Association)

Men and women recruits training together at HMS *Raleigh*. (*Life*)

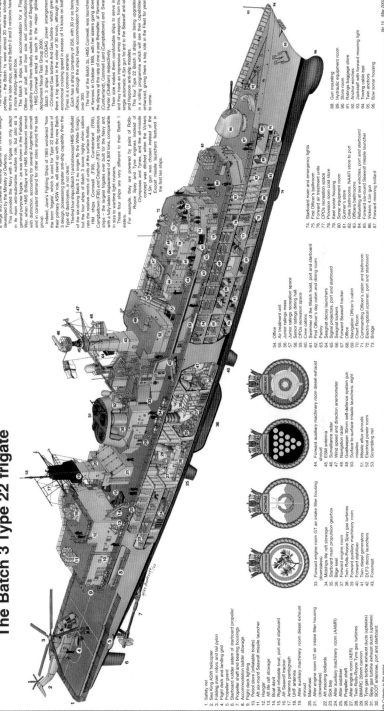

A cutaway of a Type 22 frigate, Batch 3, incorporating the lessons of the Falklands War. (*Navy News*)

The crew of HMS *Chatham* help with disaster relief after the Indian Ocean Tsunami in 2004. (Getty)

The Royal naval captives are released by the Iranians. (Press Association)

Realistic training in the Damage Repair Instruction Unit at Plymouth. (*Life*)

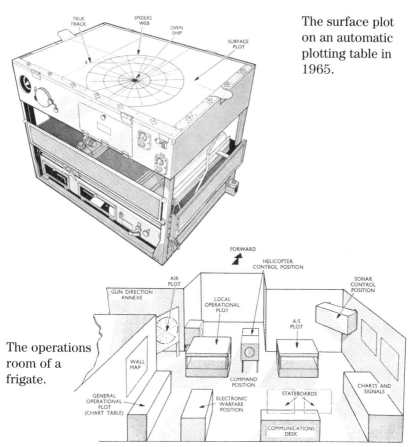

The surface plot on an automatic plotting table in 1965.

The operations room of a frigate.

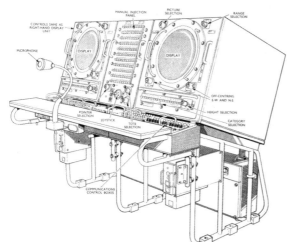

An ADA display console, an advanced system in 1965.

Images courtesy
The National Archives
ADM 239/688.

time before computers assisted the operators), which made me a favourite for exercises with other ships, where we had to work out what they were doing and report to them. We would get points for 'near' and massive points for spot on, which I could do within moments of them changing course.[38]

This was known as hand plotting, and even with Payne's skills it was far too slow to cope with modern aircraft. In some ships the radar picture was projected on to the plotting table so that the control officers could see it, but that was still not enough, so an interim system known as semi-automatic plotting, or the comprehensive display system (CDS) was developed. Highly skilled ratings known as detectors made the initial contact and identification:

CDS requires a highly trained detector rating (RP Branch) to discover the radar responses by watching a PPI. This man can maintain optimum efficiency for a period of not more than 30 minutes. During this time he can focus his attention only on a small area of the display; and he will blink about 500 times ... it is very unusual for detection to be made on the first paint; and an aircraft contact may be missed altogether. Since no human detector can examine all the possible locations scanned by the radar, the full detection potential of the set is not realised.

After that other skilled men, the trackers and analysers, fed the data into an electronic store up to six trackers were needed per watch to 'keep the course and speed measured by aligning dots of light with the echoes, a process subject to human skill and fatigue limitations'. At best a tracker was likely to lag a second behind the movements of the target. The information was fed into consoles where the fighter direction officer, force fighter officer and others could call up the data they needed. The faults of the system were recognised, and it was fitted only to the carriers *Victorious* and *Hermes* and four of the County class guided missile destroyers.

The answer was a fully electronic system in which the radar data was fed directly into a computer. For most people in 1965 these were better known in science fiction than in real life, and the Admiralty felt it necessary to explain what they could and could not do.

A digital computer cannot think like the human brain. When presented with a problem, it cannot trace out how to solve the problem. It can, however be set up ('programmed') to solve a certain type of problem whose limits are precisely defined. Having been programmed, it can solve an enormous number of problems of this type very fast indeed, in fact much faster than the human brain. This is because the computer is entirely electronic, and the timing of operations is therefore measured in millionths of seconds rather than, as with the human brain, in seconds (or, for some of us, much longer).

The new system was known as Action Data Automation. Instead of highly skilled radar plotters it needed electronics experts to operate and maintain the machines.[39]

Simulator training had always been vital to this kind of activity, and from 1970 it was concentrated at HMS *Dryad* (or 'Dryland') in the hills above Portsmouth, where replica operations rooms for different classes of ship were set up, as described in 1975:

More silent air-conditioned corridors and then suddenly – an authentic ship's Operations Room. It is all there – rows of orange radar screens, red lighting, scrambled broadcast voices all talking in Serbo-Croat ... the next room is full of Wrens, wearing headphones, bashing buttons on consoles, typing at space age typewriters, knitting or just sitting ... In yet another room a dozen or so trainee plotters are learning how to set down a simple anti-submarine tracking incident. An instructor flits from side to side, seeing that they have all got their plotting tables switched to the right scale, right time, etc. Pick up a pair of headphones, half expecting to hear the day's recipe or the latest test match score but there is only a lugubrious voice repeating the same set of numbers over and over again. Ask the nearest plotter what he is doing. He turns out to be a guttural Geordie with an impenetrable accent. His neighbour is an equally monoglot Scot.[40]

Michael Payne trained there a few years earlier:

> We learned about attenuation and super refraction, both being meteorological effects on radar. We were also taken into 'models', where we were able to put the lessons into practice by creating as near to live situations as possible without getting seasick. *Dryad*'s 'models' were mock-ups of various operations rooms, complete with radar fed from a control room. Any kind of situation could be modelled, any kind of war game could be developed ... we were firmly at the bottom of the heap, but learning fast. It is amazing how quickly you do something once you've been smashed around the ears with the heavy metal rolling rule normally used to plot 'dead-reckoning' lines.[41]

ENGINEERING

Gas turbines, originally designed for aircraft, were first fitted to small coastal craft, but it was soon realised that they could provide a boost of high power in a major warship that only needed it occasionally. They operated on the principle of the turbo-prop, in that their exhaust gases were used to drive another set of turbine blades, which in turn drove the propeller. Their greatest single advantage was the very high power-weight ratio, for they did not need boilers, condensers and all the other ancillary equipment of a steam engine. The first post-experimental application was in the Tribal class frigate *Ashanti* in 1961, a year ahead of the County class destroyers and the other ships of the class. She carried a combined steam and gas (Cosag) installation. At first there were fears about, 'the reception that the Fleet would give to the unfamiliar gas turbines and the complexities of control and interlocks which were necessary as a consequence of the combined plant'.[42]

The engine room was sealed off during operation, and the engines were monitored from a control panel. Trainees on the gas turbine simulator often suffered from culture shock. 'I came straight from training to an old cruiser, prehistoric almost, and then straight from one of the oldest ships in the navy, straight to this, so I've never seen this sort of thing before. We had automization to a level but it never worked so this has completely fangled me.' Another commented,

> With the old ships the chap was down in the machinery space actually operating the machinery manually, he had all his senses available to him, sight, touch and hearing. Quite often you just get that sort of feeling that something's wrong. With the type of machinery system we've got now, vacated machine spaces and control room panel, you've got to completely re-think your method of watchkeeping, because all your senses are being removed from you, except one and that's sight, you've got to learn to be able to diagnose, work out in your own mind, analyse what the gauges, the readings and the lights mean as to how the system is performing, whether it's performing correctly, whether you're in a breakdown situation.

Some thought it was all too easy, and one commented, 'You could number the panel and act without thinking. I've got a five year old daughter and I reckon she could learn to operate the controls. She wouldn't know what she was doing of course. But that's what we are trying to get away from I hope. The 'trained ape' approach. It's no use when something goes wrong.' There were four men in a watch on a Tribal class frigate, a chief in charge and three others: 'The only person that surveys the panel the whole time is the one in front of the throttles. The auxiliary and fuel section tend to wait for warnings and then get on with putting it right.' One trainee agreed that, 'Admittedly don't have a great deal to do but they can always sit back and see what's going on.'[43]

The gas turbine still needed a certain amount of maintenance, and unlike the steam turbine it could be opened up during its life cycle to carry this out. However, it was a classic example of 'repair by replacement', for the complete unit could be lifted out and replaced in a few hours. Eventually all-gas-turbine propulsion systems were installed, and the life of the engineering mechanic was transformed – he no longer had boilers to clean. But fears about the reaction to the system proved unfounded, and the gas turbines rapidly became popular with the ship's staff of HMS *Ashanti* and with those of other ships as they came into service.

POST-COLONIAL OPERATIONS

The British Empire was largely wound up in the post-war years. India and the new state of Pakistan became independent in 1947, not without much bloodshed and some naval mutinies. Ghana was the first of the black African colonies to achieve independence, in 1957, followed by Nigeria and Kenya in 1960 and 1963. The army fought small but much-publicised wars in Malaya and Cyprus in the hope of handing over to stable governments. Overseas bases were far less valuable in these days of world-wide alliances; Malta was independent from 1964 and the military base was given up, with much rancour, in 1979. Gibraltar was retained at the wish of the people, but less used as a naval base.

Throughout all this the navy maintained a strong presence 'East of Suez' in support of the South East Asia Treaty Organisation and based in Singapore. From the early 1960s it included an aircraft carrier and one of the commando ships carrying marines, plus some of the Tribal class frigates in the Persian Gulf and minesweepers based at Bahrain. In 1961 the Far Eastern Fleet successfully staged a demonstration by deploying ships and landing troops to support the rulers of Kuwait against a threatened Iraqi invasion. They helped relieve floods in Kenya and continued with regular anti-piracy patrols. To the lower deck, according to a recruiting pamphlet of 1963, 'The Far East had ... much to offer besides trouble, including sights and sounds more foreign to us, perhaps, than anywhere else in the world and tropical islands for which a landsman may vainly yearn.'[44]

But it looked rather different to those who served off Borneo in the mid-sixties. In 1963 the Indonesian government resisted a plan to incorporate the former British territories of North Borneo into the Federation of Malaysia and all the British services were involved in armed conflict, along with Malaysian and Australian troops. The Royal Navy provided support by helicopters (which had a high accident rate) while Ton class minesweepers such as HMS *Dartington* patrolled the coast and up the rivers, as described by radio operator 'Syd' Morris:

The usual routine was for one ship to be out at sea on patrol with the other in Kuching for rest and resupply etc. The hand over of the patrol usually took place at sea clear of the mouth of the River Sarawak, off the headland called Tanjong Po. However there was one occasion when *Dartington* was traveling up river in the early hours of a Sunday morning when round a bend ahead suddenly appeared another sweeper heading down river. Only myself and the First Lieutenant, Patrick Barton Rowe, were on the bridge. He was a very smooth and cool customer and as we generally operated in radio silence he immediately instructed me to flash to the other ship simply 'Ca va?' That was it and with a wave to each other passed without hesitating and continued on our separate ways. Very laid back!

Sometimes the sailors operated ashore, as when Jim Cook became part of the 'First Signal Assault Team' in support of the helicopter base at Nanga Gaat:

On my first stint at the Gaat I was met by my outgoing opposite number, who showed me the ropes that day and then handed over his SLR [self-loading rifle], before flying back to Sibu the following day. We were instructed to carry our weapons with us at all times and to attend firing practice every evening at dusk when we manned the perimeter trenches at 'Stand To'. There were important reasons for 'Stand To', the first being, that by firing our weapons daily we were compelled to clean them, which due to the humidity etc., was an absolute necessity, should we at any stage come under attack by Indonesian patrols, either down the Balang River, or by air, which was unlikely, due to the Indonesian's woeful lack of aircraft serviceability. The second reason was to fire at targets across the river in an old rubber plantation, and more importantly, at any driftwood floating down river from the direction of Indonesia, which could be used as cover for enemy infiltrators.

This issue was settled in 1966 after a coup in Indonesia replaced the government there. Meanwhile the British government decided to withdraw from East of Suez due to financial pressure, and that was completed by 1971.

THE NAVY AND THE MEDIA

The navy had done much to reform itself since the war, but its habit of putting new practices inside old forms made it appear increasingly old-fashioned. There was a reaction against militarism by the late 1950s, caused by the disillusionment of national-service conscripts, the fear of nuclear war and perhaps boredom with films and tales of the last war. At the same time Britain moved into the 'swinging sixties', when short hair, rigid discipline and authority were deeply unfashionable. The navy was as far from the popular *zeitgeist* as it ever was during the 'swinging sixties'. Drug-taking, even in its mildest form, was anathema in the armed services, and the navy set up its first drugs squad at Portsmouth in 1967, with one at Plymouth a year later. Homosexual acts were legalised in 1967, but the naval authorities continued to look upon them with horror. According to one officer, 'true homosexuals' were 'really perverted'; to another it was a 'disease which must be stopped from spreading'. On the contrary, Peter Cobbold wrote, 'It never ceased to amaze me how many people imagined the Navy to be full of homosexuals, for apart from a few isolated cases ... it was in fact an unusual phenomenon in the Navy of the 1950s.'[45] This is confirmed by Michael Payne in the 1970s:

I will say now, whatever anyone thinks about sailors, the incidence of queers aboard Navy ships was non-existent. I only met one during my entire career, and he was very successfully working his ticket, so we were never 100 per cent sure about him. Nevertheless it was common practice to pretend to be, to wind other people up, and I heard phrases like 'I joined the Navy for rum, bum and baccy, I've had me rum, I've had me baccy –come 'ere boy'...[46]

The national media, now dominated by television, tended to reflect and perhaps exaggerate the reaction against militarism as young producers tried to make their mark. The radio series *The Navy Lark* started in 1959 and over its long run it reinforced many of the popular stereotypes about the navy – though unlike its contemporary radio series *Round the Horne* it made no mention of homosexuality. It had a high standard of casting – Leslie Phillips as the silly-ass navigating officer ('Left hand down a bit'), Jon Pertwee as a conniving chief petty officer and Ronnie Barker as a grumbling able seaman ('I'm not 'appy'). Perhaps its best line is when someone picks up a phone and a very slow voice answers, 'This is intell-i-gence speak-ing.'

Television took little interest in the navy by this time. The editor of the *Naval Review* approached the Director of Public Relations (Navy) with some ideas:

His response was flat and final. There was, he said, not the remotest chance of interesting a TV producer, and certainly not a BBC-TV producer, in any play which showed the Royal Navy in a sympathetic light. To have any chance of performance, a TV play about the Navy would have to represent all officers as Blimps or Blighs and all naval ships and shore establishments as oppressive instruments for perpetuating class differences. I said that I thought this was a monstrous state of affairs. He said, that's show biz.[47]

This began to change in the 1970s. The drama series *Warship* ran from 1973 to 1977, using several different *Leander* class frigates as the fictional *Hero*. It dealt mainly with the captain and the officers, but in the style of its contemporary series *Upstairs Downstairs* it included many plots involving the lower deck as well. It was done with a great deal of naval cooperation and showed the navy in a favourable light. As the producer put it, 'The Admiralty thought they got as much out of WARSHIP as they put into it.' It proved highly popular with the public and ran to 45 episodes over four seasons. So too was *Sailor* in 1976, a documentary series about the carrier *Ark Royal*, headed by a theme tune sung by Rod Stewart and showing the work of the Fleet Air Arm in dealing with high-performance aircraft and something of the lives of the crew.

7

THE WAY TO THE FALKLANDS

ACCOMMODATION

By the late sixties, the authorities were becoming increasingly concerned about the future. Ratings were less and less likely to be recruited from overcrowded slums. At home they had privacy, often their own rooms, and were likely to demand it more and more from the navy. Already there was 'dissatisfaction with present standards', and changes in accommodation were among the four most important points raised by ratings, along with pay, length of engagements and separation from families. These three points could be dealt with as they arose, but it was very difficult to make radical improvements in the accommodation of a ship once it had been built. Ships being planned in 1969 might well still be in service in 2000 (and some of them were) so it was necessary to plan well in advance.

In fact, the seaman in a modern ship now had slightly less space to himself than in the past, a minimum of 20 square feet in mess deck and dining hall compared with 21 square feet; though in practice ships like the new *Leander* class frigates gave him a total of 18.9 feet in the mess deck and 2.4 in the dining hall. A man's bunk was not entirely his own: it might also serve as seating for up to three people. And his locker, the only really private area he possessed, was becoming increasingly crowded as he could now afford more than the minimum quantity of clothing, as well as civilian clothes for shore trips. The new Type 21 frigates, designed by private enterprise, had deckheads nine feet high, which allowed four-tier bunks in individual cubicles, which proved popular with the seamen but could not be applied in other ships with lower deck heights. A long-term suggestion was for CPOs to have single cabins, petty officers double cabins and junior ratings four-berth cabins. But this was impracticable, and it was planned to have only the new 'master rates' or fleet chiefs in single cabins (though without the washbasin that was allowed to a junior commissioned officer). Chiefs were to be in double or three-berth cabins, petty officers in four-to-six-berth cabins, with junior ratings in 'small mess decks' of 18 to 24 men, which would provide an 'attractive living pattern'. Some marginal improvements were to be made, including covering any pipes passing through the compartment and giving extra storage space, including hanging lockers, and putting bars in senior rates' messes. But it had to be accepted that Royal Naval accommodation would never be up to merchant navy standards, in which single cabins for all ranks were becoming increasingly common; in return, the 'shore/sea balance' was claimed to be 'in favour of the uniformed rating',[1] i.e., naval personnel.

Michael Payne describes his mess on board the frigate *Zulu*:

Our own RP's mess – with our own locker and our own pit – was like a reversed 'L' in shape. The top was the quiet area, with the whole of the side of the 'L' being right on the ship's side and the bottom being the 'mess square'. In this area we drank tea, played card games and did our socializing. Bearing in mind there were probably twenty-four men in that mess, you can get a feel for how cramped it was. So the 'three high' pits were probably five deep. In each row of three pits, the top one tilted upwards out of the way, the bottom one was therefore available for seating and the middle one, once secured properly, dropped backwards, so the sleeping part was pressed against the ship's side, with a cushion in front to act as a backrest. There would be boot lockers and blanket stowages beneath the bottom pit. If you were a junior, on the bottom bunk, you had to ensure your bed was made up properly, before sheathing it in its casing, before putting the seat cover on, so everyone could finally sit down. Now, if you wanted to go to bed early, tuff – if someone else in the mess square wanted to party, you'd have to wait till they were good and ready, before you could finally get your head down.[2]

The use of bunks had not apparently destroyed mess life as the authorities once had feared:

> The mess we were in was the 'Aft Seamen's Mess' – the whole arse-end of the ship in fact. There were all branches of sailor in there – gunners, Anti-sub and RPs, and believe it or not we all got on brilliantly. We had a messdeck lawyer, who, if you needed to know anything, would be able to tell you ... Coming from other ships, we all had previous skills and ideas, which meant we could play crib, uckers, nominations, chase the pisser – all sorts. We would sit up for hours playing while duty watch, despite pleas and threats to 'get your heads down – NOW'. That only encouraged us to post lookouts who would tell us of the forthcoming of the Duty PO on his rounds ...[3]

More efforts were made to involve the crew in mess deck design, and in 1975 it was reported in the shipping press,

> A room has been designed at Foxhill, Bath, in which the sample cards and schedules are filed in specially designed containers. Actual examples of the chairs, tables and other items specified can also be seen. It is here that representatives of officers and crew from any ship requiring a new interior treatment are invited so that they may select the individual schemes which, when put together, will cover the entire accommodation areas of a ship. This exercise can normally be completed in half a day.[4]

Later that year it was suggested that cruise ship experience was useful in the new guided missile destroyers, though the parameters were very different:

> The designers have tried to combine the practical advantages of modular furniture with layouts which make the best use of the

available space, while employing colour schemes which will appeal to the younger generation of sailors. It would be easy to do this in a fashionable brash manner by using strident colours and patterns, but such means soon become boring and unsatisfying, particularly on a ship where there is no escape until one comes ashore. The general rule in the *Sheffield*, therefore, has been to retain a reticent background and to use accent colours where considered necessary.[5]

Air Mechanic Hatcher was pleasantly surprised when he was drafted to a carrier in 1982:

The accommodation on board Invincible was more comfortable than we had ashore. We were quite surprised, as we expected it to be an all-metal tin tub. The junior rates had their own lounge with television and coffee making facilities – a real home from home ... The ship broadcast information over the television, then every night there was a video piped through to all the mess decks with a good supply of films. We were issued with three cans of beer a day, but as I'm not a beer drinker, I never drew mine. On board, you work and sleep, so running round the flight deck was a break.[6]

But none of this could get round the fact that life aboard ship was still very crowded by shore standards.

Ashore, the use of married quarters continued to increase. The new Polaris base in Scotland was planned to have 730 houses for ratings on the Churchill Estate in Helensburgh, but it turned out not to be enough; it was based on the standard ratio of other naval establishments, but a higher proportion of the Faslane men were married.[7] The navy always regarded married quarters in a different light from the other services. For the Army and the RAF, they were a way of keeping a serviceman close to his job even when off duty, and in the 1970s the authorities began to worry as increasing numbers bought houses some distance away and went to them for weekends – this might mean that bases could be undermanned during a sudden crisis. But for the navy, the married quarter was intended as 'a secure base for the family while the husband was at sea', and it was less necessary to have them near to the workplace.[8]

GUIDED MISSILES

The navy developed two guided missiles in the 1950s, both for anti-aircraft use. The inaptly named Sea Slug was for long-range use and was only fitted on the specially-built County class guided missile destroyers. It was a 'beam-rider', in that it followed a radar beam from the launching ship to its target. Each installation needed nearly 40 men to maintain and operate it, with regular routine testing of the missiles on board. These included the equivalent of 18.25 men for mechanical work, largely done by the gunnery branch, nine men from the electrical branch and 12.25 from radio electrical. Seventeen of these were highly skilled at artificer or mechanician level, and 13.5 were semi-skilled as higher gunnery, electrical or radio electrical rates.[9]

The Sea Cat was a short-range weapon. Its launching was directed by the missile-control officer, but it was guided to its target by a rating who tracked the missile and target through binoculars and guided it by means of a joystick. Actual firings were inevitably rare, but skills had to be kept in constant practice, so a simulator was developed by HMS *Excellent*.[10] The rating of Sea Cat aimer was set up in 1968 within the gunnery branch, his badge being a diagram of a missile on his right cuff. Live firings were done occasionally against pilotless target aircraft, the object being to miss slightly so that the plane could be used again. Michael Payne liked to watch the Sea Cat practice from *Tartar*:

> We did a live Seacat firing one day, against a PTA. That was always worth watching – it was a point of honour among the Seacat Aimers to totally take out the PTA. A near miss was good, but to totally wreck it was something! Standing on the quarterdeck watching while the Seacat blasted away from the launcher was a rare sight. It was even rarer when it burnt out on the launcher without going anywhere ...[11]

The Sea Cat operators of the cruiser *Blake* were tested at Portland in 1969. They had had no opportunity to practice during pre-commissioning training due to bad weather, but they did quite well in nine firings:

> Lawrence. Completed two successful shots. Control was slightly rough initially. The first missile appeared to miss just right. During the second run the camera film fouled. This shot was considered to be the best of the day ...
>
> Moss. Fired two missiles. Guidance was slightly rough with the first missile. The second was good except for a sudden jink to the left just before impact.[12]

Again the Seacat needed a good deal of maintenance, 5.5 men per mounting; almost half of these were semi-skilled men of the gunnery branch, and only the equivalent of one artificer was needed.[13] Less skilled men were needed to handle and reload the missiles, which were 'of delicate construction and must be treated with care in every stage of handling'.[14]

The Sea Dart, which entered service with HMS *Bristol* and then the Type 42 destroyers from 1973, was a replacement for the Sea Slug as a long-range anti-aircraft missile. The main task was to identify a target, which was done by the missile/gun director under the guidance of rules set by command, and the orders of the above-water warfare officer. Ideally the MGD would consult command each time a potential target was found, but that would not always be possible in a complex and fast-moving situation. It was stated that, 'His performance in assessing and coping with different practical situations will be the critical factor in determining the operational effectiveness of the SEA DART weapon system at sea.' He was assisted by two tactical indicator operators who would warn him of the appearance of new tracks on the radar and changes in the courses of old ones, using a rolling ball to indicate them to the Type 909 fire-control radar. The radar operators themselves were part of the team; in ideal situations all they had to do was make sure that their equipment was working properly, but they night also have to take account of rain, clutter, enemy countermeasures and so on, while operating 'the most delicate sensor in the ship for target evaluation'. There was also a Sea Dart controller who coordinated the reloading of the twin launchers with the needs of fire control, and a gun controller who selected the right type of ammunition for the single 4.5-inch gun and directed its firing.[15]

The Royal Navy adopted the French Exocet missile as an anti-ship system, and in the 1970s it was fitted to *Amazon* and *Leander* class frigates. Sea Wolf was the replacement for Sea Cat and was on trial by 1980. Sea Skua was an anti-ship missile launched from Lynx helicopters, which entered service in 1981. It relied on a beam from the helicopter to illuminate the target, for which a rating missile operator was carried.

All this meant that gunnery was left aside. The latest class of frigate, the Type 22, was built without any main guns at all, and HMS *Excellent* ceased gunnery training in 1974 after nearly a century and a half. A Royal Artillery officer posted to the frigate *Plymouth* in 1982 was concerned that 'she had the oldest type of gun system in the navy, and was only accurate if the crew was well practised. I'd spent some time earlier in the year at the naval gunfire range in Scotland, where *Plymouth* had shelled everywhere but the target area. The navy had neglected the art of gunnery, considering anti-submarine warfare and air defence far more important.'[16]

THE FLEET AIR ARM

By the end of the Second World War it was no longer common for battleships and cruisers to carry seaplanes, so the idea of a 'ship's flight' disappeared. It re-emerged in the late 1950s when experiments showed that a destroyer or frigate could carry its own helicopter or two. These, of course, required a maintenance crew on board the ship, and this consisted of around eight or more ratings, led by artificers. In the guided-missile destroyer *Antrim* in 1982, Chief Petty Officer 'Fritz'

Heritier had a team of 12 under him to work on an aged Wessex helicopter nicknamed 'Humphrey', including CPO Artificer Lionel Kurn, who was the number two airframe fitter, and CPO Terence Bullingham, who had held the rate since the late 1960s and worked on the flight control and armament electronic systems.[17] A Type 22 frigate had eight men, four of them senior rates.

As a seaman, Michael Payne had no respect for the 'waffoos' ('wet and fucking useless') in the frigate *Zulu* with an early and very compact hangar:

> Our shiny, navy blue helicopter lived in a little nest called a 'hangar' towards the blunt end of the ship. On the *Zulu*, and therefore all Type 81s, this hangar had a hole in the roof where the deck was a lift. Once lowered, i.e., out of sight (and mind), the idle waffoos used to do their hardest work ever – putting the covers on the hole where the helo was now sitting. This only used to take a few minutes, but being waffoos they had to work out what to do afresh, every time they did it. So their evolution could take several hours, while we sandscratchers stood laughing.[18]

Ship's flights rarely had space for specialised aircraft handlers, even on a helicopter carrier like the converted cruiser *Blake* in 1969: 'The flight deck party is drawn from the duty watch of Squadron maintenance personnel, and backed up by Squadron and ship's company handlers. With only one flight deck spot, much time is spent in ranging and striking down aircraft.'[19]

The naval airmen's belief that 'the future belongs to them' took a severe knock in 1966 when a projected new aircraft carrier, known as CAV01, was cancelled in the latest round of defence cuts. There came a further blow in 1968 when *Victorious*, last of the wartime *Illustrious* class and the first British carrier to be fitted with a fully-angled deck, was damaged in a fire at Portsmouth and it was decided not to re-commission her. The navy was now planning for a future without carriers, in which it would rely on helicopters and the support of ground-based RAF aircraft. *Eagle* was broken up in 1978, and *Ark Royal* in 1980. The confidence of the fleet as a whole was shaken. However the three new 'through-deck cruisers' of the *Invincible* class were really aircraft carriers in disguise. It was found that they could operate the Harrier vertical take-off jet, first developed for land use. In 1978–9 the Harrier was tested on *Hermes*, an old 'light fleet' carrier, which had been modernised. The tests were successful, and in 1981 the ship was fitted with a 'ski' jump so that the navalised version of the Harrier, the Sea Harrier, could carry a greater payload on a short take off. *Invincible,* the first of the new ships – now unashamedly named light aircraft carriers – was commissioned in July 1980.

THE BEIRA PATROL

The white-dominated government of Rhodesia staged a 'unilateral declaration of independence' in 1965 to avoid moves towards a multi-racial democracy], but this was recognised either by the British government nor by the international community. Economic sanctions were applied by the United Nations but were difficult to enforce while supplies could be brought in through the sympathetic regimes in South Africa and Portuguese-ruled Mozambique. So the navy had the thankless task of patrolling off the Mozambican port of Beira (the nearest port to land-locked Rhodesia) in the hope of cutting off fuel supplies. Michael Payne did not like the work in the *Zulu*:

> Our next destination was off the coast [sic] of Rhodesia, to take over as duty ship on Beira Patrol, off Lourenço Marques, to support the embargo, and stop the Rhodesians from getting any oil or supplies. 'Beira' and its connotations for Navy people can be summed up in a few words: 'misery' and 'boredom'. We did four weeks, as well as passage there, doing nothing but sailing up and down and up and down and up. We were in sea watches, one in four, but after a week or so, you became desensitized to anything but waking up, looking at your watch, determining if you had just been shaken for your

watch or if you were dreaming, going on watch, coming off watch, eating, working, sunbathing, sleeping.[20]

In 1980 Rhodesia became 'Zimbabwe' with the election of a black government and supposed guarantees to the whites, so the patrol was no longer needed.

THE NUCLEAR DETERRENT

Since the invention of the atomic bomb, and later the hydrogen bomb, it had been assumed that the RAF would be responsible for providing and delivering Britain's main nuclear deterrent with its 'V-bombers'. This was increasingly difficult by the late 1950s as intercontinental ballistic missiles became capable of wiping out the airbases, while surface-to-air missiles were likely to shoot the bombers down. There were attempts to extend the life of the bombers by fitting them with air-launched 'stand-off' bombs, but when the American Skybolt was cancelled in 1962, the Americans agreed to let the British have their Polaris missile, which could be launched from a submerged submarine. In some ways it was the ideal deterrent for a nautical nation like Britain, but it relied heavily on American technology and it was fiercely opposed in the United Kingdom by the growing Campaign for Nuclear Disarmament, and the more militant Committee of 100. New submarines had to be built, partly based on experience of nuclear boats built so far, and a base was to be constructed at Faslane on Gareloch, just off the River Clyde.

There had been some kind of naval base at Faslane since the end of the war, but it was isolated, poorly equipped and used mainly for trials of two unsuccessful and rather dangerous hydrogen-peroxide submarines, *Explorer* and *Excalibur*, known to the lower deck as *Exploder* and *Excruciator*. The base was isolated, poorly equipped and old-fashioned. One rating there saw a poster for 'Britain's modern navy' and asked how he could join it.[21] It was made clear that the new base had nothing to do with the old one apart from the site, and it would be completely rebuilt, while the naval authorities tried to boost the neighbouring town of Helensburgh as a desirable place to be –

> For a town of its size Helensburgh now offers an astonishing variety of entertainments.
>
> In addition to the usual Scottish hostelries there are:
>
> An Art Club, Wine Club (not for topers) Toastmasters Club, Horticultural Society, Flower Club, WVS, Library, Saltire Society (Scottish way of life), 35 mm Camera Club ...

It was very different from Barrow-in-Furness and Birkenhead, where sailors might be sent to stand by ships under construction. Barrow had 'very little surplus accommodation for single people', so sailors often had to live in a hutted camp. At Birkenhead 'the accommodation situation in this area is difficult' though it offered the chance of a visit to Liverpool, 'the home of certain well known musicians.'[22]

The authorities were well aware of lower deck doubts:

> Why me? – POLARIS? You're joking ... Three months at sea with no mail ... And then to Faslane for life ... Big ships nothing but flannel ... Sit at the bottom for months on end ... No runs ashore ...won't be enough schools at Faslane ... Married Quarters situation hopeless ... Don't make me laugh ...

It was conceded that many of these concerns were real, and a pamphlet of 1966 attempted to attract sailors to the Polaris fleet:

> Each submarine will have two crews of 13 officers and 124 ratings. There will be a spare crew at Faslane as well (i.e., nine crews altogether). Patrols will last eight weeks ... the submarine then returning to Faslane for a month to change over crews and maintain, after which the opposite crew will go to sea for eight weeks. NO ONE WILL EVER GO TO SEA FOR TWO PATROLS RUNNING. In two years the average person will do four patrols. The 'off patrol' crew will take leave due (standard leave rules apply), take refresher and

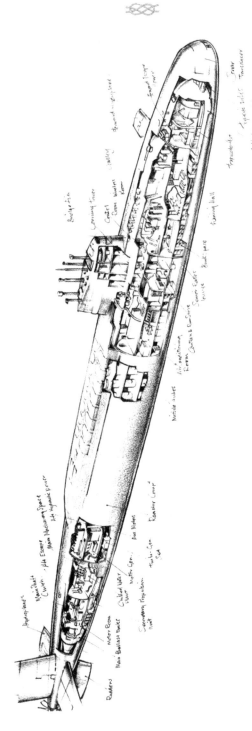

A cutaway of the Polaris submarine *Renown* produced by the builders, Cammel Laird.

214

advancement courses, break in the new boys, and work in the base at Faslane. It should be possible to tell a year in advance the exact dates of leave.[23]

The crew was organised into eight departments. The largest with 23 members was 'seamen and miscellaneous', which included a CPO Coxswain, as always the senior rating on board a submarine. Most of the others were underwater control ratings who operated the sonar, steered the ship and operated its hydroplanes. In addition there were the underwater weapons men who maintained and operated the six torpedoes. The Navigational Department was unusually large by normal standards, with 11 men, the 'nav queens' who had the duty of operating and maintaining the Ship's Inertial Navigational System, which used gyroscopes to give a very precise position without reference to the outside world – without such navigation, the Polaris missiles could not be aimed accurately. They were '(almost) immune from fire exercises, wearing Emergency Breathing Apparatus, black lighting and so on, in order that they could/can keep a close eye on this equipment.'[24] The Communications Department had eight radio operators under a chief. The Supply Department included a total of 11 stores assistants, writers, cooks and stewards. The three technical departments – Electrical, Marine Engineering and Polaris – differed very much from the traditional pyramid structure of military organisations, with a high proportion of artificers and mechanicians rated as petty officers and chiefs. The Polaris Department, the most skilled of all, had five chief petty officers and, out of 19 men, only two below the rank of leading seaman. Finally, the Medical Department had technicians and a leading medical attendant, under the command of the ship's doctor.[25]

According to the recruiting pamphlet,

Messing will be on a cafeteria system, with several choices of hot and cold dishes provided by four chefs. There is also a canteen, a washing up machine and an ice cream dispenser. Senior rates have a lounge and coffee bar over twice the size of a *Porpoise* class Petty Officers' mess, also bunk spaces on decks 2 and 3 and a dining hall. Junior rates have a recreation space abaft the fore ends, a dining hall on deck 2 and bunk space on deck 3.

A daily newspaper (with Daily Mirror cartoons) will be produced and a special news summary incorporating local news from the Faslane area.[26]

Polaris crews were often told that they were an elite: one of them had his doubts – 'Supposedly we were hand-picked from the best of the submarine trainees, other qualified submariners and a number of general service-chappies. As it turned out I think everybody got rid of their riffraff to the Polaris boats but we were soon moulded into two highly trained and motivated teams.'[27] In any case, illusions were punctured when the admiral addressed the crew of Resolution, the first boat of the class:

> He 'cleared lower deck' and told my assembled ship's company that as far as he was concerned we were just another ship in the fleet 'no different from one of the minesweepers'. Perhaps he meant well; perhaps consciously or unconsciously he was expressing the fleet's view. The comments of my ship's company, who had dedicated themselves for the past three years or more to our state of readiness, could be described as mutinous. Thank heavens, they saved them until after he had gone.[28]

Leading Electrical Mechanic Arthur Escreet volunteered for Polaris after he was shown a Defence Council Instruction showing that he would spend twice as much time ashore as at sea. After training he became a member of the first starboard crew of HMS *Resolution*:

> The Port crew fired the first of Britain's Polaris missiles and the Starboard crew witnessed this firing from the deck of an American

frigate. It was a great sight as the missile left the water and majestically rose into the sky. The crew changeover then took place and the Starboard crew fired the second missile. My operational station for the firing was Missile Trolley operator in the Missile Compartment. It was a strange sensation to feel the submarine shudder as the missile was ejected from its tube.[29]

Escreet describes the routine of life at sea aboard the boat:

The eight weeks on patrol passed through various stages. For the first two weeks the crew settled down, having just left loved ones at home and not at this stage missing them. The second two weeks became a matter of going on watch, coming off watch and perhaps watching one of the 56 movies we carried on board. The fifth and sixth weeks saw some of the crew becoming a bit bored and petty niggling took place. Midway through the patrol a 'sod's Opera' was put on. Items of ladies underwear were produced, making one wonder what sort of people you were at sea with. However, it was an enlightening opera and relieved some of the boredom.

By the seventh week morale began to improve as we realised that home was not far away. The eighth week saw the onset of 'Channel fever' and thoughts of an evening in female company. And then back alongside the wall and 'homers'. It was amusing to see many of the crew return on board the following morning with eyes in four watches.[30]

After the boat came back to Faslane there was still a great deal to do:

Very soon *Resolution* returned from patrol and all the departments swung into action. The procedure was generally always the same. The movement of Polaris submarines was highly classified and, with the exception of a limited number of officers, the first intimation of a return from patrol was when the submarine appeared at the entrance to the Clyde estuary. Included in the Port Auxiliary Service was a fast despatch boat which had started life as an RAF Rescue vessel. This despatch boat would take Captain SM 10 out to meet the returning submarine which would proceed direct to the jetty at Coulport to unload one or more missiles for routine inspection. At the Coulport jetty she was met by a contingent of Base Staff and the replacement crew. The families of the incoming crew were also allowed to attend. They had an uncanny knack of always being ready, despite the short notice. The replacement crew immediately took over and the patrol crew proceeded on leave. The work list was rapidly evaluated and the submarine came round to berth at Faslane for her maintenance period.[31]

THE HIGHER RATES

Newer ships demanded a higher proportion of petty officers. In a new Type 22 frigate of around 1980, weapons engineering had 14 men of petty officer rate and upwards, 33 per cent of the branch, while marine engineering had 38 per cent petty officers; the ship's flight needed four senior ratings as well as four junior. The operations branch, formerly the seamen, had 11 per cent officers but only 20 per cent senior rates and 69 per cent junior. The marine detachment had no officer, one sergeant who was equivalent to a senior rate, and nine men. Overall, 26 per cent of the men on board were senior rates.[32]

Sometimes the crew structure of a small ship did not allow the deployment of a suitable quantity of petty officers for disciplinary purposes. Possibly one of the problems in the notorious case of the *Iveston* in 1970 (see page 224 below) was that she did not carry any seamen petty officers apart from the coxswain, and the engineer petty officer on duty was not mentally equipped to deal with a difficult situation.[33]

A survey of electrical ratings in 1962 showed that the ambiguous position of the leading hand was still there. Some men did not seek advancement because of 'lack of interest in the service', while others cited more specifically, 'inadequate pay and privileges for increased responsibility' or 'the status of the Leading Rate – particularly the difficulties arising from sharing a mess with lower rates and the invidious "betwixt and between" position of the Leading rate'. But the difficulties should not be exaggerated: when asked, 'If you do *not* wish to become L.E.M. or L.R.E.M, why not?' 80 per cent left it unanswered, suggesting that they might go for advancement some day.[34]

THE FLEET CHIEF

With the upgrading of the old warrant officer in the 1950s, and increased cooperation with other services, the chief petty officers became aware of a gap at the top of the rating structure. The army and air force had long had warrant officers who were treated as senior NCOs rather than junior officers. In 1958 the United States Navy created new ratings of 'senior chief' and 'master chief', above the chief petty officer. In the Royal Navy there was also an anomaly in the case of the artificers. They had the equivalent rank of chief petty officer when fully qualified and were eligible for promotion to chief artificer, though there was no specific substantive rate to promote them to. As early as 1949 the Committee on Morale suggested that 'service to the age of fifty with prospects of additional advancement such as C.P.O 2nd Class and C.P.O 1st Class (similar to the Army ranks of W.O.II and W.O.I) , and a worthwhile pension are desirable'.[35] Demands began to increase for a Royal Navy equivalent to the warrant officer, but in 1960 the First Sea Lord rejected them on the grounds that there was no specific need for a new rating, and to create one would mean taking work away from officers, so there would be fewer SD commissions. At present chiefs enjoyed better pay and conditions than their equivalents, staff sergeants and flight sergeants, and their chances of promotion to commissioned officer were better. Feelings were running so high that the Admiralty felt it necessary to order captains to explain the decision to senior ratings by means of two statements – 'one "in a fairly orthodox style", the other "setting out the case in a way which is both striking and readily understandable"'.

The gap between the wardroom and the lower deck was certainly much narrower than it had been for generations, but it could still be a difficult one for a chief to bridge – crossing it meant giving up one's social circle and adopting a new lifestyle, and becoming the most junior officer instead of a senior rating with all the respect that involved. In 1965 the new First Sea Lord revived the question, this time assuming that there was a need for such a rate and ordering committees to find berths to which they could be appointed. But developments were slow, partly because the Board of Admiralty changed four times during the ensuing five years. It was eventually decided to have a single grade of warrant officer as with the RAF, not two, as in the army. The title of the rank caused much difficulty. In documents it was often known as the 'master rate' which perhaps reflected the US grade of 'master chief petty officer', but certainly not the old-style 'master' of the sailing navy, who was equivalent to a lieutenant in status. 'Warrant officer' was not considered at this point, perhaps because the old type was still within memory, though 'warrant chief petty officer' was. Furthermore the legal branch pointed out that the Naval Discipline Act of 1958 obliged seamen to obey the orders of chief petty officers and sub-lieutenants, but nothing in between. It would take some time to get an amendment through parliament, but in the meantime it would be possible to create the new rate as a grade within that of the chief petty officer. The title of 'fleet chief' was chosen. Perhaps this was also based on the US Navy, where there was a 'fleet master chief' – if so it greatly exaggerated the new Royal Navy rank's authority. By 1978 the USN only had four fleet master chiefs, one for each of the main commands, with 23 command master chiefs under them.[36] Instead the Admiralty proposed to appoint 1,100 fleet chiefs, who would come from within the 11,500 existing chiefs, so the overall numbers would not be increased.

The new rate was advertised by Defence Council Instruction in August 1970. The rank was formally titled 'warrant officer', though it was to be known as 'fleet chief petty officer' for everyday use. A fleet chief was to have managerial and divisional responsibilities beyond his normal trade ones. He was to engage for five years beyond the normal

22 years man's service from the age of 18, making a total of 27; in return he would have substantially increased pension rights. The first fleet chiefs were appointed in 1971, and in general they were held in great respect by the lower deck, very different from the old-style warrant officer in his last days.[37]

THE RUM RATION

Ever since ancient times, sailors had been issued with free alcohol on board. Rum was issued in the West Indies, and in the 1740s Admiral Vernon had the idea of diluting it with two parts of water, the original 'grog.' But wine, beer or brandy were issued on other stations according to local supply, until rum became universal during the nineteenth century. However, the sailor's 'tot' was increasingly questioned in a navy that valued technical skill more than muscle and bravado. In 1954 the captain of HMS *Osprey* experimented with the young anti-submarine ratings under training by issuing their tots at 1550, after training had finished, rather than at midday; the instructors soon found 'that the ratings are very much more receptive to teaching and that the instruction is, in consequence, of much greater value than before'. The junior ratings on the staff of the school were given the option to have the tot later but none did: 'Habit dies hard and in any case, the sailor seems to prefer his tot at 1200 before the main meal of the day.'[38]

The issue was brought up in a more general way in 1959, when it was proposed to abolish the rum issue in shore bases. Captains were sounded out but were deeply divided. It was pointed out that any compensation would have to cover the cost of a tot at commercial bar prices, which would be expensive. No one could predict the extent of discontent that would be caused on the lower deck, but the question was dropped for the moment. In July 1960 the Admiralty concluded that 'the degree of support for the abolition of the spirit ration, even ashore, does not at present justify interfering with such a long established custom'.[39]

One reaction to the demise of the rum ration.

When the issue came up again in 1968, it was politically charged. The Labour government of the time was deeply worried about seeming to be 'anti-service.' The cancellation of the aircraft carrier programme had made it very unpopular with the navy, and the recent outcry in Scotland over the disbandment of the Argyll and Sutherland Highlanders had made it very nervous about press and public reaction to any interference with tradition. David Owen, the politician now responsible for the navy, urged caution as there was no pressing need to abolish the tot now. The rum issue 'marked out the sailor as different', and the government did not want to appear as killjoys. Naval officers took a stronger line – it was said that 'the vast majority of naval officers' supported abolition. The Vice Chief of Naval Staff, who had already been troubled by the issue as Second Sea Lord in charge of personnel, claimed that 'in terms of discipline, efficiency and present day moral standards, the free rum issue was difficult to defend: following the introduction of legislation against drinking and driving, it was indefensible'. Ideas of issuing only to those above a certain age or rate were regarded as too divisive, and the board was obliged to reach a conclusion when an officer 'much higher than a commander' leaked the story to *Navy News*. This soon provoked an outcry in the press in which the *Daily Mail* ran the provocative headline, 'If the navy doesn't want a mutiny, hands off the rum.'

Whether the leak was deliberately inspired or not, it seemed to propel the naval lords towards a decision – the tot would be abolished. It was agreed that it had been appropriate 'when it was necessary to offset a harsh way of life and excessively hard physical work', but now sailors had to operate 'complex, and often delicate, machinery and systems'. Furthermore, 'The daily rum issue, being free and ready to hand, is a strong inducement to drink even on those occasions when a rating might not want to do so ...' In view of the levelling of inter-service conditions, it would not be appropriate to offer the men financial compensation, but £2.7 million was to be paid into a charitable fund for services to sailors that would not normally be supplied by the crown. Petty officers and above would be allowed to buy up to 1/12th of a pint of duty free spirits in their messes, and junior ratings could buy up to three cans of beer, though it was not to be stored or re-sold. Owen wrote to the Prime Minister early in December to warn him of a possible storm. The only remaining question was over the timing – the navy board did not want it to be confused with a coming pay review, which had nothing to do with the ending of rum, and it also wanted time to use up and then store old stocks that were held on board ship. The abolition was timed for 1 August 1970, by which time a new Conservative government had taken power. It had no plans to reverse the decision. There was plenty of criticism in the press, but mostly humorous and good-natured. And there was indeed some discontent in the fleet that year – but when it boiled over it had nothing to do with the ending of the tot.[40]

THE LAST MUTINY

The navy had been free of its old problem of mutiny since the outbreaks just after the war, apart from an incident on HMS *Wren* in 1954 when two seamen remained at the top of a ladder ignoring orders and assaulted a petty officer, while a third, who was drunk, attempted to prevent their arrest. The first two men were sentenced to six and eight years of imprisonment, the third to eighteen months' detention.[41]

Early in July 1970 the minesweeper *Iveston* was alongside at Ullapool in the north of Scotland. It was not a happy ship. There had been three first lieutenants and four commanding officers in the previous 14 months, and the new captain, Lieutenant Stephen Johnson, believed his mission was to tighten up discipline. But it seems that he paid little attention to his crew, spending too much time in his cabin and even entertaining a tramp in the wardroom. By coincidence, the ship had an unusual proportion of 'bad characters'. These included E. Griffiths, a two-badge man of 'only average intelligence, but above average strength and size' who had already served detention after getting drunk ashore. Edward Kirkbride was far cleverer but had been sentenced to 60 days in Singapore. He had 'a dislike for the service' and was 'a disloyal man.' D. Smith was even more intelligent but had once been given a suspended sentence of 28 days. B. O'Malley was a 'sea lawyer', 'too worried about his rights' and an 'inveterate grouse'. Along with Joseph Bowers, had who had a clean sheet and a good reputation, these men were drinking heavily ashore on the night of Sunday 5 July, consuming by their own account the almost incredible amount of 88 pints of beer, 34 whiskies, 20 rums, 13 cans of beer and one vodka. They were still standing when they returned on board and acted out a 'mutiny on the *Bounty*' scene as well as singing Irish rebel songs – a sore point at that time, when the troubles in Ireland were accelerating. The coxswain came out in his underpants to deal with the disturbance and was assaulted. Local police were called, and three officers appeared, which must have strained the resources of the Ullapool Constabulary. Four of the men were arrested, and the matter was reported to the Flag Officer Scotland at Rosyth, who insisted on a court martial for mutiny.

Press interest was huge, and the navy public relations department prepared a list of all the questions they thought they might be asked by the press, giving some insight into the naval culture of the time – if asked, 'Isn't it unusual for a "gentleman of the road" to be invited into a Wardroom?' the authorised reply was, 'The Navy is constantly entertaining a very wide cross-section of the community.'

At the time of the last mutiny in the Royal Navy in 1954, the words 'protest' and 'Sit-in' would have meant nothing to a group of Able Seamen. In 1970 they are household words, and they provide a vehicle for complaint which appeared attractive to an excited group of men, who had little sense and too much alcohol in them. The word 'mutiny' must have seemed very old fashioned to these young men at the time of these events.

If they were asked about 'sailors being treated like children', they were to reply,

> When men have to live in somewhat confined, close-knit conditions because of the size of ships, certain regulations have to be enforced for the benefit of the majority. These in the main are fundamental rules for the social conduct of everyone. Two examples of this – personal hygiene and lights out. It is essential to have a high standard of personal hygiene otherwise one man becomes offensive to his neighbour. When you get several men living together overhead lights must be put out at a reasonable hour so that those who wish may go to sleep, but bed-side lights are provided.

The press treated the whole matter as a farce, until the men were found guilty and sentences were announced – 12 to 21 months' detention followed by dismissal with disgrace. The affair was simply a drunken prank gone wrong, and it found no echo in the rest of the navy. But it gave the navy an image of hard-drinking seamen and aloof officers, exactly what it was trying to avoid.

THE COD WARS

Britain fought three 'cod wars' with Iceland between 1958 and 1976, as the islanders attempted to conserve their fishing stocks by extending their limits successively to twelve, fifty and 200 miles. British trawlers were encouraged to resist and were protected mainly by naval frigates, which involved long days in rough and cold seas.

Icelandic patrol boats would attempt to cut the nets of the trawlers, while frigates would move in to stop that, often getting into a ramming situation.

> We would ride off the gunboat's assault on our defenceless trawlers by getting between it and the trawler. Our skipper was brilliant at this, and could make the gunboats look totally foolish. On this occasion, though, the *Baldur* thought he'd get in the way. The boss thought much differently, For about an hour we rode off its attacks, and we both sailed about gesturing and posturing – keeping the thing away, as ordered. The *Baldur* finally got close, and we warned her by radio that we were rigged with stabilisers, stretching '2 to 3 feet' out of our sides. It got closer and our Jimmy did a running commentary on the situation over the ship's broadcast. He reported the impending collision so precisely that it was exactly on the third 'now' in 'standby now, now, now' that the actual impact was felt and heard by us below decks. The impact reeled us, but our port stabiliser unfortunately pierced the *Baldur*'s hull, necessitating her extremely rapid return to Reykjavik. We laughed like buggers, especially when, while closed up, we heard about ourselves on the BBC World News. The stabilisers actually extended about [6] ft out ... it was his fault – he started it.[42]

THE WOOLY PULLIE AND THE BERET

The appearance of the sailor changed rather suddenly in the mid-1970s:

> It was about this time [1975] that the Admiralty decided we could all have two new wooly pullies [pullovers], similar to those worn by the Army and Air Force, but ours were a deep, navy blue. They had epaulettes on each shoulder, ready to put our new rank/rate badges on. We wore them self-consciously at first, but gradually got used to them, and threw away those bloody awful itchy things from all those sunrises away at *Raleigh*. We were also issued with berets, not that we knew how to wear them – we needed lessons for that. We wore these even more self-consciously than the woollies, as we all looked

really ridiculous. They did, though, stay on our heads better in roughers, and could be jammed in the pockets of our foulies, along with the rest of the stuff we carried, so from that point of view they were an improvement.

The more traditional caps, the 'ice-cream hats', were only used for 'being on duty and for being trooped and appearing before the skipper'.[43]

Good conduct stripes were not worn on the pullies; attitudes to them had been reversed. According to Michael Payne, 'Badges made you look like a silly old git – you would be called 'grand-dad' or worse if you had them. I ended up with two, but kept forgetting to sew the second one on.'[44] With the growth of the conflict in Northern Ireland, service personnel were subject to attack and were positively forbidden to wear uniform on leave, so the appearance of naval towns like Portsmouth and Plymouth was changed. The traditional square and fore-and-aft rigs were only worn on ceremonial occasions, as some officers had feared in the 1950s. Square rig was simplified again in 1975. The lanyard and black ribbon were abolished, and the trousers now had more conventional vertical creases, instead of five horizontal ones to allow them to be stowed in a locker.

THE FALKLANDS WAR

In 1979 the Thatcher government came to power and increased service wages to match civilian standards. These gains were soon accompanied by navy cuts under the unpopular Defence Secretary John Nott, including a plan to sell the carrier *Invincible* to Australia and the scrapping of the Antarctic survey ship *Endurance*. This led to a growing crisis in the South Atlantic: Argentine scrap merchants landed illegally on South Georgia, while their government in Buenos Aires became increasingly militant in pushing their long-standing claim to the Falkland Islands. As the crisis built up, Petty Officer Graham Libby of the nuclear submarine *Conqueror* was on leave in Portsmouth:

I had only been there a few days when there was a knock on the door and this policeman stood there saying, 'You've been recalled. Make your way back to the boat.' It was the morning of April the first he knocked on the door, and I thought it was a wind-up, April fool, so I phoned the boat up in Faslane, and they said, 'Yeah, it's true – you're recalled.' When I got there it was just a hive of activity. There were stores on the jetty, there was a complete new weapons load, everybody was running around, and I thought this is not a wind-up, this is not an exercise, something is going on here.[45]

On 2 April, Argentine forces landed on the Falkland Islands and quickly overwhelmed the small Royal Marine force there. Armed forces leave was cancelled and all available ships were quickly got ready for a sudden and unexpected war. To CPO Alan Taylor of the carrier *Hermes* at Portsmouth,

Initially, the main activity was storing ship. We took in as much food as we could cram in, from first thing in the morning until late in the evening and sometimes into the night. Convoys of civvy and Naafi lorries were queuing up for delivery. For other stores, the departments on the ship were 'looking inwards', deciding what they wanted and asked for it. Someone else was sending stuff they thought we should have; if we forgot anything, they had already thought of it. I have never seen the supply system work so well, so quickly, and most of it was the correct stuff.[46]

The carriers *Hermes* and *Invincible* sailed past the Round Tower at Portsmouth on 5 April, with crowds cheering. They were accompanied by the assault ship *Fearless,* two frigates and four landing ships. They would be joined by other ships that were already at sea or would leave later, including merchant ships taken up from trade (STUFT) such as the liners *Queen Elizabeth 2* and *Canberra* with troops, and the container ship *Atlantic Conveyor* with a cargo of helicopters and military stores.

Like almost everyone in Britain and the world, the crews found the situation very unreal. In the destroyer *Sheffield*, 'The various feelings around the ship were funny, some of the lads were really excited at the prospect of going to war, the other lads were more subdued understandably. Everyone was frightened although no one showed it ...'[47] John Leake was one of several men who joined the lower deck by an unusual route on the way south. He had served in the army and then became civilian Naafi canteen manager in the frigate *Ardent* – 'It was the best of both worlds, like being a civilian in the services.' On the way to the Falklands the canteen managers were offered the choice of leaving or enrolling in the navy – he chose the latter and was rated a petty officer. He soon found a use for his experience in operating the ship's machine-guns. As *Sheffield* approached the operational area ahead of the task force,

> All carpets on two decks and below were to be removed and stowed or ditched. All loose furnishings were to be fully secured, all pictures removed from the bulkheads. The only things we were allowed in our lockers were a number one suit, changes of underwear and socks, and some warm clothing in case we had to abandon ship. Everything else had to be stowed in the various store rooms around the ship.[48]

HMS *Antrim* was sent south to help expel the Argentines from South Georgia, and extreme weather created problems for the crew servicing her helicopter, which they nicknamed 'Humphrey.'

> Eleven of us went out, and even in full foul weather gear, anorak, trousers, overalls under that, plus full Number eight action working dress and thermal underwear, it was as if you were naked – the wind just went straight through the lot. Anybody falling into the sea wasn't going to survive. We got ourselves round the helicopter by hanging on to each other's lifelines, and put on as many lashings as we could to make sure the helicopter stayed there.[49]

When the weather cleared it was decided to rescue some SAS troops trapped on the islands, 'so we stripped out all the dunking sonar equipment and ripped the guts out of the cabin to cut the weight right down. The Wessex 3 wasn't designed to carry troops. It was a big operation.' As Humphrey returned, CPO Heritier showed proprietorial concern. 'I was stunned; here were seventeen people in the aircraft; sitting in the door, lying on top of each other, biggish people. I was very concerned about the damage we'd done to the aircraft to carry all this.'[50]

Then it was found that an Argentine submarine had escaped from South Georgia and was a threat to the operation. Humphrey was re-converted to the anti-submarine role, which 'involved a lot of red-eye from the maintenance crew'. It was loaded with two depth-charges, though 'Handling these things is not for when you're tired, at three o'clock on a Sunday morning.' The helicopter observer found the submarine, *Santa Fe*, on the radar and attacked her, the first ever live attack on a submarine by a helicopter. She was damaged and brought into Grytviken in recaptured South Georgia. CPO Bullingham found that one of the men had lost a leg in the attack. 'I felt guilty that it had been our depth charge, and deliberately kept out of the way to avoid seeing him. I'd been one of the people loading the depth charge into the helicopter ...'[51] the Argentines on South Georgia soon surrendered, leading to great relief among the government: Mrs Thatcher proclaimed, 'Rejoice, rejoice'.

On joining the rest of the task force, the maintenance crew still had to work hard on the 21-year-old helicopter:

> Keeping Humphrey going required a lot of improvisation, but one day the engine blew all its oil out, just managing to land. Changing the engine on a Wessex 3 is a very long job, and a guided missile destroyer is very cramped. All the helicopters were needed for cross-decking, so we had to get this done really fast. It normally takes four days – ashore in Portland. We worked forty-eight hours non-stop, while the other trades ran around doing the checks, getting supplies

and feeding us with food and coffee. After thirty-six hours we got it on to the flight deck to test and adjust at full power with the aircraft screwed down in a special rig. We were very tired, doing stupid things like forcing in oil without realising the tank was already full.[52]

Air raids were launched on the airfield at the Falklands capital of Port Stanley on 1 May. On the flight deck of *Hermes*, Naval Airman First Class Andrew Wroot waited for the aircraft to return:

We stood around, waiting and hoping they would all come back. Then we got the order, 'Stand by to receive two Harriers.' They came over; in the distance we could see a couple more, then others for other directions until the air seemed full of them. We tried to land them on as quickly as possible because we knew they were short of fuel. It was controlled panic. If you were there you would think that everything was going wrong – everyone running about all over the place – but really it was all under control. I think they were all down within about six minutes of the first sighting.[53]

Petty Officer Arthur Balls was the Sea Skua missile operator in a Wessex helicopter off Port Stanley, waiting to attack enemy ships that might try to escape:

The firing continued, lots of puffs of brown smoke with bright flashes inside. Then one of the flashes got bigger and I saw it coming towards us, about half a mile from us. I thought it was a shell exploding at first but then I realized it was a missile. Two or three minutes later, I saw another one; this one came high towards us from out of the middle of the anti-aircraft fire. I lost sight of it from the front cockpit but the men in the back reported it coming much closer; they were getting quite excited. So it was time we did something; we turned round and ran away. The missile disappeared into cloud but then reappeared again. The men in the back got really excited then; they thought it was going to hit us ... The missile didn't hit us; we thought it reached the end of its flying time and fell into the sea.[54]

Meanwhile the nuclear submarine *Conqueror* was tracking the Argentine cruiser *General Belgrano* and was given permission at the highest level to attack by torpedo. Petty Officer Graham Libby was the senior sonar operator:

> It's a funny feeling because you weren't nervous because this is all you'd ever trained to do. As time went on, you were constantly passing to the captain the bearings and updating the captain on its position – it was constant updates and the chatter back and forth was tremendous. And even then we were still going, 'It's never going to happen.' Then I thought, 'Fuck me – we are going to fire.' And people looked at each other and went, 'Fucking hell.' I'll never forget it, never forget it. And then the boat vibrated, the first one went, you're moving your cursor around and you hear the fish running away, there's two, three's three, all three are running. And you hear the captain asking, How long to run? So the periscope goes up at the last minute and the scope goes up and he puts his eyes to it, bang.[55]

Belgrano sank with the loss of more than 300 lives, and the Argentine navy stayed in port for the rest of the war. As *Conqueror* withdrew from the scene, Libby continued to listen through his sonar:

> It was a noise we'd never heard before, and we couldn't understand what it was. It was a tinkling noise, like someone wafting their hand through a big glass chandelier. And it wasn't until the analysis of the tapes afterwards that they realized, following the explosion and fires and all that hot metal, it was like dousing a piece of hot metal in a bucket of water. That's what it was as it was going down.[56]

There was some very inappropriate triumphalism in the press at home, but that was not reflected in the navy. The Chaplain of the frigate *Broadsword* reported, 'When *Belgrano* was sunk there was no elation in our ship, as we could be in the same situation ourselves.' And in *Hermes*, ITN correspondent Michael Nicholson found, 'No sailor aboard our ship is celebrating. Sailors do not rejoice in the deaths of other seamen, no matter who they are.'[57] However, the issue remained controversial, as *Belgrano* had been outside the exclusion zone at the time and was heading away from the action.

The feeling of triumphalism did not last for long in any case. Two days later the Type 42 destroyer *Sheffield* was on radar picket duty, though she had no short-range Sea Wolf missiles for close-range defence. In *Invincible* 20 miles away, David Forster was on duty in the operations room, as he reported 18 years later:

> As I was the long-distance air surveyor, I operated 1022 radar which covered 258 miles down to 18 miles radius from the ship. I was sitting at my display when a contact appeared at 180 miles. So I waited for the next sweep – and there it was again. I logged it into the computer and reported it as I'd done so many times before. But this time [an officer] said there was nothing there. The next sweep of my radar came and there it was, now at 160 miles. I reported it again. But the same thing happened. Precious time was passing us by, we did not alert the fleet. We did nothing. The next sweep of my radar, it was at 130 miles, so I reported it again. This time [the officer] became annoyed and told me 'You're chasing rabbits'. My mate now reported a contact at 120 miles and closing. I changed my display down to watch it closer. The contact was now at 80 miles and closing. The radar swept again but this time there were two contacts. The second contact was only on our display for two sweeps when it disappeared under radar coverage. This indicated that we were dealing with an Exocet missile designed to skim above the waves. My mate and I reported the double contact and the fact that one had suddenly disappeared. [An officer] told us that we were 'riding a bike'.[58]

Forster thought he should have shouted, 'There is a fucking contact, there's something coming in, believe me, alert the fleet!', but naval discipline asserted itself and he said no more. For whatever reason, *Sheffield* was not at full action stations that afternoon and PO Medical Assistant G. A. Meager was resting:

At about 1400 I was asleep in my bunk, I woke up and looked at my watch and decided that I had another hour in bed before I had to get up for my watch at 1600. A pipe was made 'AWO Ops Room AWO', with a sense of emergency, this was followed by a loud crump and the ship shuddered violently. Realising we had been hit by something I fell out of bed, landing on a fellow comrade who was to die later that afternoon.[59]

She had been hit by an Exocet missile, which failed to explode but nevertheless set off fires and explosions throughout the ship. Meager went to the area of the worst damage.

The sight that next hit me is one I will never forget as long as I live. The whole of the port waist was covered with junior rates fighting the fire with buckets of water on lengths of rope so as to cool the superstructure. I made my way forward to the flight deck where I found the worst of our casualties, one Chief Petty Officer with 60 per cent burns and shrapnel wounds, obviously in terrible pain but amazingly he still had his sense of humour.[60]

The order came to abandon ship. 'This was when there was? the first signs of panic. Throughout the whole thing it was noticeable that calmness reigned supreme, maybe all that training at Portland and other exercises had paid off in the long run.'[61] Meager had timeless feelings of loss after that:

When we abandoned ship and had time to sit and reflect everybody suffered from some form of shock, some deeper than others. Fear of a strange ship. Sadness of losing friends, a ship and all personal belongings. It's an incredible feeling to see nearly everything you own going up in smoke, the only things you've got left are the clothes you stand in, it is a very strange feeling.[62]

Andrew Wroot was one of the flight deck party on *Hermes* as the *Sheffield* casualties arrived:

The first one came in by helicopter, arms covered in plastic bags, face all black. He seemed confused. I had never seen anything like it before – horrific. There were many more after that and a lot of hard work to be done. We all thought the *Sheffield* would be saved; we never thought a single missile could knock out one of our most modern ships.

Later, when they piped that the *Sheffield* had been abandoned and should be considered lost, all of us in the junior ratings dining hall became completely hushed, perhaps the odd whisper and a murmur, but mainly general disbelief.[63]

On 21 May the navy landed marines and soldiers at San Carlos Bay and the ships suffered heavily in 'bomb alley' as the Argentine Air Force launched attack after attack. In *Antrim*, CPO Terry Bullingham froze as the Skyhawks came in, while the rest of the flight deck crew retreated. 'Time stands still on these occasions, and realizing the aircraft were pointing at me like the proverbial finger of fate, I got myself down and went into the foetal position, as everyone on the flight deck was spreading out ...then I felt a sickening impact like smashing your head in a car crash .. colleagues told me my helmet was full of shrapnel. If I hadn't been wearing it, I would have been dead.' In the medical station Bullingham could see nothing but was reassured – 'You've just got a pair of black eyes, Steve' – but he already knew he had been permanently blinded.[64]

Antrim survived, but the Type 21 frigates *Antelope* and *Ardent* were both sunk by bombing that day, followed by *Coventry*, sister ship of *Sheffield*, and the container ship *Atlantic Conveyor* on the 25th. As soon as she arrived from the West Indies, *Exeter*, the only Type 42 fitted with the new Type 1022 radar, led the defence and shot down four aircraft during the campaign. After the losses, there were no qualms about firing back and it was reported of one Sea Dart operator. 'On the way down, this chap had been saying that he would never be able to press the button when the time came; he could never kill someone like that. Later, after his first Sea Dart firing, someone asked him how he felt. 'Bloody marvellous.' That was the post-*Sheffield* feeling.'[65] But this was not enough to defend the landing ships *Sir Tristram* and *Sir Galahad*, which were attacked in Fitzroy Cove and the latter sunk, with heavy losses. Eventually the British forces prevailed on land and the Argentines surrendered on 14 June.

It was a dramatic demonstration of naval power, deployed 8,000 miles from home and with virtually no advance planning. The navy's prestige was at its highest since 1945, and crowds turned out again to welcome the ships as they came home, one by one or in small groups. As wives and children were filmed greeting their loved ones, the public became aware for perhaps the first time how much the navy had become a family institution.

8

THE MODERN NAVY

Recruiting

The navy basked in the afterglow of the Falklands War for some little time, but it could not last for ever. Once it was over, the public had the impression of waking from a dream, and some seemed embarrassed about their enthusiasm during it. Politicians mostly denied that it was a major factor in Mrs Thatcher's second, and more decisive, election victory in 1983. Certainly the war was hardly ever mentioned during that campaign, but it did restore her fortunes, from being a deeply unpopular leader to an election winner. The war was also reflected in naval recruiting – in 1983 more than 30,000 applied for 4,000 vacancies. Interestingly, however, officer recruitment remained slow that year.[1]

From 1982 ratings were signed on for the 'open engagement'. They would join for 22 years' full pensionable service, but could leave with 18 months notice after they had completed 2½ years' adult service, in other words after four years. It was hoped that this would take advantage of the inertia of some on the lower deck, as they would have to *positively* resign well in advance, rather than leaving by default by not making a 'conscious decision to re-engage'. Bonuses were available to those who did progress through their time.[2]

Recruiting remained strong in 1983–4, and targets were met even though they had been increased, except in the case of artificer apprentices, where there was strong competition from industry. According to the recruiting staff in 1985, 'Every weekday brings an average of twenty would-be sailors into the Greater London careers office. If, at the end of the week, five out of a hundred are accepted into the Navy, it is a very good week indeed.'[3]

By the 1980s, it had become far less common for a son to follow his father into a particular career. In 1985, 17 per cent of recruits at HMS *Raleigh* joined because they had a father in the navy or another service. They were outnumbered by 28 per cent who saw travel as the greatest advantage, even in the age of the cheap flight, and 19 per cent who joined for the career prospects. 14 per cent more joined because they had been sea cadets, 8 per cent because of ambition, 9 per cent because of a liking for the sea, and the same number for the traditional (but negative) reason of unemployment.[4]

By 1985 many thought that the young men were of a higher standard than in the past: 'The fleet master-at-arms thought the Navy was now attracting a more intelligent and aware type of person. This had its implications on the discipline side.'[5] The new, smaller navy could afford to be selective, and thorough tests were carried out at recruiting offices. For example, after a series of stiff tests and an interview in the central London office in 1985, a lieutenant concluded of one candidate, 'His record at work is unstable and he is not progressing in any aspect at all. His motivation is very, very weak. But I think in twelve months time he could make the Navy, if he does as he is told. I have advised him to go to the Royal Naval Reserve. Physically there are no problems at all.'[6] By 1986 applications were 8 per cent down on the previous year, though all targets were achieved including that for apprentices. Figures remained adequate until almost the end of the decade, when two contradictory factors began to take effect – the decline of British industry and the end of the Cold War.

TRAINING

Raleigh, near Plymouth, was now the only training establishment for new entrants apart from male officer candidates. By 1984 it had undergone a transformation from the 'hutted camp' of war years:

A complete rebuild over the past 10 years had transformed RALEIGH into a modern attractive purpose built establishment with a very wide range of facilities unsurpassed anywhere in the Royal Navy. These include 3 Loyal Class ships in the Inshore Training Squadron, the Harbour Training Ship SALISBURY and some 120 power boats and sailing craft. There is also a comprehensive range of sport facilities including a splendid indoor swimming pool ... On the more leisurely recreational side there is a modern NAAFI complex including a club and diso [sic] and the largest collection of space invader machines anywhere in the three services![7]

Training was much abbreviated compared with the past, as the captain of *Raleigh* said in 1986:

In the old days when the young boy seaman went to H.M.S. *Ganges*, he was there for a year. Twenty years ago at *Raleigh*, he was here three or four months. Now we do it in six weeks. We have been squeezed. That means ever-greater demands on the motivation and expertise of the staff ... the old British taxpayer has got his pound of flesh out of the Navy today, in terms of value for money.[8]

Entrants were given the chance to reconsider their choice of career. In the 1987 documentary *Nozzers* the training lieutenant agonised over a Scottish lad who wanted to leave after the long journey from home. By 2004 the navy had no need to take unwilling recruits. One class was addressed by a petty officer:

If you don't want to join the Navy, then don't ... It must be your decision. If you are here because your dad pushed you into it, or because someone else pressured you, then you should leave. We don't do press gangs any more. OK? We want you if you want us – simple as that. It costs £30,000 to train each one of you over the next eight weeks, so we want to know if you are a good investment ... Later on tonight you will be invited to sign your naval contract. If you are sure, then sign it. If you want to sleep on it, do so and tackle the decision tomorrow morning. Plenty of people do that – we call them 'sleepers'. Any questions?[9]

However, the wastage rate was not large: in 1983, 45 out of 544 people had been given Premature Voluntary Release or PVR. Less than ten of these were young men the navy would have wanted to keep anyway.[10] If they did sign, they had to stay for six weeks before the next opportunity to leave would come. They were issued with working dress, once known as Number 8 and later as Number 4, with an orange flash for their epaulettes, 'the sign of their rank, or should I say absence of rank?' They started to learn the basics of naval life. Foot drill has often proved controversial in the navy in the past, and some have seen it as a waste of time, something imposed by the army and HMS *Excellent*. Today *Raleigh* tends to regard it as more essential than ever with a generation of teenagers who are not used to obeying orders:

> These recruits are coming from a society which doesn't have any discipline either, and they are full of ideas about their rights – all pink and fluffy political correctness. Sometimes, if we shout at these people, we get a bollocking for giving them a bollocking. If someone is late they are in trouble as far as I am concerned but then we are told, 'Go easy, they probably have underlying problems.' Sorry, they are late – that is their underlying problem![11]

After the first week spent in isolation, 'the remaining six weeks of training at H.M.S. *Raleigh* are a careful balance of one hundred and one topics of training and talks'.[12] On another course,

> The recruits, continuing their Phase One training, have had a busy week. They have been attending lectures on kit maintenance, history of the naval uniform, naval law, ship's safety and team building. Today they have been learning about the mechanism of the rifle, and now they are on the rifle range for the first time.[13]

Only male ratings had to be able to swim until 1990, when Wrens went to sea. By the 2000s, all recruits had to be able to jump from a high diving board wearing full safety kit – three failures in this would lead to dismissal. The petty officer instructors were very different from those who had tyrannised *Ganges* half a century or so earlier. In *Nozzers* they consistently addressed the recruits in a firm but gentle tone. During a very unsatisfactory kit inspection in 1984 one recruit was told, 'General presentation, one out of ten. And I think I'm being generous there.' But again the tone was not oppressive. 'Many of the devastating judgements were delivered in a helpful tone of voice, suggesting more sorrow than anger; sorrow that the recruit hadn't come up to the high expectations entertained of him.'[14]

The instructors at *Raleigh* still take huge pride at the passing-out parade at the end of the course, in seeing parents amazed at the transformation of their shambling, apathetic children into smart and disciplined sailors:

> They are lined up in their ranks – resplendent in their Number Ones and shouldering SA 80 rifles with bayonets fixed. The Royal Marine band is playing stirring marching music and everyone's families are here to witness the occasion. There are many cheeks wet with tears of pride and emotion.[15]

In the supply and secretariat branch, HMS *Pembroke* at Chatham closed in 1983, and training was moved to *Raleigh*. Until 2001 stewards and chefs often spent a long time ashore before joining a ship. After basic and professional training at *Raleigh*, stewards would spend four months and chefs ten months at a shore establishment as 'part four' of their training. A chef might spend two years in the service before joining a ship. The last part of the training was abolished and the rest concentrated more on fitting a trainee to Operational Performance Standard to become suitable for a billet on a destroyer, frigate or submarine.[16]

One of the lessons of the Falklands War was that damage control was found to be inadequate, and as a result Damage Repair Instruction Units were set up at Plymouth and Portsmouth. The one in HMS *Excellent* simulated the decks of a frigate with the lower deck half-filled with water while the whole assembly rocked in a realistic manner. The task was to use plugs and props to block up holes in the bottom and sides, making both temporary and longer-lasting repairs. All this training was vindicated, not in action, but when HMS *Nottingham* ran aground off Australia in 2002: 'Despite the severity of the flooding, the Ship's Company pulled together in impressive style.' Within 25 minutes the flooding had been limited, partly by crew swimming through diesel-contaminated water, or standing in up to five feet of water. Shores were erected despite some faults in those supplied, and electrical supplies were re-instated so that pumps were in use. 'It was reported that morale remained high throughout and teams were cheerful and enthusiastic focussing on their tasks. A good deal of ingenuity was evident in solving shoring problems, running ad hoc cable supplies and stemming water ingress. When questioned all felt that their training [had] prepared them well for this incident.'[17]

THE SHIPS

There were no new principles in ship design after the 1980s except to reduce the radar signature by means of 'stealth'. Gas turbine was established as the main motive power of larger surface warships and diesel of smaller ones, while all submarines were eventually nuclear-powered. The gun made something of a comeback after the Falklands experience, with 4.5-inch weapons being fitted to the foredeck of each of the third batch of Type 22 frigates, and close-range anti-aircraft guns such as the Dutch Goalkeeper as a last ditch defence. Their guns made the 'Type 22s, batch 3' very useful in any operation with the potential need for naval gunfire support (or NGS) – the earlier Type 22s carried no main guns, the *Leander*s had mostly given them up, the Type 42 destroyers were mainly reserved for air support, and the new Type 23 frigates were not yet ready. As a result *Chatham* and *Cornwall*, in particular, would feature in many of the navy's most memorable deployments over the next decades.

In the mid-1980s the *Leanders* were still the mainstay of the fleet, though some suggested the bottoms were falling out of them, and by modern standards they were expensive to man. From 1988 onwards they were sold overseas, scrapped or used as targets. The 'stretched' Type 42 destroyer was already planned before the Falklands War, and four of these were launched with increased close-range defences. The most important new design to enter service was the Duke class, the Type 23 frigate. After the rising expense of the Type 22, the Type 23 was designed as a low-cost ship; although costs rose yet again as the ships were built, they still cost 25 per cent less than the Type 22s. Their greatest advantage was that they were designed for 'stealth', to

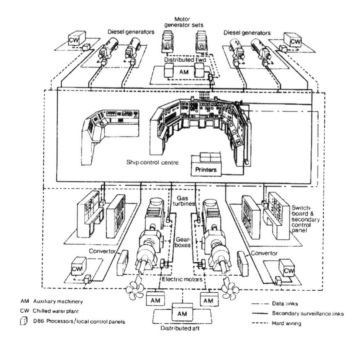

The machinery layout for Type 23 frigates, using the combined diesel-electric and gas (CODLAG) arrangement.

present a low radar signature, but their elegantly-curved hull lines were spoiled by a great square funnel, which took some getting used to. In the early stages they were dogged by computer problems, and operations room crews had to communicate verbally as they did in the days before automation took over. The Type 23s had far smaller complements than their predecessors. Compared with 259 on a Type 22, a Type 23 carried 185 men and women, made up of 17 officers, 57 senior rates and 111 junior rates. The high proportion of chiefs and petty officers tended to make it more necessary to persuade men to stay on for longer, and on board ship it meant there were fewer hands to do menial duties. There were plans to subcontract some of the cleaning, but that was difficult in many foreign ports where there were security risks, and it was impossible at sea.

Three new classes of mine warfare vessels were built, though in far smaller numbers than the 'Ton' class of the 1950s. The 12 River class ships were designed for use against Soviet deep-water floating mines and were built in the mid-1980s. They were mainly used by the RNR until the end of the Cold War made the concept obsolete, and they were sold in the 1990s. The 12 Hunt class mine countermeasures vessels of the 1980s were also used with the Northern Ireland Squadron. They fulfilled the dual role of minesweeping and minehunting, whereas earlier vessels could only carry out one of these roles. The *Sandown* class of the 1990s were smaller, 450 tons compared with 685. The 49-ton training ships of the *Archer* class had originally been designed for the use of the Royal Naval Auxiliary Patrol Service until it was disbanded with the end of the Cold War. Some were used for patrols off Gibraltar, but the majority joined University Royal Naval Units, carrying a crew of five regular RN and 12 students – they were unusual in that the accommodation for the regular RN ratings was better than that for URNU midshipmen.

OVERSEAS CONTRACTION

The British Empire might be said to have ended formally with the withdrawal from Hong Kong in 1997. Two hundred sailors paraded that April as the base, HMS *Tamar*, was closed. As early as 1985 a marine engineering mechanic had commented,

> We seem to go [to] fewer and fewer places. The runs [ashore] are decreasing all the time, it seems. The chaps feel this generally. There is not so much to balance the boredom of long periods afloat, when it seems that the only time you get off is for cleaning the ship ... If you go to interesting places, you tend to forget that, but not otherwise.[18]

The West Indies guard ship, renamed the Atlantic Patrol Task (North), was a popular posting. In the 1980s the Dominican historian Lennox Honychurch asked visiting ships such as *Rhyl, Glamorgan* and even the Royal Yacht *Britannia* to haul old cannon back into place at Fort Shirley, an important historical site being restored in the north of the island. In 1991 the naval attaché at Barbados replied humorously to the effect that, 'Well I don't think we have the men with the stamina for such things at present, everything aboard ship nowadays is done by pressing computer buttons!' However, in 2010 HMS *Manchester* was asked for men to help raise a flagpole, and they were inundated by volunteers; unfortunately the ship was diverted to relief work when Hurricane 'Tomas' hit St. Lucia.

In cooperation with the much larger US Navy presence, the West Indies guard ship patrolled against drugs and assisted in natural disasters. From December 1995 to April 1996, for example, HMS *Brave* made three major drugs seizures with a street value of more than £125 million, while a helicopter identified drug plantations for destruction by the civil authorities.[19] In 1997 the frigate *Liverpool* anchored off Little Bay on the north-western coast of Montserrat to supervise the evacuation of the population.[20] In 2010 there was a gap in coverage as ships were no longer stationed there outside the hurricane season, and there was no ship to help after the Haiti earthquake.

Defence of the Falklands (Atlantic Patrol Task (South)) was a standard commitment after 1982, but not a popular one:

> I think that last year I had seven hours off the ship in four months. In that seven hours, I just walked around for a bit of fresh air; it was so nice to get off the ship. There is nothing to do in the Falklands. A couple of hours I spent on South Georgia, just throwing snowballs. I was glad just to stretch my legs on land.[21]

Gibraltar remained a British possession. The naval base was less used than in the past but was still popular:

> Practically the whole ship's company are ashore and enjoying the facilities, shops and restaurants of their beloved Gibraltar. With its Marks & Spencer, Woolworths, W. H. Smith and the densest collection of pubs in the world, it is Jack's home from home. This hallucination of England clinging to the edge of Spain is a sailor's paradise and although many complain that the mood of the place has changed with the depletion in the British naval presence and the opening of the border with Spain, it has retained much of its bizarre English charm.[22]

Despite the much publicised withdrawal from East of Suez in the seventies, continuing crises in the Middle East and East Africa caused ships to spend a good deal of time there. Mombasa in Kenya was a popular run ashore, though,

> The town itself is somewhat on the grubby side, with streets full of potholes and buildings crumbling. Nevertheless, it has a character all of its own and the local people were invariably friendly. At the roadsides were hundreds of small stalls, their owners constantly trying to sell things to visitors. When the ship sailed, there were enough carved wood elephants, giraffes, impalas and warthogs onboard to start a zoo.
>
> The best thing about Mombasa was the weather, although there was a torrential downpour on Christmas Day! Most people took

advantage of the tropical sunshine to visit the beautiful, white, sandy beaches, or just to sit by the pool in the Mission to Seamen. Some went further afield, to the idyllic hotels along the coast to enjoy a few days station leave.

The Seychelles turned out to be less attractive;

> The Seychelles, idyllic tropical islands set in an azure sea, proved to have a similar climate to Devonport in the summer, except that the rain was warmer. Port Victoria itself did not seem to be the best place to break down as not only were the engineering facilities sparse but we threatened to take the very flimsy jetty to sea with us when the wind got up. With this in mind we flashed up and headed north through the Indian Ocean to the Gulf.

The crew of *Glamorgan* found, 'Bahrain was a different run ashore. Only the expatriates could afford the prices, but they looked after the ship's company well judging by some of the headaches in the morning.'

> By the following morning the news had travelled round the ship's company that the organised runs ashore were the only way to have a good time. Some of them had fallen foul of the local hotels bar prices (£3 for a small beer) and were still in shock. ... As well as attending the sporting and social functions many of the ship's company took time off to visit the local town market (The Souk) hunting for the few shops selling local curios amongst the hundred selling Japanese Hi-Fi. Others visited the American Administrative Support Unit (ASU) where a cheap beer, a few laughs and a re-fight of the War of Independence could be guaranteed.

Dubai was a favourite place during deployments in the Gulf, with 'many and varied delights that make modern Dubai, that oasis of hedonism set like a sparing jewel in the arid deserts of the Arab Emirates, one of the most popular destinations for a sailor wanting to let his or her hair down."Look at that!" says Rab, focussing his binoculars on Dubai's dramatic skyline. "A sailor's paradise and no bleedin' mistake."'[23]

EARLY PLANS FOR WOMEN AT SEA

The idea of sending Wrens to sea had already occurred during the Second World War. They served as crews of harbour craft in October 1941 and also in Naval Control of Shipping, which involved boarding merchant ships. The more general question was raised in the Navy Estimates debate of 1943, and the First Lord was briefed by the Director:

> D.W.R.N.S. points out the impracticability of employing 'mixed' crews. The additional refittings that are constantly being developed for use afloat make a double demand upon the limited space and weight permissible in warships, both by reason of the fittings themselves and the extra personnel to work them. It is becoming increasingly difficult to fit an adequate complement into existing ships, and it is impossible to spare space and weight for separate female accommodation.
>
> To 'man' a warship wholly by a female crew would be impossible owing to lack of expertise.[24]

Clearly the role of women was changing in civil society by the 1970s, though never as fast as some of them wanted. The Sex Discrimination Act became law in 1975, but the armed forces were specifically exempted from it. Naval recruiters and presentation teams were regularly asked, 'When will Wrens serve at sea?' Moreover, the act was likely to increase the expectations of women in the long-term. The authorities looked into this seriously in 1976. The use of women offered several advantages, including a better career pattern for the small number of ratings who would be affected, a potential reduction in manning problems, and the navy showing 'a positive and progressive attitude in its treatment of women', which in turn might be 'a morale and recruitment booster'. There was no question of them joining combatant ships, but several other possibilities were looked at. The Duke of Edinburgh dismissed any idea of them serving on the Royal Yacht, and in any case there was no mess deck suitable for them. There were several old trials ships, but all were near the end of their lives and it would not be economic to convert them to take women. This left survey vessels, and a very detailed report was made on the possibility of employing two petty officers and nine junior rates in HMS *Hydra*. One mess deck was to be converted for the POs and another for the junior rates, with lockers carefully arranged to prevent any view of the bed spaces from the door. It was noted that 'women appear to accrue more personal possessions than men of an equivalent age group'; conforming to the stereotype, the messes were fitted with suitcase racks, tea lockers, mirrors and ironing boards. An official commented, 'The seagoing sailor will have to accept some adjustment to his normal daily life – moderation in the use of certain expletives, more discretion perhaps in his mode of attire on his way to and from the bathroom.'

But the Hydrographer of the Navy in charge of the vessel concerned dismissed the idea out of hand. The Hydrographic Service was about to begin a major reorganisation which would damage morale enough without any new experiments. The ships in question were mostly employed in the Persian Gulf, where shore facilities for women were non-existent. A seabed operations vessel was suggested as an alternative, and this had the advantage that it only went to sea for 21 days at a time from UK ports, but it was on its own and stationary for much of the time so it 'did not offer ideal shipboard experience'. More generally, it was feared that there would be protests from sailors' wives, who resented the presence of Wrens even on shore. In 1978 the whole idea was dismissed by an official who was 'unmoved' by the suggested advantages, and believed that, 'The time to decide to send WRNS to sea will be when we can discern (perhaps in our studies of the manpower difficulties that we expect to encounter in the 80s) a clear-cut and tangible advantage to the Navy in WRNS progressively taking over a substantial part of the non-combatant sea-going task.'[25]

Subjection to the Naval Discipline Act in 1978 had implications for the status of women as combatants because the Geneva Convention stated that all members of armed forces party to a conflict, except medical personnel, had 'the right to participate directly in hostilities'. According to the British government view in 1988,

> In these terms, members of the WRNS would be combatants in the event of a conflict involving the UK. However, it has long been Government policy that servicewomen shall not be employed in 'combat roles'. As the Royal Navy classifies all seagoing billets in naval hulls as 'combat', Naval servicewomen do not qualify for regular sea service and they do not serve in complemented sea billets.[26]

Women were, however, allowed to go to sea for short periods in civilian-manned Royal Fleet Auxiliaries. A hundred and fifty of them were taken out in the appropriately-named frigate *Amazon* in 1988, and that appeared satisfactory. But by 1989 it was the shortage of men that was the main driver of change. The dip in the birth rate by the early 1970s was beginning to take effect on recruiting figures – it was estimated that there would be a million fewer school leavers by the mid-1990s. There were already 300 gaps in manning requirements afloat and 2,000 ashore. Admiral Sir Brian Brown was ordered to look into the matter and soon rejected a suggestion that women should be employed afloat in peace but withdrawn if war started. The effect of this on a 'worked up team would be very bad, and the practical transfer arrangements could delay an appropriate response in a crisis'. Moreover, the women would be seen as 'fair weather sailors' by the rest of the crew.[27] There would also be difficulties in employing them in a warship:

> It is a fact that most men are physically 30% stronger than most women. It is also a fact that with the advent of computer assisted

technology the modern Navy is considerably less physically demanding than previously. However, day-to-day life at sea does demand more stamina than life ashore and there remain specific areas where above average strength is required; replenishment at sea, action stations, stretcher- bearing, negotiating some hatches.

Women's training would need to build on these areas, but experience with women in the fire and ambulance services was encouraging.[28]

THE FIRST WOMEN AT SEA

In February 1990 it was announced that women would be allowed to volunteer to go to sea in warships. The first batch served in HMS *Brilliant* and formed about 6 per cent of the complement during the First Gulf War in 1991. Commander C. S. Hadden reported,

Fifty-something days at sea and in defence watches (much of it inside the potential Iraqi area of operations), regular SCUD alerts, and a

Tugg's less official view of women on board ship.

significant length of time at minewarning red with messdecks below the waterline cleared was certainly long and stressful enough to expose any potential weakness in men or women.

Were we less aggressive, less dangerous to the enemy? No, with women in the ops room, MCO and on the bridge we were at least as effective, and (given women's greater aural acuity and better powers of concentration) arguably more so. When we spent a dangerous 17 hour-long night fighting a major merchant ship fire shortly after the war's end were we less effective or did we fight the fire less aggressively? No, women were employed equally with men, including the business end of firefighting hoses.[29]

From September 1993, male ratings and all women who had joined after September 1990 were on the same advancement roster, and the proportion of leading hands and senior rates would not depend on gender but on merit. By this time, women had truly joined the lower deck. Recruiting of women did indeed increase, so they made up 5.6 per cent of the navy in 1990 and just over 7per cent by 1992, but that level remained fairly steady throughout the decade, and predictions that they might reach 20 per cent at some stage were never realised.

Full acceptance was not so easy, however. In *Brilliant* in 1994 one woman said, 'Because we are on deployment the workload is much greater and you always feel that you are resented by a lot of the men. I think they feel it is a man's world and that we are in the way. It'll take a long time for them to get used to Wrens at sea – if ever'.[30]

When the crew had their SODS [ships opera and dramatic society] opera the Wrens took the chance to state their case, which was not appreciated by the men.

'Gentlemen, before we entertain you with a song I have a few words of introduction.' She pauses.

'I would just like to say thank you for the superb welcome and hospitality you gave us when we arrived on the ship ... NOT!'

Some sailors at the back of the audience start to hiss.

'You have at all times treated us not as splits but as equals ... I DON'T THINK!'

The hissing gets louder.

'Your kindness, tolerance, and lack of prejudice has not gone unnoticed. THANKS FOR NOTHING ONE AND ALL! This song is dedicated to you.'

A section of the audience has now broken into a chorus of hisses, jeers and catcalls. The officers in the front row look uncomfortable.[31]

A report by the University of Plymouth in 2000 showed that after ten years there were a thousand women serving in 47 naval ships. Seventy-three per cent of posts were open to them, but still not in submarines and small vessels or on mine-clearance diving. They were generally accepted on board, and only 13 per cent of males expressed a preference for all-male ships, down from 47 per cent in 1993 – though 50 per cent of ratings still had some doubts about mixed crewing, and this was prevalent among the junior rates, who tended to believe that women were not given their share of physically demanding tasks. It was found that women were more likely to shorten their careers than men. Nor was the navy compatible with motherhood. There were few sea-going female senior rates to provide role models, and the 'management of relationships' caused problems. Unlike couples in army or RAF bases, sailors at sea had no chance to get out of their confined environment. It was difficult for a heterosexual couple to conduct a relationship on board as a 'no touching' rule was in force:

My boyfriend, Paul, was actually on this ship – that's how we met. Having him on board was terrible.

It was one of the hardest things I have ever had to cope with because the environment of a warship doesn't allow a show of emotions. When we were on board we just had to be regular shipmates, no different from anybody else. Then, on shore we could be normal and very 'lovey-dovey' for a while, but the next day back to being shipmates again.[32]

Sometimes, it was claimed, a ship became known as a 'love boat' – 'One can identify them immediately by the string of love-struck, heterosexual sailors locked in passionate embrace on the quarterdeck, in warm ports away from home.'[33]

ACCOMMODATION AFLOAT AND ASHORE

Ashore, the navy started the 1980s with a long-standing deficit in the provision of married quarters, but that tended to reduce due to the decline in overall numbers and to economic factors. In line with national trends, a large proportion of the navy owned their own homes by the end of the millennium, including single people. A survey of 2001 showed that 82 per cent of married personnel were homeowners, and nearly all had property within 20 miles of a port area.[34] This tended to reduce the importance of married quarters; in 1996, 13,000 out of 55,000 were empty across the three services. They were privatised by selling them to Annington Homes Ltd, to be leased back to the Defence Housing Executive. Upgrades were still planned on many of them, including 630 at Faslane.[35]

For single ratings, there was increased demand for single living accommodation – 'a room of one's own'. Ashore, the problem could be solved given money and time. Project EMMA at Portsmouth was planned to deliver 584 units by 2003–5, Project ARMADA at Plymouth was for 1,650 in 2004–8, and FASLAR at Faslane was to produce 2,432 between 2003 and 2010.[36] Afloat, the ocean survey vessel HMS *Scott* was unique in providing a single cabin for every officer and rating, including en suite facilities. But this was not practicable in the fleet at large. In the new Type 23 frigates,

> The mixing of branches and specialisations within Junior Rates messdecks is a welcome departure from the traditional keeping of 'dab-toes', 'stokers', 'greenies' and 'white mafia' apart. Mixing has delivered a real esprit de corps and been highly successful in promoting greater inter- and intra-departmental understanding – particularly since the introduction of the Warfare Branch Operator/Mechanics.[37]

But accommodation was still cramped in submarines, such as the new *Trafalgar*:

> My accommodation, I was told, would be roomy for a T-boat ... In fact, I could almost fully extend my right arm before I came into contact with a 30-ft Sub-Harpoon anti-ship missile. Also sharing the weapons storage compartment were eight of the newest members of the crew of 120, and a good deal of high explosives.'[38]

HOMOSEXUALITY

The increasing acceptance of homosexuality in society at large created new problems for the navy. At first it continued to try hard to keep it out of the navy, but by 1999 it was clear that this could not last for ever. A petty officer accommodation manager highlighted the problems it might create:

> At present in all ships' Standing Orders, no females are allowed in male accommodation and vice versa. Therefore, how can I regulate single-sex accommodation? ... it is hard enough segregating the non-smokers from the smokers, never mind gay personnel. Will I have to create heterosexual floors and gay floors? If so, can Wren Smith and AB Jones now live in the same mess? If not, then surely it is discrimination.[39]

After a century or so of jokes and popular myths, the navy at last had to confront the issue of homosexuality. In the 1990s it was still actively driving gays out of the service. Though it was no longer illegal under military law, they could be administratively discharged – one sailor was dismissed because a list of Portsmouth gay clubs was found in his locker, without any evidence that he had taken part in any homosexual practices. Several cases came before the European Court of Human rights, including one brought by John Beckett, a weapons engineering mechanic who had joined in 1989 and had done well in his assessments, being considered an officer candidate. In 1993 he saw his chaplain about a personal matter and told him that he was gay. He was interviewed by his officer, then his locker was searched by the service police. He was questioned about his relationship with women, whether he bought pornographic magazines and whether he had been abused as a child. They demanded details of his homosexual relationships, and whether he was 'butch' or 'bitch.' He was then given an administrative discharge. In 1999 the European Court of Human Rights ruled the behaviour of the naval authorities was illegal, along with the cases of three other ex-service personnel.

The services were obliged to reverse their attitudes. In January 2000 the Secretary of State for Defence announced, 'There is no longer a reason to deny homosexuals the opportunity of a career in the Armed Forces.' The only test was to be: 'Have the actions or behaviour of an individual adversely impacted or are they likely to impact on the efficiency or operational effectiveness of the service?' This caused surprisingly little controversy, perhaps because the sailor had traditionally been tolerant of homosexuals. By the end of the year the Ministry of Defence found the new policy had had 'no effect on morale' though early in 2001 very few gays had publicly come out and one seaman said, 'My private life has never been embroiled in my working life. If I'm asked, I'll answer, but I don't walk around with a big flag saying "I'm gay".' By 2005 the navy was the first of the armed services to positively target gay recruits through Stonewall's Diversity Champion's Programme. Gay personnel were allowed to share married quarters if they had registered as a civil partnership, but the 'no-sex afloat' policy was to apply to them as it did to heterosexual couples. It was reported that 'a substantial majority' of naval personnel had taken the recognition of gays 'in their stride.'[40]

ENGINEERS

In 1983 the mechanicians were merged with the artificers and the rating system regularised so that there were no longer artificers first, second and third class but petty officers, chiefs and charge chiefs. The

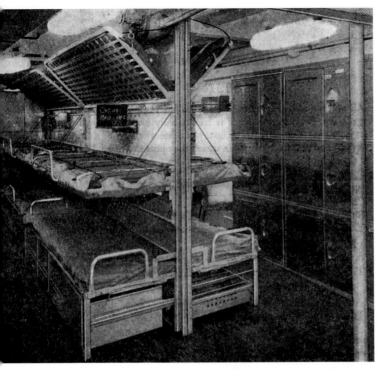

Left: 6 Bunks on a messdeck in the 1960s.
Below: A wren works with a male rating to service a Dragonfly helicopter in the late 1950s. (Fleet Air Arm)

Above: A float at the Notting Hill Carnival attempts to boost the multi-racial profile of the navy. (Broadsheet, 1998–99)
Below: Seamen plotting with the grease pencil.

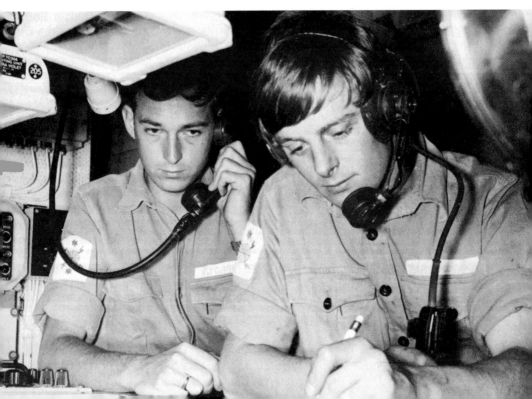

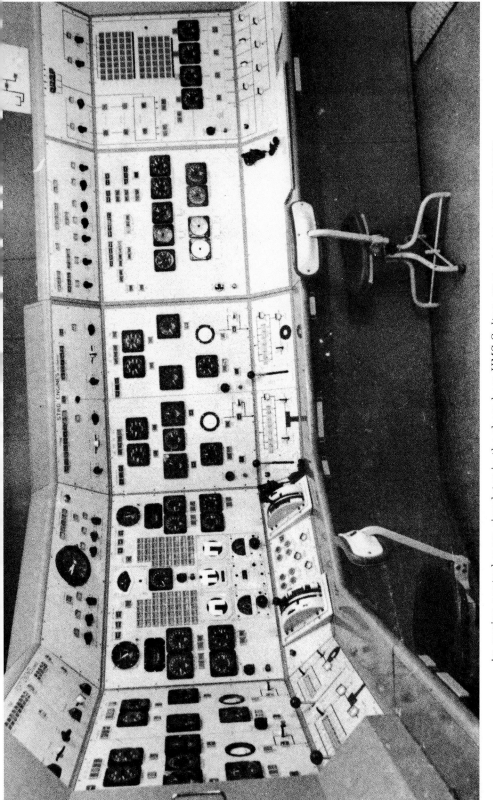

An engine control room simulator in the shore base HMS *Sultan*. (National Archives ADM 204/3553)

Above: The Messdeck of a *Leander* Class frigate. **Left:** Manhandling a Seacat missile, securing the canister base to the launcher platform in 1961. (National Archives 1/27992)

The chief petty officers' mess in a *Leander* Class frigate.

The Icelandic patrol boat *Thor* rams the frigate *Andromeda* in January 1976 (Press Association)

HMS *Conqueror* returns to Faslane after sinking the *Belgrano* – the pirate flag was traditional for successful submarines, but did not help British public relations at the time. (Alamy)

A casualty from HMS *Sheffield* is helped on board the *Hermes*. (Getty)

authorities wanted to reduce the basic grade for an artificer from chief to petty officer, but that met strong opposition, as the artificers and ex-artificers (who were prominent among the engineering officers) closed ranks against them. The Directorate of Naval Manning replied, 'The proposal to set the base rate for artificer at PO is not, nor ever has been a device for saving money but is aimed at ensuring that military rank is used appropriately.'[41] A former artificer predicted a retention crisis among serving members of the branch. 'The serious proposal that the Artificer structure should in the future be based on the Petty Officer level and not on the Chief Petty Officer level as at present and the news that Artificer Apprentices for the first time ever are to be downgraded to be dressed in square rig has left me wondering whether there could have been two changes more likely to depress serving Artificers, to make retention that much more difficult and to work against recruiting; this in a manpower area where neither was ever buoyant.'[42]

In any case the role of the artificer was changing, though he was no less important: 'Although modern technology has removed the historical requirement for artificers to manufacture replacement parts for machinery, their role remains pivotal as systems engineers and diagnosticians in every area of naval technology.'[43] In 2004 the new rank of warrant officer second class was introduced, specifically to cater for charge chief artificers, who until then had 'poor standing' among their other artificers and no formal military authority over them.

Half a century after the term was expunged from the official vocabulary, and nearly three quarters of a century after it had been common to shovel coal, the rank and file of the engine room department were still known colloquially as 'stokers' and often relished it:

Nobody loves a stoker! It's because we're never seen and inhabit this mysterious underground netherworld full of pipes, dials, pistons and oil leaks. They all take us for granted. I mean, we're responsible for the obvious things like the engines that drive the ship through the water but we're also responsible for the production of water through the desalination plants that produce two tons of fresh water per hour, the electric generators, the sewage plants, the air conditioning – the list is endless. Of course there are more glamorous positions, like in the op's room or on the upper deck with the gunners, but you try running this ship without the stokers. They only realize we're here when something goes wrong and we have to fix it.[44]

Life on Board

Arriving on board ship, new crew members might be welcomed by the captain:

> OK. Well, erm, welcome on board. I always like to meet everyone who joins the ship just to say one or two things. First of all, what I always stress is that you must very quickly develop a really good knowledge of the ship ... because only when you know the ship will you be a safe member of the ship's company, and only then will you be able to contribute in areas other than your own specialist areas. ...
>
> The other thing is that you are all members of a single team. Just because you are all able rates and I've got four rings on my shoulder does not separate us but combines us. It just signifies that we've all got our parts to play.[45]

Food became very much more sophisticated over the years as the British palate improved. On board *Brilliant* in 1994, 'Leading Cook Mark Warburton is busy preparing lunch. On the menu today is corned beef pie, chicken and vegetable curry, liver, bacon and sausage casserole and seafood pasta, with baked and boiled potatoes, leeks, carrots and baked beans.' And in a nuclear submarine four years later, one of the cooks explained,

> We do not have a menu rigidly planned months ahead ... We vary it as we go along – you cannot re-store on a patrol, so we like to see what's left and go from there.

The occasional dish doesn't suit everyone, but for what they get and what we have to work with I think it's pretty good.

Chinese and curries and that sort of thing go down well ... You always have the steak night Saturday, and fish on Friday. And there's roast lunch on Sunday otherwise people get upset, and Yorkie duff with it.[46]

Visiting HMS *Galatea* at that time, one public school boy noticed 'the different life between the officers and the ratings. ... The ratings are much more boisterous and jolly, whereas the officers are very much more serious.'[47] The seaman now had far more regular contact with the shore, and like almost everyone came increasingly under the influence of modern media. Surgeon-Commander Rick Jolly feared for his culture:

What worries me much more is the prospect of our Naval slang and usage falling into oblivion as a direct result of neglect. In the good old days of the tot, messdeck conversation was witty and vital, stimulated by a daily infusion of bubbly. Nowadays, that inevitable glass nipple in the corner projects its mind-numbing videos and game shows to an equally-glazed audience, and four hundred years of living, dynamic, unique and constantly-changing spoken exchange is in danger of withering by atrophy.[48]

Not everyone agreed that the screen was so important. In 1984, 'No, the video was not worth the money, since few people were watching it. (At sea the routines and the limited space available are not conducive to video-watching; while, alongside the jetty at Rosyth, the sailors would spend as much time as possible ashore.)'[49] However, on long patrols such as off the Falklands that year, it took on much greater importance. 'We have lots of videos aboard, and watch the box all the time. I watch some of the videos four times. It gets that bad down there in the Falklands, especially in defence watches.'[50] Ten years later the crew of HMS *Brilliant* were watching tapes of *EastEnders*, *Big*

Break, *Tomorrow's World* and *Pop Quiz* on the ship's closed-circuit TV system, though they continued to play the traditional game of uckers, 'one of the few recognisable features of life for someone who last served at sea in the 1960s':

> Moves may resemble Ludo but anyone who adopts a simplistic style is accused of 'Ludo playing' in tones of great disparagement. The subtleties are in the extra rules, for pairs playing with 'blobs' and 'mixy blobs', for attacking opponents through 'suck backs', 'blow backs' and 'side swipes' and for dealing with cheating by 'timber shifting', 'number rolling' and 'six-throwing bastards'. The ultimate sanction against blatant cheats is to 'up board', a toddler's tantrum tactic much admired by artificers, which involves scattering the board, the pieces and the players to the four corners of the mess.[51]

By 2000 it was planned to allow crews at sea to watch TV in real time using satellite systems, but that was very expensive and only had limited use. More realistically, they could watch it in non-real time using the SCOT (Shipborne Communications Terminal) system. Money was allocated for dockyard infrastructure at Devonport and Portsmouth so that crews alongside could watch cable TV, while the Royal Naval Film Corporation, which had entertained the navy since the 1930s, began to issue DVD viewers instead of 16mm film projectors.[52]

Traditional branch 'demarcation' was increasingly difficult to maintain in a smaller navy with smaller crews. In 2001 multi-skilling was positively encouraged and extra pay was given to those who carried out a multitude of duties, for example in replenishment at sea and fire-fighting parties.[53] Multi-skilling was already common on submarines by 1998 as the *Navy News* correspondent found:

> 'Everybody gets involved with the general running of the boat.'
> As he spoke the boat's radio supervisor was poring over the navigational charts and a junior officer was getting some gentle

ribbing from a couple of senior ratings – a not unusual state of affairs in *Trafalgar*.[54]

One officer claimed that 'From our ABs all the way up, they know the submarine intimately. You would not be surprised to see a cook close up a bulkhead in a fire.' Another spoke of a steward who was 'one of the best planesmen for throwing it about when required'.

9
AFTER THE COLD WAR

With the demolition of the Berlin Wall in 1989 and the collapse of Soviet Communism two years later, the navy no longer had a clear potential enemy. The government used the opportunity of the 'peace dividend' to cut the armed services with its policy as described in 'Options for Change'. This resulted in a reduction of naval strength from 60,000 to 40,000 men and women, which was achieved by 6,000 voluntary releases, 12,000 redundancies and by reducing recruitment by 2,000. However, as in the 1920s, this proceeded too rapidly, and serious 'gapping' or undermanning began to develop in many sectors. This ran at a manageable rate of 3 to 4 per cent from 1992 to 1996 but shot up to 11 per cent in 1997.[1]

The decline of industrial Britain was reflected in increased interest in the navy as a career. As one sailor put it in 1994,

> I didn't fancy the mines so I joined the navy. All my cousins and friends were down the mines but they're all out of work now. Mines 'ave all closed down. So I reckon I made the right decision putting on a blue suit but I'll be glad when me time is done. It's not what it was in the navy. I mean they used to be cryin' out for people to join up and then they would train you from scratch – teach you everythin' you wanted to know about ships, damage control, fire fightin', ropes, knots – everythin'. But now they've got very choosy an' only take people with O levels an' GCSEs so you've got youngsters comin' in as senior rates 'cos of their bleedin' exams who can order people like me around ...[2]

The return of boom times made recruitment more difficult, for example in 1997–8:

> The climate in which the Royal Navy and Royal Marines recruit gets no sunnier. Demographic and attitude surveys show that there is a fairly static pool of young people which is unlikely to enlarge until after the year 2010, an increasing trend for youngsters to be attracted to further or higher education, and continued concerns by potential recruits that the service has not seen the last of downsizing.[3]

From 1999 two-year engagements were available for men and women aged between 17 and 32, with the chance to transfer to longer engagements by mutual agreement.

Management Style

The navy is far more integrated with society today, and that is reflected in its methods as much as anything else. For decades it has been recognised that a man leaving the navy at a relatively early age will need some help to find a job ashore, but today that is incorporated in naval training with national vocational qualifications. In 1993 one CPO complained that for skills such as management he needed documentary evidence from his superiors in past ships, but, 'In my case all the ships I have served on have now been scrapped, and the ships' companies scattered to the four winds.'[4] From 1996 the navy took part in 'Investors in People', a national scheme intended to encourage employers to train and develop their staffs, with a trial on HMS *Invincible*. (In fact, since Victorian times the navy had always devoted a certain amount of attention to the training of its men, which was made easier by the fact that it often had control over their labour for some years to come and could therefore benefit from the training.) Not everyone was impressed with such schemes: 'I am now just as tired of waiting for uniform that is fit for the purpose as I am of reading glossy brochures continuing a multitude of different types of management plans. Just about all of which comment on our commitment to the "most important single factor" in the form of such initiatives as Investors in People and Duty of Care,' wrote one officer to *Navy News* in 2005.

'Topmast' – Tomorrow's Personnel Management System – was designed in 2000 to 'provide a flexible and responsive manpower system that would deliver the manpower component of Operational Capability while providing attractive employment and career progression for Naval personnel:

> The TopMast plan is that when an enhanced manning regime is required, ships will operate a squad system in a fashion similar to a top sports team. In simple terms, each operational unit will be complemented with a higher number of people than there are billets to be filled. The precise number will be calculated so that the unit can always deploy with a full team, whilst leaving some ashore to meet guaranteed harmony, leave, training and augmentation requirements ...
>
> There will no longer be a manning and training margin. People placed in the margin will now be contained within the manning regime and be the responsibility of the employer at the Waterfront. This will mean that there will be increased delegation to the Commanding Officer of the front line unit: no longer will the manpower be 'owned' by 2SL.[5]

Since time immemorial there had been a wide difference between the career management of officers and ratings, summed up in the fact that officers were 'appointed' to ships while ratings were 'drafted.' In 1998 the navy rejected the idea of a sudden 'big bang' change in which all ratings were suddenly 'appointed', but instead began a gradual process of change. Warrant officer candidates were given written assessments of promotion prospects, and forthcoming job vacancies were to be advertised in *Navy News*:

> Ratings who wish to volunteer for a particular course or draft should reply to [the Naval Drafting Directorate] by the 15th of the month, but it is stressed that applications will only be considered where

fairness in drafting can be maintained.

Ratings due sea service will not be considered for a shore service billet, but ratings due shore service may volunteer to go to sea under the current out of turn (EOOT) arrangements. Volunteers should normally:

Be due the appropriate type of service (sea/shore) in the stated timescale

Be of the same rate as that required

Have the right experience to meet the stated job details

Have sufficient time to serve to provide continuity requirements.[6]

A local drafting office was set up at Devonport: 'This is not a return to the old days of "Base Port drafting" but it will enable Devonport ratings to have direct access to drafting representatives who can offer first hand advice and guidance.'[7] 'Continuity drafting' was first tried with the Sixth Frigate Squadron based at Devonport in 1998. It aimed to give the chance to serve for an extended period in the same squadron or even the same ship, though at first it applied only to junior rates in the warfare branch. In 2001–2 Waterfront Manning Organisations were set up at Devonport, Portsmouth and Faslane. Each was headed by an experienced warrant officer to advise ratings on their careers and to liaise with the Naval Drafting Directorate in HMS *Centurion* at Gosport. From 2003 executive warrant officers were appointed as shipboard personnel managers, starting with WO Allister Woodward on HMS *Chatham*. He too used the football analogy:

I was put on board as like the old football team. The co-ordinators are the coaches, and they run their team. Now they've got X amount of players that play for their team but they can only put 11 on the field at any one time.

I sit back there in the grandstand as a manager, and make sure that the co-ordinators aren't taking the Michael out of some players by playing them every time, getting them really tired, and other players are sat on the sidelines for months on end not getting the chance to play.

With 133 per cent drafting for the ship, he had some flexibility with leave:

> One instance is this young girl, it's her sister's graduation from university. Now she said 'I'd like to attend it because the whole family are going.' And I've said 'Well, let me put it in the plan, let's see what we can do. We've sat down with her and the co-ordinator and said, 'Yeah, we can figure that one out, we can get you home for that.'[8]

Advancement rosters were abolished from 1999, and ratings now faced promotion boards instead. Ratings with less than three years' service were allowed four travel warrants per year to their homes to help them as they became established in their careers. The time-honoured rating of ordinary seaman was merged into able seaman. The period of notice to leave the service was reduced to 12 months for officers and ratings. Restrictions on alcohol in shore accommodation were reduced to bring the navy into line with the other services. It was felt that 'in the modern Navy, in which the Management makes increasingly complex demands on very junior personnel, this should be matched by treating them as responsible citizens off duty'.[9]

By 2000 after numerous closures, training was concentrated in a few bases. Apart from *Britannia* at Dartmouth, which dealt with all officers, *Raleigh* included all initial training as well as the School of Seamanship and the Submarine School. Whale Island in Portsmouth had long given up gunnery but had *Royal Arthur* to teach leadership to petty officers as well as the fire-fighting and sea safety schools. Engineering training, including aircraft and nuclear, was now concentrated in HMS *Sultan* at Gosport, the largest naval training establishment in Europe. *Collingwood* in nearby Fareham did most of the computer training, while *Dryad* in the hills above still trained individuals and teams of the warfare branch to man the operations rooms (but soon this would be closed and its facilities moved to *Excellent* and *Collingwood*).[10]

The rating structure did not become any simpler, and in 2005 a letter in *Navy News* complained that

> many civilian – and indeed ex-Naval readers of your paper (and possibly even some serving matelots!) might be out of touch with the current names and abbreviations such as CCPOWEMSM(C) and WO[1] (CS(C) or whatever ... In the other armed services, the junior personnel have simple titles like 'private' and 'gunner'. Even in the Royal Marines a technical specialist is just referred to as a marine. Why can't the Navy simpl[if]y things and call people by ancient, honourable and comprehensible titles like seaman and stoker?[11]

THE ROLE OF THE SEAMAN

As early as 1983 the traditional seaman was being missed in certain quarters. It was pointed out that 'the reserve of knowledge and experience is currently vested in a rapidly dwindling group of senior ratings, many of whom were trained under the former system of Boy entry, with long periods at HMS GANGES, ST VINCENT and RALEIGH. A strong emphasis was placed on seamanship in these establishments, followed by a career which emphasised it as an advancement requirement.' After surveys in 1973, 1977 and 1979, a seaman sub-branch was formed for leading hands and above of the operations branch, and seamanship was to be regarded as a three-level skill. All new entries, regardless of branch, would learn the rudiments. Most operations branch men would be brought up to the second level, with the members of the new sub-branch forming a skilled nucleus. [12]

It was only by about 1985 that the operations branch was beginning to acquire a sense of identity, while preserving that of the individual sub-branches of radar, sonar, gunnery and so on.[13] But soon that would change yet again. The operations branch and the weapons engineering branch were seen to be moving in different directions. The former needed fewer low-skilled people, since routine tasks such as missile loading and gun aiming were becoming more and more automated, while the weapons engineering branch needed a greater proportion of junior rates than before. There was also a need to raise the technical awareness of the operators, to make more efficient use of manpower in ships that were having to make do with ever-smaller complements, and to provide rewarding careers for everyone involved. The answer, it was finally decided in 1989, was to merge the operations and weapons engineering branches to form the warfare branch. Weapons artificers would remain intact to carry out high-level servicing.

Recruiting for the two separate branches ceased early in 1993, and recruiting for the new one began soon afterwards. Entrants would be known as operator mechanics after their Part 2 training at HMS *Dryad* and would wear the missile, torpedo and lightning-flash badge of the old weapons engineering branch. Initially they would wear the letters 'AW' under the badge until they were categorised in above water tactical ('AWT', formerly the radar branch) above water weapons ('AWW', formerly the missile branch), underwater ('UW', formerly sonar), 'MW' for mine warfare, 'EW' for electronic warfare or 'C' for communications. Those going into the submarine service would have the letters 'SM' prior to categorisation, then they were divided into 'SSM' for submarine sensors, 'TSM' for submarine tactical, 'WSM' for submarine weapons and 'CSM' for submarine communications. Members of both the old branches would be given the chance to cross-train to take up the new ratings, though some would refuse or be unsuitable, in which case they would have to serve in the assault ship *Fearless* or the ageing Type 42 destroyers, which would retain the old structure.

The Second Sea Lord explained the position to the chiefs on board the frigate *Brilliant* in 1994:

> Undoubtedly, there are some jobs that can be streamlined. And other jobs that can be combined. This will mean, in some cases, after appropriate cross training, that one man will be able to do the jobs that two men are currently doing. Logically, this must mean that some people will end up without a job. I do not believe in hiding that fact and I will tell any man the same thing.[14]

This was enough to make Leading Seaman Micky Goble fearful about his future:

> He was on about 'leaner manning' and the combining of operators and maintainers. You know, instead of having one bloke to operate the radar and another to maintain it they're now goin' to have one poor sod to do the lot. But then there's an even poorer bleedin' sod who's out on his ear. Guess who? They're looking for youngsters now because the kid out of school is a better investment on the cost o' training.[15]

Officers regretted the loss of the old weapons engineer, who was often a 'character' in contrast to the young artificers whose 'management skills are usually immature and many of them see themselves as technicians first and managers/senior ratings a poor second'. A chief WEM, on the other hand, usually acted as the department's coordinator on board ship and was the weapons engineering officer's right-hand man. Such men would eventually die out under the new system, but that could not be helped. In the meantime the warfare branch, like all new branches in the navy, struggled for 'respectability', which was only achieved in 1999 when the first senior rates went to sea to give it a proper hierarchy.[16]

From 2006 ratings could enter the seaman branch at AB level instead of leading hand, and the facilities of the School of Seamanship at *Raleigh* were augmented to cater for this. As a warrant officer put it, 'We're not a small cog in a big wheel, but a big cog in that machine. A RAS [Replenishment at sea] is one of the most dangerous evolutions at sea in peacetime, and it cannot be done without us.' Apart from that, the men of the branch would handle ropes on entering and leaving port, supervise the lowering of seaboats and carry out work on ropes. They would learn the craft of the sailmaker to work on awnings, flags and fire curtains and of visual signalling by lamp or flag, whose messages could not be blocked or overheard. 'What we are talking about here are specialist seamen. With the creation of the new branch, we are re-focussing on traditional skills – skills which served us well at Trafalgar and remain hugely relevant today.'[17]

THE FLEET AIR ARM

Invincible, having proved her worth in the Falklands, was kept on in the navy and joined by her sisters *Illustrious* in 1982 and *Ark Royal* in 1985. With the sale of *Hermes* in 1986, these three ships formed the British aircraft carrier force until *Invincible* came out of service in 2005 and *Ark Royal* was finally decommissioned in 2010. Two larger carriers are expected to be ready in 2016 and 2018, but only one will be used as a carrier. The Sea Harriers are to come out of service before that, and the navy will have no fixed-wing aircraft for around ten years, so a great deal of Fleet Air Arm expertise in aircraft handling is likely to be lost.

The base at Portland closed in 1999, and the Sea Harriers moved to RAF Cottesmore when they were not at sea. Only Yeovilton and Culdrose in south-west England remained as Fleet Air Arm bases, the former dealing with Lynx helicopters and the Royal Marines Commando Helicopter Force, the latter with Sea Kings and Merlins. Much shore-based maintenance is now done by civilian personnel, and Yeovilton employed 2,000 civilians alongside 1,675 service personnel in 2006 – maintenance was organised by the Naval Aircraft Repair Organisation until 1999 when it was merged with the RAF's servicing group to form the Defence Aviation Repair Agency.

There was still plenty of work for the flight deck crews, for example during the threat of an attack by sea off Bosnia.

Out on the flight deck the aircraft maintainers have wheeled the low-slung yellow trolleys that cradle the Sea Skua missiles out to the waiting Lynx. Quickly and efficiently they hoist the blue and grey projectiles up to the launching arm of the helicopter on the port side. The air crew look out to their left incredulously – they have never taken off on an attack mission with live ammunition before. Within seconds the deadly missiles are hooked up, wired up and primed. The maintainers scuttle back to the hangar and wait.[18]

The meteorology branch of the Fleet Air Arm added oceanography to its duties, and from 1993 the letters 'METOC' were carried under the branch badge. Naval Airman Stuart Parkes served in HMS *Campbeltown* in 1997:

> My meteorological tasks include providing timely and accurate weather observations for the safety of the ship's flight, and to provide the Command with details of the effect of the environment on the ship's weapons and sensors. In areas where there is little information about current weather conditions, my observations are of great use to the Commander in Chief's Weather and Oceanography Centre (CINCFLEETWOC) and to the national Meteorology Office at Bracknell. During normal cruising watches, I work a routine so that I can fully support the forecaster. My work involves gathering data from any different sources, including gale warning signals and satellite pictures from CINCFLEETWOC.[19]

SUBMARINES

The old diesel-electric submarines of the O class, the mainstay of the fleet in the seventies, were scrapped or sold by 2000, with no less than seven surviving as museum ships in some form. A new class of four, the *Upholder* class, was ordered with a view to clandestine operations, but the end of the Cold War removed that need. They were laid up then sold to Canada in the early 2000s. Thus the submarine service became an all-nuclear force. The historic site at Gosport was no longer needed, and submarine basic training moved to Plymouth, with most of the boats based at Faslane.

Again there were no radical changes in technology, except that increased electronics allowed a slight reduction in manpower (for women were still not allowed to go to sea in submarines). In HMS *Trafalgar* in 1998,

> The helmsman becomes the planesman as soon as the hydroplanes start to bite, and is responsible for steering the ship with the rudder and maintain depth.

Alongside him, seated at the 'snakes' wedding', is the panel watchkeeper, who monitors the trim and ballast of the submarine, represented by a tangle of lines and sights.

Behind and between them sits the ship control officer of the watch.

Crew members on ship control duties do six hours about, depending on the speed of the vessel, with the planesman and panel watchkeeper swapping more frequently than the ship control officer of the watch.

'In *Trafalgar*, depth is usually automatic, and course is manual, though at periscope depth it's the other way round,' said CPO Ian Hurst.[20]

In the nuclear deterrent force, the Polaris boats were replaced by larger ones carrying the Trident missile in the mid- and late-1990s. The Trident boats are 20 metres (65 feet) longer and have almost twice the submerged displacement of the Polaris boats, with a slightly smaller crew of 140. The manoeuvring room only needs four watchkeepers instead of five. The Trident submariners made at least one small gain from the 'peace dividend' at the end of the Cold War in that they were now allowed the occasional run ashore overseas, though both opportunities and locations remained limited. This began with a six-day trip to Gibraltar in November 1998, where they received 'a tremendous Gibraltarian welcome'.[21]

PROMOTION

As always, the supply of senior rates depended partly on recruitment a few years before. In 1989,

Promotion prospects for ratings are more directly related to changing requirements. Whereas career planning does take account of reasonable expectations of advancement it is inevitable that the length of time in any given rate will depend on the rate of exit from the one above it. For example in 1977 advancement to Leading Hand took on average only 3.7 years, which was rather too fast to achieve the required quality in the higher rate, while in 1987 it took 5.9 years, which is a little too slow![22]

The biggest change in the promotion system came in 1999, when the rosters were abolished and ratings came before promotion boards, as officers had done for some time. The first boards for promotion to petty officer were held in July that year, with the actual promotions taking place in October. For promotion to leading hand, the boards would first sit at the end of October, for promotions to take effect from May 2000. Roadshows toured the naval bases to explain the changes.[23]

Another dip in recruiting in the mid-1990s led to a 'black hole' as 2,000 fewer people joined than would have been expected in normal times. In 2001 the warfare branch was short of 344 leading hands and was a quarter under strength in some specialisations.[24] By 2003 there was a 20 per cent deficiency in leading hands at sea, which was likely to lead to a similar shortage of petty officers in a few years time. It was not a new problem, of course, and the Second Sea Lord was echoing many of his predecessors when he wrote, 'Leading hands are, and will remain, in short supply. Bringing the most able rates from all branches forward earlier requires careful preparation, timely promotion and ongoing development. In my view, the leading hand really is the first superior officer – a fact that many appear to have overlooked in recent years.'[25]

OFFICERS AND RATINGS

In a sense a warship was always a cross-section of the nation, but that was more true than ever by the 1990s, as both officers and ratings were drawn from wider social groups than in the past. According to Micky Goble of *Brilliant*,

This ship is like a little England floating around the oceans of the world. You got every type on board that you would have at home:

brainy types, brawny types, nice ones, 'orrid ones. You got doctors, cooks, mechanics, sparks, chippies. You got mad scientists, village idiots, high class toffs and then a few bog-common dregs to make up the numbers ... like the Royal Marines![26]

Relationships between officers and ratings were now less formal:

'Ah, Leading Seaman Goble. Going off watch?'
  'Yes sir.'
  'Get some shut-eye then. Don't start watching your Star Trek videos.'
  'Don't knock the Trekkies sir. For we shall inherit the earth!'
  'Even more reason to catch up with your sleep then. It's a tiring job running the planet so I'm told ... '
  'Don't worry – I'll get to my pit sir. But I'm going to get some scran first and then the leading regulator is going to cut my hair.
  'OK. See you tonight.'
  'The idea fills me with great joy sir,' says Goble leaving.[27]

Early in the twentieth century ratings used to complain about young officers who had little contact with the lower deck and showed great arrogance. In the 1960s complaints were usually about their insecurity and inexperience after Dartmouth training. By 2000 they were likely to be about young graduates with a good general education who had no experience of service discipline or routine and had to be backed up by senior rates.

In 1999 the promotion structure for ratings becoming officers was streamlined, and the distinction between upper yardsmen and special duties was abolished – those over 26 were now senior upper yardsmen, and they did not face the restrictions of special duties officers. The upper limit for commissioning was raised from 34 to 46, and soon four very senior warrant officers and two CPOs were selected. By 2001 the Second Sea Lord was proud of what had been achieved:

The other thing, in terms of building careers, which I like to tell people about is that 30 per cent of Naval officers joined the Navy as ordinary sailors.

So this is a real meritocracy – this is an organisation which talent-spots. We don't care where you went to school or who your dad was – we're just interested in what you can do and how far you can go.

I've got people who joined as ordinary seamen who've gone on to command the Navy's destroyers as captains – and that is just fantastic.[28]

In 1994 it was acceptable for a master at arms to dine ashore with the captain and first lieutenant, though one showed a certain amount of social insecurity in a Cretan restaurant:

The two officers have ordered taramasalata to start, followed by lobster and prawn Creole and are waiting for the master-at-arms to make his choice from the menu. He is tempted by one of the more familiar dishes such as fish and chips, but thinks better of it.

'Very good choice sah's. I think I'll have the same. Yes indeed. Very tasty I'm sure.'[29]

Class seemed to dominate as much as ever in a formal dinner in *Brilliant*'s wardroom in 1994, in an age when only the very rich ashore could afford personal servants. Petty Officer Tony Lilley explained,

I consider these officers to be my 'gentlemen'. I look after them. See to their needs. Get to know their little ways. Some people say this is all wrong them having special service and that it's too 'upstairs downstairs' but I don't agree. I reckon officers deserve a little better. It's their right. If we go to war we look to them to do right by us so they should get the rewards in peacetime.[30]

OPERATIONS

In the 1980s, the problem of Islamic militancy was beginning to surface. The Armilla Patrol began in 1980 as troubles mounted in the

Middle East due to Russia's war in Afghanistan, followed by the Iran-Iraq War. At first the patrol consisted of a destroyer and a frigate, with one extra ship from 1987 plus three or four minesweepers. Patrolling was carried out in cooperation with various other navies, both global and local. When sent there in 1983, some of the crew of HMS *Glamorgan* saw it as an interruption to the sports programme – 'Due to the fact that the ship was sent on Armilla Patrol instead of to the Far East as originally planned, fewer games of rugby could be played and the standard of play was generally low except in the Gulf States.' On the way the ship stopped briefly to help with another crisis:

> Lebanon proved to be a busy interlude: the flight performed a magnificent task; while lookouts continuously scanned the skies, weapons crews stayed closed up all day; and some of the department went ashore, helping to rebuild the British base in Beirut. At night we were able to relax our vigilance a little, but not so the communicators, ops room, crews and 'Gollies' [electronic warfare specialists]. For them the endless watchkeeping round never slackened for a second: even as we turned away towards Suez, the radars and EW equipment continued to scan the horizon – alert for any threats – while the ROs kept the radio links open.

Once on station, there was still plenty of work to do; as CPO Richard Gough of HMS *Boxer* put it,

> One of the primary tasks of the Armilla Patrol in 1988 was to escort British Shipping through the Straits of Hormuz, the access waterway from the Gulf of Oman into the Persian Gulf. The reason for the escorted passage was to protect these ships from [potential] attack by Iranian shore-based missiles. In addition, the Iranians were also using Swedish Boghammer boats, capable of harassing shipping in hit-and-run attacks ...[31]

The anti-submarine function of frigates was not needed in such operations; instead, CPO Gough made special arrangements in *Boxer* to keep the guns, missiles and decoy systems manned:

> To ensure I could effectively man these weapons, I had negotiated
> for a number of Radar and Sonar operators to supplement my missile
> team. This enhancement made complete sense to the ship's
> command, as these Ops ratings would not be used in their anti-
> submarine role while we served in the Gulf. HMS *Boxer* was now a
> ship with ears and a bloody big bite ...[32]

Glamorgan continued with anti-submarine training in 1983–4:

> Unfortunately for the Sonar crews, there were few submarine targets
> to 'ping' against, so they had to make do with a training target we
> carry. It is suspended beneath a buoy and the entire contraption is
> called the 'Ship Laid Underwater Target Transponder' or 'SLUTT'
> for short. So if you ever hear that the Ops Department laid a slut on
> deployment you will know what they are talking about![33]

Sea time remained high, and in 2001 the Second Sea Lord said,

> For the majority of our people, I think the operational tempo of the
> navy is higher today than it was in the middle of World War II – we
> work them very hard. Because our ships, although they still break
> down from time to time, are much more reliable than they used to
> be. And that's partly why the operational tempo is high.[34]

The collapse of the Soviet Union was not the 'end of history' that had
been predicted, and it did not lead to a peaceful world. In 1994 the
Royal Navy cooperated with 13 navies in support of United Nations
Resolution 820 to prevent arms from reaching the warring parties
in former Yugoslavia. That too involved long periods at defence
stations:

> This means that everybody works for six hours and rests for six hours
> around the clock, that permanent watches are kept through the high-

powered binoculars on both sides of the bridge wings in addition to constant surface, sub-surface and air radar/sonar surveillance, and that everyone carries their battle bags at all times. These white canvas bags slung around the shoulder contain the all-important anti-flash gear – hoods, gloves and overalls – that are designed to prevent the terrible flash burns that occur in the vicinity of an explosion.[35]

Though *Brilliant* never came into contact with any Yugoslav force during her deployment in 1994, there were many ships and aircraft that had to be identified.

It is 0900. Micky Goble is at his place in the operations room. His job is to monitor the surface radar screen and keep a constant look-out for ships coming into the area. His eyes dart constantly over the screen, stopping every now and again as they fix on a fresh blip. Is it a merchantman trying to break the embargo? Is it a Yugoslavian warship? Is it an Albanian speedboat carrying refugees to southern Italy? Or is it merely an innocent fisherman from Dubrovnik trying to catch a few red mullet to sell at this evening's fish market?[36]

Technology now allowed the operator to mark the identity of each contact on the screen.

Back on the surface radar Micky Goble has identified the newcomer on his screen as the Adriatica, an Italian ferry. He marks it with a reference number, sits back and presses the scan-change button that increases the reach of the radar map from 15 miles to 96. He notes the reassuring blips and code numbers that mark the other Sharp Guard ships patrolling the neighbouring sea areas. There is USS *Deyo* in one area and the Spanish ship *Victoria* in another.[37]

Two days later Leading Seaman Wiggy Bennet, the electronic warfare director, reported the situation to a heads of department meeting:

Captain, sir, gentlemen. It's been relatively quiet on and under the water today, sir. All Yugoslavian submarines and frigates have remained in port over the last twenty-four hours. One patrol boat conducted a routine coastal patrol and then returned to port. Air activity, on the other hand, has been busy again, sir. There were seventy-one tactical flights across the region and one episode of bombing practice on the southern ranges. In the actual conflict, sir, according to the press, UN aircraft were hit by small arms fire at Sarajevo airport. The airport went on alert following the incident, sir. The Russian special envoy has urged the West to lift sanctions on the Serbs without imposing conditions ...[38]

At home, meanwhile, the navy was still needed to aid the civil power, as for example in 2000 during a foot-and-mouth epidemic: 'The call came on 5th April, with deployment just 2 days later, for 60 people to reinforce 43 Wessex Brigade in Devon and another 80 to assist 160 Brigade in South Wales.' In the same year naval teams were deployed during a fire service strike on Merseyside. 'The RN crews were kept exceptionally busy. Over the 11 days of intermittent strike action Service teams answered 856 call outs which was more than double the usual rate because of hoax calls and many small-scale incidents of arson. Some serious fires had to be tackled but fortunately there was no loss of life to civilians and no serious injury to Service personnel.'[39]

HMS *Chatham* already had a BBC film crew on board when she was diverted to help with the Indian Ocean Tsunami in 2004. Despite missing seasonal festivities, the crew was pleased to be doing something useful. 'Yeah, well, it's a bit of a bugger missing out on New Year as well as Crimbo, but the job's there to do. Frankly, most of us just want to get stuck in – and I'll tell you something else, it'll beat the hell out of the patrolling malarkey we've been doing.' Another rating agreed: 'I'm pleased we're going down there. Makes me feel useful. Just hope we make a difference. It'll do my head in if we just arrive and float around for days, doing nothing.'[40] They did indeed have to sail around Sri Lanka looking for an opportunity to intervene – 'Everybody's itching to get stuck in. We can see the coast just a few hundred metres on our port side. I reckon if they don't get off soon, they're gonna bust'. CPO Rick Bennett went ashore with the captain to negotiate with various authorities. 'You can't even imagine what these people have been through, can you? ... We have lots of skills on board, you know ... Not just Navy skills, but skills people have brought with them from Civvy Street. We have carpenters, electricians, engineers, tailors, brickies. All sorts. It's amazing, when you ask round, what you find you've got at your disposal. Add to that a bit of military discipline and organisation, then Bob's your uncle!'[41]

The crew soon found work in repairing houses and fishing boats, clearing wells and in medical assistance.

DISCIPLINE

As always, the older hands lamented the decline in discipline since they joined, though perhaps with more justice than in earlier ages:

> I mean in the old days if my hooky said 'jump!' I would say 'How high?' but now with me and Mark both being hookies and we say 'do something' to these youngsters they just look at us and say 'Why?' And I'll tell you summat else. When we first joined an' we didn't do somethin' right we'd get a clip round the 'ead. An' we learnt fast. Today, if you touch 'em you're up on a bleedin' charge![42]

But this kind of indiscipline was very low key, so it was rarely reflected in punishment returns. As a leading seaman put it in the 1980s,

> People today can't afford to lose their rate status or be fined. It is bad for their career. So behaviour is better in the Navy, without a lot of heavy-handed discipline. I think now is very fair, not severe. For the people who do actually get into trouble, whatever they have done, they deserve what they get.[43]

To some extent the system was self-policing on board:

> Ratings, senior and junior, are expected to keep their behaviour
> within bounds manageable by the mess; it is only if they hawk their
> offences to a wider audience that serious trouble may be expected.
> If they come back aboard late at night the worse for wear, and
> enliven the mess with full and frank opinions on matters sporting
> and racial, it may be tolerated. If they start broadening their audience
> by staggering down passageways with their conversation stuck in
> the same groove, the honour of the mess will have been impugned.[44]

It was on the run ashore that trouble might arise as groups of sailors
released their pent up frustrations:

> The British sailor, generally speaking, can drink for Britain – and
> in a sense he does. I remember my time with Scouse Ashton, the
> regulator back in Plymouth, when he told me that the British sailor
> seeks out alcohol wherever he is. That is largely true. It seems to
> be part of British naval culture, but that is not to say that all sailors
> are drunkards. In some ways it is quite ritualised behaviour; it's
> what sailors do en masse to underscore and emphasise their
> comradeship.[45]

Often the local people were more to blame than the sailors. According
to a leading regulator in the 1980s, 'You get some very nasty assaults
around in Portsmouth. It is about 70 per cent civilians assaulting our
men, and about 30 per cent our men attacking others. Most of it we
call "Rate Bashing". They wait until they get a *matelot* on his own, and
then have a go at him.'[46] And in Istanbul in 1994, the crew of *Brilliant*
were taunted by Galatasaray football fans:

> 'You know Pincher,' says Goble, his words slightly slurred, 'if that
> had kicked off the news would have been "British thugs on rampage
> in Istanbul". "British football hooligans start trouble again ..." *The
> Sun* and the *News of the World* would have lapped it up.'

'Yeah, they were just dying for us to react. But there was no point was there? If we had flashed we might 'ave given them a hidin' but then we'd be in the slammer. Lose pay. Lose leave. Lose rank.'[47]

When there was trouble in Istanbul, it was between two members of the crew, which tested the fairness of the naval justice system. Leading Weapons Engineering Mechanic Gladman was accused of assaulting a petty officer in a pub and agonised about whether to take the case to court martial or accept the captain's judgement.

I just don't know what to do. Really I think I should go for a court martial when we get back so then I can get a barrister and really put up a good defence. I mean I'm being really stitched up here as far as I'm concerned. You know I 'ad a bleedin' shoutin' match wiv' the geezer but he's the one who says I put one on 'im. I'm saying I never touched the bloke. There's no witnesses who saw me 'it 'im. There's only people who saw us arguin'.[48]

In the end he opted to be tried by the captain, who dismissed the charge of assault but fined him £150 for using provocative language. The lower deck regarded this as a fair result.

In 1995 the Detention Quarters at Portsmouth were closed, and punishment was now carried out on a joint service basis in the Military Corrective Training Centre at Colchester under RN staff. Ten years later the Regulating Branch moved its training into the former HMS *Dryad* at Southwick to share it with the army and air force police services. There was some concern that they might be overwhelmed – the navy had only 300 regulators compared with the RAF's 1,800 policemen (partly to guard the perimeters of airfields) and the army's 3,500.[49] But the old charge, dating from the late nineteenth century, that the navy relied too much on the ship's police was clearly no longer valid.

In 2000 a new Armed Forces Discipline Act was needed to conform to the provisions of the Human Rights Act of 1998. The main changes for the navy were that a naval Judge Advocate had to approve the keeping of a sailor in custody for more than 48 hours before trial; there was to be a right of appeal against summary conviction; and when a defendant elected to go before a court martial the sentence was capped at the maximum that could be awarded by the captain.[50]

THE GULF WARS

In August 1990 tensions in the Middle East reached a new level when Saddam Hussein of Iraq invaded Kuwait, causing the Western nations to mount a campaign that would become known as the First Gulf War. A US-led coalition was rapidly established in the region, to which the Royal Navy sent around 25 ships. Mike Brodie was a radar operator in a Type 42 and spent almost the whole of February at defence watches, 'Constant night time, when you are in 8 hour defence watches you forget actually when it is day and when it is night.' With the constant threat of attack by Iraqi aircraft and Silkworm missiles – as well as chemical warfare – there were frequent false alarms, as he recorded in his diary:

> Defence watches! At 0150 Local whilst asleep off watch the chemical alarm sounded. Whilst shitting mayself I had my respirator on in two seconds and then got dressed as quick as is possible amongst all the panic! I made my way to the senior rates dining room where all the upper deck gun crews were to go. Everybody believed it was real and the adrenelin was fast flowing. I started to think I could smell something in my gas mask, then I felt dizzy and extremely worried. When you are in that kind of situation all kinds of things happen to you. Your mind plays tricks on you but to me it wasn't a trick this was for real. At approx 0235 a false alarm was called and I went back to my bed still a bit shaky. At 0240 the bloody alarm went off again, my god my heart can't take any more of this, went through the exact same procedures except false alarm was called before I left the mess.

Part of the problem was the lack of communication between the different navies and air forces conducting the war:

> A couple of times we got to the stage of full alert and locked the target up with our fire control radar preparing to shoot it out of the sky. It could have been a missile coming straight for us!! You know what happened ... the decision was made on all those times NOT to fire. Now I tell you now, yes they were friendly aircraft but what if they weren't??? Those bastards flying should have flown as to the rules agreed and exited at the agreed points. If it were a missile we would have what 45 seconds to lock it up and get a missile off before it would reach the point where nothing could be done.[51]

In fact the British ships suffered no serious damage. HMS *Brazen* was fired on without result, an attempted air attack was foiled by Allied fighters, and *Gloucester* fired two Sea Dart missiles and destroyed a Silkworm missile, while Lynx helicopters from the frigates and destroyers destroyed 15 Iraqi ships and vessels, including five by HMS *Cardiff*'s Lynx alone. In addition the Royal Navy swept 2,500 mines. When the Iraqis surrendered at the end of the month, Mike Brodie had mixed feelings as he lived under the huge clouds created by burning oil wells. 'Fires still burning in Kuwait and the sky is still black at midday. Rain fell today and it was black! I wonder how long this pollution and blockage of the sun will go on? Iraq agrees to the terms and apart from small details to be finalised the war is over! HOORAY!' But unlike the Falklands it was overwhelmingly a land war, in which the navy's role was secondary.

In August 1990 tensions in the Middle East reached a new level when Saddam Hussein of Iraq invaded Kuwait, causing the Western nations to mount a campaign that would become known as the First Gulf War. The country was invaded by Allied countries in 2001, with support from the Royal Marines and the Fleet Air Arm. It is a landlocked country, but about a thousand Royal Navy personnel serve there every year, mostly operating helicopters and as medics. All personnel are sent on pre-operational training, with two weeks at *Raleigh* familiarising themselves with infantry kit and the SA80 rifle. They spend the next week at *Nelson* in Portsmouth learning the laws of armed conflict and the rules of engagement, followed by a final week at the army's Longmoor camp carrying out realistic exercises. Once in the country, many of them do not leave the bases at Camp Bastion and Kandahar, though Medical Assistant Natalie Chinniah won an award for teaching a group of Afghan nurses trauma management: 'The tour has been a real experience. I've been shot at and have been on the receiving end of rocket attacks. I have been able to put my medical training to good use; on one hand I have used it to treat people who have been injured in battle and on the other hand I have used it to help train the local nurses in trauma management.'[52]

The Second Gulf War of 2003 was even less of a maritime affair than the first, because Iraq without Kuwait had only a very short coastline. Nevertheless the navy deployed the aircraft carrier *Ark Royal*, the assault ship HMS *Ocean*, three destroyers, three frigates, seven minesweepers, two submarines and 13 Royal Fleet Auxiliary vessels as well as about 5,000 personnel in support of the US-led overthrow of Saddam Hussein. But it was the long aftermath of the war that led to the navy's most embarrassing incident for many years.

On 23 April 2007 two rigid inflatable boats from HMS *Cornwall* were conducting routine searches of shipping off the Iraqi coast. They were manned by one naval and one marine officer, one woman and six male seamen and six marines – but no senior ratings or NCOs who often provided mature and experienced leadership on operations. They were confident of their position inside Iraqi waters, for they were using Xerxes navigation equipment and a handheld GPS, one of which was operated by Operator Maintainer Arthur Batchelor. After getting information from the ship's Lynx helicopter, they boarded and searched a merchant vessel at anchor, having already conducted 66 operations of this kind in the last four weeks. They had the cooperation of the crew of the vessel and found nothing suspicious. After a search of more than an hour they left at 0919, when two speedboats were seen approaching about 400 metres away. They blocked the two RIBs in and the Iranian Revolutionary Guards on board threatened them with weapons including heavy machine-guns and rocket-propelled grenades. The Lynx had already left and *Cornwall* was some miles away, partly because the water was too shallow for her. More Iranian boats arrived and according to Batchelor, 'Captain Air [of the Royal Marines] told us to put our weapons down and cooperate. I think he saved our lives that day. We were boarded by very aggressive Iranian soldiers. One of them was huge and kept staring threateningly at me. They ripped off our communications pieces and grabbed our weapons.' Leading Seaman Faye Turney tried to conceal her sex by keeping her helmet on but was eventually forced to take it off. 'When the guard saw her face, his jaw dropped so far it practically touched the bottom of the boat. He just started and pointed at her chanting "Woman, woman, woman, woman!"'

The captives were taken ashore and subjected to psychological torment. They were kept in separate cells and Faye Turney and others were told that the rest had been released. They were told they would face years in jail unless they confessed to invading Iranian waters. When they were eventually allowed to come together they were filmed and shown on world television looking surprisingly content. Some of them made a conscious decision to agree they had been in Iranian waters, in order to secure their release. After 13 days they were issued with shiny grey suits and taken to meet Iranian President Ahmadinejad before being sent home.

Clothes were important during the affair – apart from the suits, the Iranians made sure that Leading Seaman Turney's head was covered with a scarf. It was probably not by chance, therefore, that when the freed captives appeared before a press conference they were dressed in Number 4 uniform with light blue shirts and berets, rather than the square rig that would have emphasised difference in rank from the officers, and perhaps symbolised imperialism. (Square rig is almost entirely reserved for formal occasions now, as some had predicted in the 1950s.)

Up to this point the captives' decisions – not to resist capture and to confess to the Iranians – were controversial but could be justified as preventing a serious international incident when several trigger-happy nations were active in the region. It was far more controversial when they were allowed to sell their stories to the press. At first Faye Turney's account in the *Sun* tended to reinforce the stories of psychological warfare against them. She had been isolated, measured and heard the sound of sawing and hammering which made her believe the Iranians were making her coffin. She had promised her three-year-old daughter that she would be home for her birthday in a few days time, and that also caused her to admit the incursion. But the press had already turned against them and Arthur Batchelor's account happened to mention that the Iranians had called him Mr Bean, they had confiscated his iPod and he had cried in his cell. Soon questions were being asked. Even the First Sea Lord considered that it was not appropriate for iPods to be taken on active service. Faye Turney's promise to her daughter was used to suggest that that women were not suited to front-line operations, as they were more loyal to family than to country. The mother ship *Chatham* had been too far away to help, and the boat crews had not been trained in counter-interrogation techniques. A Parliamentary report on the incident was not allowed to quote a secret Ministry of Defence report in full, but it concluded among other things that, 'there needed to be improvement in training for particular tasks, including boarding, and specialist teams should be deployed for this task'. In addition, 'There was a lapse in operational focus in the front line, and a widespread failure of situational awareness.' As a result, 'formal administrative action has been taken against a number of people across a wide spectrum of ranks'.

It was also concluded that servicemen should never be allowed to sell their stories again, but the damage to the navy's prestige had already been done. The army was taking quite serious casualties in Iraq and Afghanistan by this time and at an army-navy football match the solders chanted, 'What shall we do with the captive sailors?' The answers were all deeply insulting to the navy –

> Take away his iPod and make him blubber
>   Ear-lye in the morning
> Put him in a suit and make him smile
>   Ear-lye in the morning :
> Give 'em forty grand and hear them snivel
>   Ear-lye in the morning.

TERRORISM AND PIRACY

During the 'troubles' in Northern Ireland from 1969 onwards, the army played the primary role, and the navy was deployed to prevent gun-running with three Hunt-class minesweepers on station as late as 2005. Only one member of the Royal Navy, a recruiting officer, was killed during Northern Ireland operations, out of a total of 763 deaths from all services. So far the Royal Navy has not been subjected to a terrorist attack like the one that crippled the USS *Cole* off Yemen in 2000, when the world first got to know the name of Al-Qaeda. But the rise of Islamic terrorism, and Britain's participation in the wars in Iraq and Afghanistan, means that it can never feel totally secure against it, which places extra stress on the crews. ' We 'ave to repel all comers so need to keep a good look-out,' says Rab, pointing to the high-powered binoculars around his neck, 'and we 'ave to be armed to the 'ilt, because you never know when some silly bugger's going to come along and try to ruin our day. I don't mean other warships, but the suicide bomber bearing down on us in a bleedin' pedalo or somink. That's the sort of thing we 'ave to be ready for these days.'[53]

When first detailed to go on anti-piracy duty from HMS *Avenger* in 1983, Richard Gough was bemused: 'At first I assumed it must be a wind-up and laughed at the request. Pirates are something from

Hollywood aren't they? But they weren't joking as I quickly discovered from the briefing.'[54] In fact, containing piracy has now become a major operation for the navy, in cooperation with others. In 2009 it led to another controversial incident when, by following the rules of engagement, it failed to prevent the kidnap of the yachtsmen Paul and Rachel Chandler by Somali pirates. But unlike the Iran hostage incident, this did not reflect on the lower deck as such.

The Navy and the Nation

The Royal Navy has done its best to foster public interest in the last few decades. Navy Days held in Portsmouth and Plymouth in alternate years attract vast crowds. In Scotland, Faslane had far shallower roots in the local community than Portsmouth and Plymouth – it was politically controversial and its nuclear facilities posed exceptionally high security risks. But the Faslane Fair grew from humble enough beginnings as a street fair in the married quarters, and then moved to the sea front at Helensburgh as a kind of military tattoo. In 2001 boat and bus trips were organised to the base a few miles away.[55] In 2005 the celebration of the 200th anniversary of the Battle of Trafalgar off Portsmouth was a huge success, involving people all over the country with, for example, the planting of woods in memory of each of Nelson's ships. The main event at Portsmouth attracted media coverage and thousands of people, but by its nature it emphasised the past rather than the present, and it could not conceal the fact that the modern navy could not fill the Solent as it had done in 1914 or even 1977, without calling on foreign navies and merchant ships.

On the whole, television continued to be kind to the navy, which placed public relations much higher in its priorities than ever before. The 1987 documentary series *Nozzers* gave a sympathetic view of training at HMS *Raleigh*. In 1995 *HMS* Brilliant – *In a Ship's Company* was filmed during the campaign in former Yugoslavia. As well as several of the officers it focused on Leading Seaman Micky Goble, radar operator, ship's comedian, and 'in some respects an unlikely sailor. Chubby and balding, he walks with the rolling shuffle of a veteran prop forward, sports the beer belly of a veteran hooker and talks with the nasal twang of a scrum half who has had his nose kicked once too often.'[56]

The ITV drama series *Making Waves* was in production from 2002 and had a good pedigree – a producer who had worked on the highly successful military series *Soldier, Soldier* and several actors who were well known from television appearances. It had good and experienced scriptwriters, full cooperation from the navy and was given a strong build up in the press. It had already been rescheduled several times before it appeared in July 2004, up against Channel 4's hit *Supernanny*. It used the rather inaccurate slogan, 'Life at sea is never dull' and indeed it tried to cram a great deal of action into every episode, its characters including a mixture of officers and ratings and a budding romance across the great divide. But it failed to engage the viewers and was pulled after three of its six episodes had been shown. To add insult to injury, it was replaced with the repeat of an outtake show, *It Shouldn't Happen on a TV Soap*. One naval source was quoted as saying that it was 'a kick in the teeth to our sailors'. It is difficult to say exactly what caused the disaster. Was it a poor storyline, or a script dismissed by one reviewer as a 'collection of clichés and stilted dialogue'? Or was it the problems of scheduling? Or did it show that the public had fallen out of love with the navy?

Not everyone connected with the navy was happy about the 2009 fly-on-the-wall series *Warship*, which showed HMS *Bulwark*. A retired officer complained,

> Senior officers are shown as desperately wanting to be seen as one of the boys. A ship's commander has been reduced to 'Eks Oh' and junior officers have all the bearing and authority of Winnie the Pooh. Petty Officers either simper 'Hi guys' like holiday camp attendants, or bellow pointless, foul-mouthed inanities like wannabe parade sergeants.

He concluded, 'The Royal Navy has had to suffer some utter tripe in the past, but this lot beats it all.'[57] It is impossible to tell how much the people concerned were putting on a show for the cameras and how much editing presented a distorted picture, but the fact remains that they *did* behave that way in real life.

Today films and televisions series deliberately mocking the armed forces, such as *The Navy Lark*, are in the long distant past. Though the popular press loves any scandal involving naval personnel, the bulk of the British media is almost excessively deferential to the armed forces, especially to the army, which has seen the great majority of the recent action in Iraq and Afghanistan. But that does not necessarily mean the navy gets the prominence it deserves.

In an age dominated by the media, the navy and the whole of the British seafaring sector have to live with the fact that the public is less aware of the sea than in the past. People travel much farther on holiday, but nearly always by air unless they take their cars with them and use ferries. If they only know the beaches of the Mediterranean, they are sometimes unaware of the rise and fall of the tides in British waters. The British merchant navy is no longer a significant factor in world commerce. The docks no longer employ large numbers of men, and they are often situated in relatively remote places such as Felixstowe and even Shetland rather than close to the centres of cities such as London, Liverpool or Glasgow. British seapower is no longer dominant in the world, and in a sense the British no longer want to know about it.

The picture is not all bleak. Water sports in various forms, including dinghy sailing, yachting, angling and scuba diving are all highly popular. Naval fiction, from Horatio Hornblower to the works of Patrick O'Brian, remain in print and are represented in film. And with the rise of ancestor research, many ordinary people find that seafarers are among the most interesting of their forebears.

Beyond all this is a much greater reality. The waters around Britain are far from empty, as ferries, cargo ships, oil tankers and container ships go across and along the waterways. Mineral exploration often conflicts with the protection of wildlife, while leisure sailors such as yachtsmen, scuba divers and water-skiers compete with the other interests, and often with each other. The fish within the seas are the constant subject of conflict and regulation, and our taste for seafood is far more sophisticated than in the past, but undiminished. The country is more dependent on the sea than ever with huge imports of oil, and the standard of living depends on cheap goods imported by container ship from the Pacific Rim. Whether we like it or not, sea transport is a vital factor in globalisation – today ideas travel electronically, people largely by air over long distances, but goods mostly by sea. With the concept of 'just in time' delivery, any disruption to supplies, because of war or any other factor, would soon lead to distress. It is the navy's job to prevent this happening, and to referee the conflicts between the different interests.

·

CONCLUSION

What can we learn from five hundred years or so of lower-deck history that is still relevant in the present age? Some complaints about the lower deck are perennial – that petty officers are closer to the lower deck than their officers or too absorbed in their technical skills to pay any attention to discipline; that seamen are brave and patriotic in action but feckless when left to their own devices. Perhaps the most recurrent is that seamen are not what they used to be. After several decades of fast and unprecedented change, how can we assess whether this is really true?

There have always been negative aspects to lower deck culture. Though constant swearing is probably no more common on the lower deck today than in society at large, the aggressive style of mess-deck conversation, once it was understood, was as legitimate a way of expressing feelings as any other. Violence against shipmates, other crews or the public, is far less common than it once was. On the whole, the seaman is still generous and often sentimental, but with shorter service and greater contact with the shore, his character is much less marked than in the past. Today it is difficult to identify a strong lower-deck culture, and it is no longer possible to say of seamen, as Dr. Thomas Trotter did more than 200 years ago,

> Excluded by the employment which they have chosen from all society but people of similar dispositions, the deficiencies of education are not felt, and information on general affairs is seldom courted. Their pride consists in being reputed a thorough bred seaman; and they look upon all landmen, as beings of an inferior order.

Unless something is badly wrong, a sailor is unconditionally loyal to his messmates, his ship and his country. His officers have to earn that loyalty, and they are not always successful. Naval officers tend to believe that they alone create the ethos and skills of the rank and file by training and discipline. This is partly true, but the culture of the lower deck has always tended to promote fearlessness and applaud real, valuable skills, which is what motivates seamen in battle. Moreover, it is often the seaman who has to take the initiative in identifying the enemy with eye, sonar or radar, or in attacking him with gun or guided missile.

Officers, and often historians, tend to assume that sailors fight well in battle because of loyalty to their officers. There is some truth in this, and they will certainly be inspired by good leadership. But it is not the whole truth. Sailors have at least as great a loyalty to their messmates, their ship, the navy as a whole and their country. They do not cheer their side on at a football match, for example, because they love their officers. Likewise in battle, their courage is inspired by patriotism or group loyalty, or by the respect of the population.

As we have seen, the Second World War was the zenith for the initiative of the lower deck seaman, when the determination and intelligence of landing-craft coxswains, asdic and radar operators, sick-berth attendants, anti-aircraft gunners and artificers might have a decisive effect on an operation. British sailors fought well, not just because of their training and the naval ethos, but because the lower deck has always had its own pride and standards. The lower-deck seaman has always added value to the naval effort beyond anything that is put into him by his officers.

The navy today has coped reasonably well with most of the divisive factors in society. It is far less class-based than it was in Victorian times, and since the 1950s lower-deck seamen and women have had a good prospect of rising to commissioned rank. It tries hard to give women a fair chance, and it seems on the face of it to have integrated homosexuals quite well. It does its best to recruit members of ethnic minorities, and there is no evidence that such recruits are seriously discriminated against once they are in. It might be argued that in the past it coped with these issues informally in any case – James Cook, the son of a farm labourer, was able to rise to captain and gain world fame more than 200 years ago. Dozens, perhaps hundreds, of women were on board Nelson's ships at the Battle of the Nile in 1798. There were plenty of non-white men in the navy at that time, as can be seen in prints and paintings as well as crew lists. And sailors have traditionally been tolerant of homosexuals even when society at large persecuted them. In that sense the navy has arguably returned to its true character after the repressive Victorian years.

The one issue that is outstanding, it might be argued, is a role for the disabled. Again, there is a past history here. Nelson rose to prominence after he had lost an arm and the sight of an eye, while ships' cooks up to about the 1870s usually had at least one limb missing. It might be argued that these people were injured in the service after they already had some experience, but nevertheless they found roles afterwards. One wonders if blind people with a highly developed sense of hearing might make especially good sonar operators, though of course they might be a liability if the ship were in danger.

For the future, there are many issues that might have to be resolved. Scottish independence is on the agenda again, and if that happened it would probably deprive the United Kingdom of its main submarine base at Faslane. It is difficult to see where it could be moved to; the use of Milford Haven would probably drive the Welsh along the same road as the Scots towards independence. The separation of Scotland would also deprive the navy of what is now quite a fertile source of recruits, and at the same time it would involve the setting up of a relatively small Scottish navy.

In the past the navy had a large working-class base to recruit from. This has changed due to the decline of British industry and by the fact that a large proportion of young people do university level courses, and have higher expectations of life. Not many graduates are likely to be satisfied with the relatively low status of the lower deck. They are unlikely to join the navy, and if they do so through lack of opportunity elsewhere, they would be of almost equivalent education to the officers set over them, and greater than their petty officers. This would provide an unstable element. One way round this would be to expect most or all of the new entrants to do some time on the lower deck before officer training. This is not unlike the system that was used for CWs in the Second World War, and parallel to that of the police force, where even the chief constable has done time on the beat. But ultimately this might mean the end of a separate lower-deck culture. It would mean that petty officers would be selected from those who did not rise to commissioned officer status though lack of educational qualification, ambition or ability, or perhaps inverted snobbery. But throughout history good petty officers have been essential to provide mature and experienced leadership. In the age of sail most of them had been press-ganged into the navy, which caused difficulties. Nineteenth-century officers constantly complained about the difficulty of finding good petty officers. The Invergordon Mutiny of 1931 was partly put down to the lack of support by the petty officers, showing how dangerous it can be for the Admiralty to alienate them. In more recent times, the *Iveston* Mutiny of 1970 may have been partly caused by the shortage of petty officers on board. And in the 2007 debacle off Iran, it is perhaps significant that no petty officers were involved.

Perhaps it is also significant that practically all the armed forces in the world, even those that started off as revolutionary, have the same three-part structure – privates or able seamen; NCOs or petty officers who are promoted from the lower ranks; and officers who mostly enter with the prospect of a commission. This reflected the organisation of a rural society with landowners, tenant farmers and labourers, or an industrial one with managers, foremen and workers – but it implies class and educational distinctions that are not found in modern working or social life. No other armed forces seem to see the need to grasp this particular nettle, and there is no reason to expect the Royal Navy to do so at the moment. But it may well become an issue in the future.

The rise of electronics also means a change in culture, though it is not clear how far that revolution has still to go. Like so many people on shore, sailors now spend much of their time looking at computer screens, whether to detect enemy activity or to monitor their own machinery. Could the completion of the electronic revolution mean that skilled work is less needed and all decisions are made at officer level, leaving the lower deck only domestic duties? So far there is nothing to show that is likely to happen, and there is a counter tendency. The Royal Navy as we know it was formed mainly to fight large-scale wars, against the French, the Germans and potentially against the Soviet Union. It has always had to cope with surprises, such as the Falklands War. Conflicts against organised naval powers would be fought mainly by radar, sonar, computers and guided missiles, but much of naval work in the future is likely to be against pirates and terrorists, which will require large numbers of relatively low-skilled people and will rely much more on human vigilance, cunning and bravery.

Naval history tends to be regarded as conservative on several levels. Those of a radical or socialist disposition are not inclined to join the service in peacetime, though as we have seen, it was very different in a world war. A ship is a hierarchical organisation, in which democracy can play very little part even if the crew members are ostensibly serving to preserve it in a larger sense. The navy in the past spent a large part of its effort in maintaining the British Empire, which is now deeply unfashionable except for a conservative minority – though academic study of it is not. Naval history has nearly always been written by officers or those who read their papers or interviewed them, so the lower deck view is rarely represented. Sandwiched between conservatism and radicalism in this way, the history of the lower deck is less well covered than it might have been. The 200th anniversary of the mutinies of 1797 provided some stimulus to study the subject, though the overheated context of a major revolt is not necessarily to best way to find generalisations. And the lower deck of the later nineteenth century, when many of its habits were formed, is very little covered.

It is generally agreed that we are losing contact with the sea, and the media are no longer interested, but the headlines in a single week or two early in 2012 show how much it still affects us. The *Costa Concordia* case, a cruise liner wrecked in the Mediterranean, is no longer on the front page of the newspapers, but it will continue to attract attention for some time as the wreck is removed, more bodies are found and the enquiry continues. And the conduct of its captain, Francesco Schettino, becomes increasingly difficult to justify. In contrast, the achievement of 16-year-old Laura Dekker in becoming the youngest person to circumnavigate the world is controversial, but admirable – *The Guinness Book of World Records* looks rather mean-spirited in not entering it as it is considered 'unsuitable.' The raising of the wreck of HMS *Victory* (lost in 1744) promises to be controversial as the archaeological community questions the motives and methods used. On a far more serious note, there is a real threat of a devastating maritime war in the Strait of Hormuz, which only highlights our dependence on seaborne oil supplies.

Behind it all, it is worth remembering that 95 per cent of world trade goes by sea, and we in the United Kingdom are more dependent on imported goods than ever. Imagine the effect if the load of a container ship, say the equivalent of 8,000 road vehicles, was put on the roads all at once – a traffic jam of 50 miles?

Despite all this, the navy's prestige today is far lower than in the past. It has been overshadowed by the army in recent conflicts in Iraq and Afghanistan, though it is just by chance that Britain's last two wars were mostly land-based. It has suffered more dramatically than the other services from financial cuts, and it is unlikely that its aircraft carriers will be in operation for some years. So far it has not distinguished itself in the fight against piracy.

The navy has suffered bad moments in the past. It was a national disgrace when Admiral Byng was shot for the loss of Minorca in 1756, but the Royal Navy went on to its greatest era. It lost several frigate battles in the War of 1812 with the United States, but soon recovered. It under-performed in the First World War, and the mutiny at Invergordon seemed to show serious weaknesses to the public, but the navy went on to a 'finest hour' in the Second World War, in which its achievement was at least as great as any of the other services, or the civil population. It has always recovered from bad times and gone on to greater things. But there are important questions to be asked. Is it true, as one captain joked in the 1980s, that 'the men do not have the stamina for such things at present, everything aboard ship nowadays is done by pressing computer buttons'? Or does the naval rating still believe as he did in 1942, 'I am a British Sailor. The British Sailor has always been the best seaman, the finest fighter, the hero of the people. Therefore, I am a hero.'?

GLOSSARY

Able Seaman (AB). A skilled seamen with at least one year's experience. Later, the lowest rating on the lower deck

Admiralty. Until replaced by the Ministry of Defence (MoD) in 1964, the government body that administered the navy, headed by the Board of Admiralty

Admiralty Fleet Order (AFO). Orders to ships and stations from the central authority, of varying importance

Aft. Towards the stern in a ship

Air Mechanic. A semi-skilled maintenance rating

Artificer. A highly skilled man, originally in the engine room, rated as chief petty officer when fully qualified.

Artisan. A skilled man in a trade that can be learned ashore, for example a plumber or painter, usually rated as petty officer.

Asdic. Echo-sounding equipment used to detect submarines underwater The term was later replaced by sonar

Badge. Specifically, a good-conduct badge or chevron

Barrack Stanchion. A seaman who contrives to avoid sea drafts

Bilges. The lower part of a ship, where water might accumulate

Berth, Birth. The position of a ship at anchor, or a man's sleeping accommodation, or the space for a mess between two guns

Boat. A small craft usually with open decks; a ship's boat is one that belongs to the ship and can be hoisted on board or towed behind

Boatswain. Originally, a warrant in charge of the rigging and mustering the crew

Branch Officer. The successor to the old style warrant officer, replaced by the Special Duties officer

Captain. A naval rank, equivalent to a colonel in the army. Also a courtesy title for the commanding officer of any ship, especially naval

Chief petty officer (CPO). The most senior rating, until the new style of warrant officer was introduced

Class I, II, III uniform. Class I was with collar and tie, worn by chiefs and later petty officers. Class II was the traditional seaman's uniform worn by junior ratings. Class III was an inferior version of Class I, worn by writers, stewards, etc.

Clubs. Nickname for the physical training instructor, based on his badge

Continuous Service (CS). Service for a term of 12 years

Coxswain. A petty officer who steers a ship's boat and leads its crew, often under the charge of a midshipmen. The senior rating in a small warship such as a destroyer or submarine

Demob or demobilisation. Release from the armed forces, usually at the end of a war

Dhobying. Washing of clothes

East of Suez. The policy of keeping a substantial naval force in the Indian Ocean

Engineering Mechanic. Originally a skilled man who had not served the full apprenticeship needed for an ERA. Later a semi-skilled man or woman in the engineering department, the replacement for the stoker

ERA. Engine room artificer

Fish. A torpedo

Flashing up. Igniting boilers

Fleet Air Arm. The naval air service, which bore that title officially from about 1950

Fore-and-Aft Rig. Originally, sails used by cutters, schooners, yachts, etc. in which the sails run fore and aft in their neutral position. Later, the dress of the seamen who were not in square rig, with peaked cap and collar and tie.

Gas turbine. A jet engine, used to power a turbine and propellers in a warship

Good conduct badge. A chevron awarded to a seaman after a specific period of good conduct

Handraulic. By hand or muscle power, a corruption of 'hydraulic'

Handsomely. To work slowly and carefully, especially when lowering an object

Heads. Naval term for toilets

Home port. The three home ports to which warships were attached were Chatham, Portsmouth and Plymouth. These became manning divisions late in the nineteenth century

Hostilities Only (HO). A rating enlisted for war service only

Instructor. A highly qualified man in the gunnery or torpedo branches, for example. He did not necessarily spend a large part of his time in instruction

Joss Man. The master at arms

Jumper. The main outer garment in square-rig dress

Killick. Originally a small anchor, later used to describe a leading seaman because of his anchor badge

Leading Seaman (LS) or Leading Hand. Originally a skilled seaman, who gradually took on executive authority, which was formally recognised by the 1950s. Usually the leading figure in a mess

Master at Arms. The head of a large ship's police and the senior rating on board

Mate. A petty officer and assistant to a warrant officer, e.g., master's mate, gunner's mate

From 1912 a man selected for the lower deck for training as a commissioned officer

Mechanician. A man recruited from among the stokers and trained to be almost the equivalent of an ERA

Mess. The seamen's main living space, usually centred on a table

National Service. Compulsory service in the armed forces, usually referring to the post-Second World War period

Non-substantive rating. A seaman's status in a skill such as gunnery, largely independent of his 'substantive rating' as a leading seaman, petty officer, etc.

Ordinary Seaman. A man with less than a year's experience, less skilled than an able seaman

Port. The left-hand side of the ship, looking forward

Pulling. A naval term for rowing

Rate, Rating. As applied to a seaman, his rating in a particular level of skill as a seaman. Also a man holding a rating, i.e., a member of the lower deck

Retention. Keeping men on beyond their original engagement in the navy

Roster. The system by which seamen were promoted according to their place on a roster in the home port concerned

Roundly. Quickly, the opposite of 'handsomely'

Royal Fleet Reserve (RFR). Seamen who had already served with the fleet, kept up some training and were liable to recall

Royal Naval Reserve (RNR). Professional merchant officers and seamen who trained with the Royal Navy and could be called on to serve in wartime

Royal Naval Volunteer Reserve (RNVR). Amateurs who did some part-time training as seamen. During the Second World War temporary officers were commissioned in the RNVR, though most of them were not volunteers.

Sea Dart. A short-range anti-aircraft missile

Sick Berth Attendant (SBA). A medical rating, who might be the only medical personnel on a small ship, or specialise in one of various fields

Sick Berth Tiffy. Slang for 'Sick Berth Attendant'

Sonar. Anti-submarine echo-sounding, the replacement term for 'Asdic'

Special Duties Officer. From the mid-1950s, an officer commissioned from the lower deck, with limited promotion opportunities.

Special service. Short service for ratings, usually involving a period of seven or five years with the fleet and then with the reserves, adding up to 12 years in total

Square off. To tidy up

Starboard. The right-hand side of the ship, looking forward

Stoker. Originally a man employed to shovel coal into a furnace and tend the water in a boiler. Later a semi-skilled engineer. The term was still used colloquially by the lower deck long after its official replacement

Stoker Mechanic. Originally a stoker who had picked up a certain amount of mechanical skill. In the 1950s the stoker's replacement.

'Swain. Lower deck term for the coxswain of a ship

TAS. The Torpedo and Anti-Submarine Branch

Three Badge AB. A long service seaman who has not been promoted beyond able seaman

Tiffy. Lower deck term for artificer

Tot. The seaman's allowance of rum

Two-and-a-Half Ringer. A lieutenant-commander

Type 42. A class of destroyer that entered service from the 1970s, named after towns

Upper Yardsmen. Lower deck seaman selected for officer training

Warrant Officer. Originally an officer such as a boatswain or gunner appointed by warrant rather than commission. Treated like a junior commissioned officer rather than a senior petty officer, he was replaced by the branch officer then the special duties officer. When revived in 1971, the warrant officer was more like a senior petty officer, which was reflected in his original title of 'Fleet Chief'.

Watch. A period of two or four hours during which particular seamen are on duty; or a group of seaman who form a watch

Woolly pullie. A woollen pullover worn by all ranks from the 1970s

Wrens. Acronym for the Women's Royal Naval Service, also used as a rating title

Writer. A naval clerk

Y-Scheme. A scheme that gave pre-entry training to selected young men during the Second World War with a view to their becoming either officers or technicians

NOTES

1. Training for the People's War

1   A. D. Divine, *Destroyers War*, London, 1942, p 3

2   See B. Lavery, *Able Seamen*, London, 2011, p 303

3   John Whelan, *Home is the Sailor*, London, 1957, p 103

4   Imperial War Museum, documents, G. T. Weekes, 1445

5   Imperial War Museum, documents, Coombes, 91/7/1

6   John Palmer, *Luck on my Side*, Barnsley, 2002, p 26

7   *Brassey's Naval Annual*, 1906, p 1

8   National Archives, ADM 1/10088

9   Mass Observation Archive, University of Sussex, Report nos 886–7

10   Ken Kimberley, *Heavo, Heavo, Lash up and Stow*, Kettering, 1999, p 10

11   National Archives, T 161/1042

12   John Davis, *The Stone Frigate*, London, 1947, p 6

13   National Archives, ADM 1/21955

14   Davis, op cit, p 24

15   Alec Guinness, *Blessings in Disguise*, London, 1987, p 155

16   Kimberley, op cit, p 17

17   Davis, op cit, p 39

18   James Callaghan, *Time and Chance*, London, 1987, p 58

19   Hannen Swaffer, *What Would Nelson Do?*, London, 1946, p 93

20   Davis, op cit, pp 99, 129–39

21   Albert H. Jones, *No Easy Choices*, Upton upon Severn, 1999, pp 22–3

22   J. P. W. Mallalieu, *Very Ordinary Seaman*, London, 1944, p 34

23   Admiralty, *Royal Naval Handbook of Field Training*, London, 1920, p 19

24   *Naval Review*, November 1954, pp 452–5

25   Ibid, January 1955, pp 80–3, 128–9

26   Kimberley, op cit, p 18; John L. Brown, Diary of a Matelot,1942–1945, p 9, *Jack – the Sailor with the Navy Blue Eyes*, Bishop Auckland, 1995, p 16, Roy Fuller, *Vamp Till Ready*, London, 1982, p 142

27   F. S. Holt, *A Banker all at Sea*, Newtown, Australia, 1983, p 32

28   J. Lennox Kerr and David James, *Wavy Navy, by Some Who Served*, London, 1950, p 194

29   National Archives, ADM 1/16774

30   Admiralty Fleet Order (AFO) 277/1940

31   AFO 882/1941

32   *Hansard*, col 1441, 26/7/39, 47

33   National Archives, ADM 1/17944

34   Davis, op cit, p 112

35   *Hansard*, vol 378, cols 1088–9

36   AFO 1163/1943

37   Whelan, op cit, p 178

38   Ibid, p 185

39   AFO 277/1940

40   Whelan, op cit p 221

41   George Melly, *Rum, Bum and Concertina*, London, 1977, p 8

42   National Archives, ADM 1/17944

43   John Davies, *Lower Deck*, London, 1945, p 78

44   Whelan, op cit, pp 146-8

45   Personal communication to the author

46   Peter Bull, *To Sea in a Sieve*, London, 1956, p 25

47   J. P. W. Mallalieu, *On Larkhill*, London, 1983, p 203

48   Piers Paul Read, *Alec Guinness*, London, 2004, especially Chapter III

49   Robert Burgess and Roland Blackburn, *We Joined the Navy*, London, 1943, p 9

50   Ibid, p 7

51   Mallalieu, *Very Ordinary Seaman*, p 109

52   S. Gorley Putt, *Men Dressed as Seamen*, London, 1943, p 31

53   Mallalieu, op cit, p 139

54   Ibid, p 173

55   Ibid, p 171
56   Ibid, p 161
57   Gorley Putt, op cit, p 34
58   Mallalieu, op cit, p 98
59   Burgess and Blackburn, op cit, p 7
60   Gorley Putt, op cit, pp 89–90
61   Mallalieu, op cit, p 163
62   Davies, op cit, p 91
63   Mallalieu, op cit, p 127
64   Ibid, p 147
65   Gorley Putt, op cit, pp 80–1
66   Paul Lund and Harry Ludlam, *The War
      of the Landing Craft*, Slough, 1976,
      p 78
67   H. P. K Oram, *The Rogue's Yarn*,
      London, 1993, p 229
68   Tristan Jones, *Heart of Oak*, 1984,
      reprinted Shrewsbury, 1997, pp 29, 44–5
69   National Archives, ADM 1/12133
70   *Hansard*, col 2015
71   Mallalieu, op cit, p 121
72   National Archives, ADM 199/788A

2. The Branches

1   Admiralty, BR 224/45, *Gunnery Pocket
      Book*, 1945, pp 2–3
2   Ibid, p 104
3   L. C. Reynolds, *Motor Gunboat 658*,
      London, 2002, p 22
4   John Campbell, *Naval Weapons of
      World War Two*, London, 1985, p 76
5   Sir Roderick Macdonald, *The
      Figurehead*, Bishop Auckland, 1993,
      p 99
6   Reynolds, op cit, p 70
7   *Gunnery Pocket Book*, op cit, p 162
8   John W. Davies, *Jack, The Sailor with
      the Navy Blue Eyes*, Bishop Auckland,
      1995, p 41
9   Leonard Charles Williams, *Gone a Long
      Journey*, Havant, 2002, pp 133, 144
10   Phillip E. Vernon and John B. Parry,
      *Personnel Selection in the British
      Forces*, London, 1949, p 211
11   John Davies, *The Stone Frigate*,
      London, 1947, p 112
12   Nicholas Monsarrat, *Corvette
      Command*, London, 1975 edition, p 189
13   George Luscombe, *Total Germany*,
      Edinburgh, 1999, p 1
14   Ibid, p 8
15   National Archives, ADM 1/14110
16   Roy Fuller, *Vamp Till Ready*, London,
      1982, p 142–3
17   National Archives, LAB 29/249
18   Admiralty Fleet Order (AFO) 2214/42
19   Donald Macintyre, *U-Boat Killer*,
      London, 2002, p 25
20   National Archives, ADM 199/241
21   Macdonald, op cit, p 43
22   J. P. W. Mallalieu, *Very Ordinary
      Seaman*, p 153
23   National Archives, ADM 1/15871
24   John Whelan, *Home is the Sailor*,
      pp 153–4
25   Imperial War Museum Documents,
      92/27/1
26   Fred Kellet, *A Flower for the Sea, a
      Fish for the Sky*, Dellwood, 1995,
      pp 43–4
27   AFO 4496/42
28   John Winton, *Sink the Haguro*, London,
      1979
29   National Archives, ADM 1/12133
30   National Archives ADM 1/17685
31   National Archives, PREM 4/55/3
32   John Gritten, *Full Circle, the Log of the
      Navy's No 1 Conscript*, Dunfermline,
      2003, p 34
33   Albert H. Jones, *No Easy Choices*,
      Upton upon Severn, 1994, p 17
34   National Archives, ADM 1/17685
35   Ian Hawkins (ed), *Destroyer*, London
      2003, pp 233–4
36   Tristan Jones, *Heart of Oak*,
      Shrewsbury, 1997, p 195
37   Gritten, op cit, pp 42–3
38   Hawkins, op cit, p 234
39   Nicholas Monsarrat, *Three Corvettes*,
      London, 2000, p 44
40   National Archives, LAB 29/249
41   National Archives, ADM 101/563
42   Admiralty, *First Aid in the Royal Navy*,
      BR 25, 1943, p 3
43   Ibid, pp 51, 57
44   J. L. S. Coulter, *The Royal Naval
      Medical Service*, London, 1954, vol II,
      p 48 ff
45   Ibid, vol II, p 339
46   National Archives, ADM 239/335
47   Chris Howard Bailey, *The Battle of the
      Atlantic*, Stroud, 1994, p 101
48   Alan Brundett, *Two Years in Ceylon*,
      Lewes, 1996, pp 44, 46
49   John L. Brown, *Diary of a Matelot,
      1942–1945*, Lowesmoor
50   Derek Hamilton Warner, *A Steward's
      Life in the Royal Navy*, Ilfracombe,
      p 15
51   Brown, op cit, pp 19, 27, 33
52   Nicholas Monsarrat, *HM Frigate*,
      London, 1946, p 16
53   Brown, op cit, p 26
54   Imperial War Museum Documents,

86/61/1

55   National Archives, ADM 1/12114
56   R. 'Mike' Crossley, *They Gave me a Seafire*, Shrewsbury, 2001, pp 48–9
57   Jones, op cit, p 133
58   Godfrey Winn, *Home from the Sea*, London, 1946, p 89
59   Whelan, op cit, p 100
60   Jones, op cit, p 88
61   George Melly, *Rum, Bum and Concertina*, London, 1976, p 7
62   Joseph Wellings, *On His Majesty's Service*, Newport, Rhode Island, 1983, p 67
63   Sidney Greenwood, *Stoker Greenwood's Navy*, Tunbridge Wells, 1983, p 58
64   'Officer's Aide Memoire', in B. Lavery (ed), *The Royal Navy Officer's Pocket Book*, London, 2007, p 24
65   D. A. Rayner, *Escort – The Battle of the Atlantic*, London, 1955, p 66
66   Monsarrat, *Three Corvettes*, pp 187–8

3. Navies Within the Navy

1   G. G. Connell, *Jack's War*, London, 1985, p 78
2   Alexander McKee, *Black Saturday*, London, 1960, pp 67–8
3   Max Arthur, *Lost Voices of the Royal Navy*, London, 2005, pp 230, 232
4   Ibid, pp 296–7
5   *Navy News*, May 1991
6   Malcolm Brown and Patricia Meehan, *Scapa Flow*, London, 1968, pp 173–4
7   John Whelan, *Home is the Sailor*, London, 1957, p 109
8   Tristan Jones, *Heart of Oak*, Shrewsbury, 1984, p 251
9   Chris Howard Bailey, *The Royal Naval Museum Book of the Battle of the Atlantic*, Stroud, 1994, pp 12–13
10   Fred Kellet, *A Flower for the Sea, a Fish for the Sky*, Dellwood, 1995, p 31
11   Personal communication to author
12   Peter Gretton, *Crisis Convoy*, London, 1974, pp 37, 170–1
13   Max Arthur, op cit, p 308
14   Ibid, pp 530–1
15   National Archives, ADM 1/17685
16   Paul Lund and Harry Ludlam, *The War of the Landing Craft*, London, 1976, pp 15–16
17   Brian Macdermott, *Ships Without Names*, London, 1992, p 28
18   J. Lennox Kerr (ed), *Wavy Navy*, London, 1950, p 223
19   Lund and Ludlam, op cit, pp 158–9

20   John W. Davies, *Jack, The Sailor with the Navy Blue Eyes*, Bishop Auckland, 1995, pp 25, 91
21   Imperial War Museum documents, Coombes, 91/7/1
22   Peter Scott, *The Battle of the Narrow Seas*, 1945, plate following page 168
23   Royal Institution of Naval Architects, *British Warship Design*, London, 1983, p 124
24   National Archives, ADM 1/17685
25   Davies, op cit, p 51
26   L. C. Reynolds, Motor Gunboat 658, London, 2002, p 116
27   Vivian A. Cox, *Seven Christmases*, Sevenoaks, 2010, p 43
28   Godfrey Winn, *Home from the Sea*, London, 1946, p 32
29   National Archives, ADM 1/17685
30   National Archives, ADM 1/11361
31   National Archives, ADM 239/14
32   Keith Nethercoate-Bryant, *Submarine Memories*, Hadley, 1994, pp 65–6
33   Hannen Swaffer, *What Would Nelson Do?*, London, 1946, p 36
34   Quoted in Piers Paul Read, *Alec Guinness*, London, 2004, p 135
35   Whelan, op cit, p 175
36   Ibid, p 172
37   George Melly, *Rum, Bum and Concertina*, London, 1977, p 57
38   National Archives, ADM 1/22967
39   National Archives, ADM 1/15685
40   Bill Glenton, *Mutiny in Force X*, London, 1986, p 124
41   G. G. Connell, *Jack's War*, London, 1985, pp 175–6
42   Ibid, p 177
43   Ibid, p 149
44   Glenton, op cit, p 20
45   Stuart Eadon (ed), *Kamikaze, The Story of the British Pacific Fleet*, 1995, p 419
46   Ibid, p 243
47   Glenton, op cit, p 219

4. The Age of Austerity 1945–55

1   National Archives, ADM 1/14111
2   National Archives, ADM 116/6420
3   Alan Allport, *Demobbed: Coming Home After the Second World War*, Yale, 2010, p 35
4   Ibid, pp 189–90
5   Hannen Swaffer, *What Would Nelson Do?*, London, 1946, pp 22–3
6   David Phillipson, *Band of Brothers: Boy Seamen in the Royal Navy*, Stroud,

2003, p 133

7   B. R. Mitchell, *Abstract of British Historical Statistics*, Cambridge, 1962, p 66

8   Eric Leggett, *The Corfu Incident*, London, 1974, p 49

9   National Archives, ADM 1/21943

10   Ibid

11   National Archives, ADM 1/22474

12   Swaffer, op cit, p 89

13   National Archives, ADM 1/24093

14   *Brassey's Naval Annual*, 1947, p 297

15   Brasseys Annual, 1955, p 78

16   Peter M. Cobbold, *The National Service Sailor*, Wivenhoe, 1993, pp 6–9

17   Ibid, p 34

18   Jack Rosenthal, *An Autobiography in Six Acts*, London, 2005, p 83

19   Ibid, p 88

20   Cobbold, op cit, pp i-ii

21   Trevor Royle, *The Best Years of their Lives, The National Service Experience 1945-63*, London, 1986, p 319

22   Cobbold, op cit, p 286

23   Leonard Charles Williams, *Gone a Long Journey*, Havant, 2002, pp 133, p 205

24   *Naval Review*, 1946, p 51

25   National Archives, ADM 167/131

26   National Archives, ADM 205/103

27   *Admiralty Manual of Seamanship*, vol 3, 1967, p 383*ff*

28   Leggett, op cit, pp 73–4

29   Ibid, pp 88–9

30   Leslie Frank, *Yangtse River Incident*, Uckfield, 2006

31   S. P. Mackenzie, *British War Films*, London, 2001, p 147

32   National Archives, ADM 1/21943

33   Ian Buxton, *To Sail No More*, Liskeard, 1997, p 2

34   National Archives, ADM 1/20820

35   Cobbold, op cit, pp 264–5

36   National Archives, ADM 1/21943

37   Phillipson, op cit, p 79

38   Ibid, p 83-4

39   Ibid, p 45

40   National Archives, ADM 1/26226

41   National Archives, ADM 1/21943

42   National Archives, ADM 1/24093

43   National Archives, ADM 1/20810

44   National Archives, ADM 1/25714

45   National Archives, ADM 1/25688

46   National Archives, ADM 1/22602

47   National Archives, ADM 1/22602

48   National Archives, ADM 1/26614

49   National Archives, ADM 1/22613

50   Denis Sherringham, *Swing the Lamp, Jack Dusty*, Thorpe Bay, 1998, pp 12, 22

51   National Archives, ADM 1/21951

5. The Navy in the Affluent Society

1   Admiralty Fleet Order (AFO) 56/519

2   David Phillipson, *Band of Brothers: Boy Seamen in the Royal Navy*, Stroud, 2003, p x

3   AFO 56/616

4   National Archives, ADM 116/6371

5   National Archives, 1/26796

6   Eric Grove, *Vanguard to Trident*, London, 1987, pp 161–3

7   National Archives, ADM 1/27731

8   *The Times*, 22 January 2007

9   *The Herald*, 22 April 2009

10   National Archives, ADM 1/26226

11   Ibid

12   National Archives, ADM 1/25714

13   National Archives, ADM 298/341

14   *Navy News*, 3 March 2010

15   Denis Barker, *Ruling the Waves*, London, 1986, p 29

16   *Royal United Services Institute Journal*, vol 113, p 217

17   National Archives, ADM 1/21943

18   AFO 55/530

19   'The Nassau Connection' in *Brassey's Annual*, 1966, p 134, p 97

20   Leonard Charles Williams, *Gone a Long Journey*, Havant, 2002, pp 213, 221–2

21   Sherringham, Denis, *Swing the Lamp, Jack Dusty*, Thorpe Bay, 1998, pp 133–51

22   National Archives, ADM 239/584

23   Rory O'Conor, *Running a Big Ship*, Portsmouth, 1937, p 99

24   National Archives, ADM 1/21699

25   For example BR 25, *First Aid in the Navy*, 1943, contrasted with BR 67(1), *Admiralty Manual of Seamanship*, vol I, 1964

26   Peter M. Cobbold, *The National Service Sailor*, Wivenhoe, 1993, p 26

27   National Archives, ADM 1/24180

28   Cobbold, op cit, p 190

29   National Archives, ADM 1/17258

30   National Archives, ADM 1/20381

31   National Archives, ADM 1/20678

32   National Archives, ADM 1/22594

33   BR 1927(52), *Naval Airman Branch Qualifying Courses*, in National Archives, ADM 234/460

34   National Archives, ADM 1/28718

35   BR 1927(52), *Naval Airman Branch Qualifying Courses*, in National Archives, ADM 234/460

36 National Archives, ADM 1/22602
37 Ibid
38 National Archives, ADM 1/20375
39 National Archives, ADM 1/28793
40 National Archives, ADM 1/21943
41 Ibid
42 National Archives, ADM 1/22602
43 Ibid
44 National Archives, ADM 1/25714
45 National Archives, ADM 1/22602
46 National Archives, ADM 1/28718

6. The Electronic Navy

1   *The Royal Navy as a Career*, 1963,
    pp 20–1
2   National Archives, ADM 1/21943
3   National Archives, ADM 330/89
4   Michael Payne, *When I was on the
    Tartar*, Stroud, 1999, p 110
5   Brassey's Annual, 1962, p 310
6   Rick Jolly, *Jackspeak*, London, 2000,
    p 295
7   *The Royal Navy as a Career*, op cit,
    passim
8   National Archives, INF 13/272
9   Denis Barker, *Ruling the Waves*,
    London, 1986, p 247
10 Diesel Weasel website,
    www.dieselweasel.co.uk
11 National Archives, DEFE 49/85
12 Diesel Weasel website
13 National Archives, ADM 1/27088
14 National Archives, ADM 1/28605
15 National Archives, ADM NA
16 National Archives, ADM 1/20318
17 National Archives, ADM 1/27822
18 Ibid
19 National Archives, ADM 1/24046
20 Ibid
21 National Archives, DEFE 24/280
22 Ibid
23 National Archives, DEFE 24/257
24 National Archives, DEFE 24/280
25 Broadsheet, 1997–8, p 46
26 Broadsheet, 2001–2, p 39
27 National Archives, DEFE 69/397
28 National Archives, ADM 331/8
29 Payne, op cit, Stroud, 1999, p 3
30 Ibid, p 9
31 National Archives, ADM 1/28245
32 Payne, op cit, p 133
33 Ibid, p 128
34 James D. Ladd, *By Sea, By Land*,
    London, 1998, p 529
35 National Archives, ADM 330/48
36 Payne, op cit, p 75
37 Ibid, p 73

38 Ibid, p 142
39 National Archives, ADM 239/688
40 B. B. Schofield, *Navigation and
    Direction: the Story of HMS Dryad*,
    Havant, 1977, p 156
41 Payne, op cit, pp 32–3
42 National Archives, ADM 281/287
43 National Archives, ADM 204/3553
44 *The Royal Navy as a Career*, p 22
45 Peter M. Cobbold, *The National Service
    Sailor*, Wivenhoe, 1993, p 189
46 Payne, op cit, pp 46–7
47 *Naval Review*, 1970, p 304

7. The Way to the Falklands

1   National Archives, DEFE 49/53
2   Michael Payne, *When I was on the
    Tartar*, Stroud, 1999, p 60
3   Ibid, pp 144–5
4   *Shipping World and Shipbuilder*,
    April 1975, p 324
5   Ibid, September 1975, p 853
6   Hugh McManners, *Forgotten Voices of
    the Falklands*, London, 2007, pp 44–5
7   *Brassey's Naval Annual*, 1966, p 134;
    Peter Nailor, *The Nassau Connection*,
    London, 1988, p 97
8   National Archives, DEFE 49/18
9   National Archives, ADM 239/584
10 National Archives, ADM 234/948
11 Payne, op cit, pp 189–90
12 National Archives, ADM 330/48
13 National Archives, ADM 239/584
14 National Archives, ADM 1/27992
15 National Archives, ADM 220/2171
16 McManners, op cit, p 117
17 Ibid, pp 117, 33
18 Payne, op cit, p 82
19 National Archives, ADM 330/48
20 Payne, op cit, p 99
21 Geoff Feasey, *Very Ordinary Officer*,
    Fisher, Australia, p 213
22 Chief Polaris Executive, *Polaris and the
    Royal Navy*, London, 1966, pp 6–7
23 Ibid, p 1
24 Rick Jolly, Jackspeak, London, 2000,
    p 295
25 Cammel Laird, *HMS Renown*, nd,
    *c.*1969, Birkenhead
26 Chief Polaris Executive, op cit, p 3
27 J. E. Moore (ed), *The Impact of Polaris*,
    Huddersfield, 1999, p 255
28 Ibid, 248
29 Ibid, p 252
30 Ibid, p 252
31 P. G. La Niece, *Not a Nine to Five Job*,
    Yalding, 1992, p 210

32 Leo Marriott, *Modern Combat Ships 4:*
    Type 22, Shepperton, 1986, p 49
33 National Archives, ADM 330/89
34 National Archives, ADM 204/3395
35 National Archives, ADM 1/21943
36 US Naval Institute, *The Blue Jacket's*
    Manual, 1978, p 159
37 National Archives, DEFE 49/96
38 National Archives, ADM 1/25830
39 National Archives, ADM 1/27165
40 National Archives, DEFE 13/791
41 National Archives, ADM 330/89
42 Payne, op cit, p 174
43 Ibid, pp 175–6
44 Ibid, p 176
45 Mike Rossiter, *Sink the Belgrano*,
    London, 2008, p 17
46 Martin Middlebrook, *Operation*
    Corporate, London, 1985, p 72
47 'Doc', *100 Year History of the Sick*
    Berth Branch, Portsmouth, 1984, p 160
48 Ibid, p 160
49 McManners, op cit, p 118
50 Ibid, p 120
51 Ibid, p 125
52 Ibid, p 129
53 Middlebrook, op cit, p 129
54 Ibid, pp 131–2
55 Rositer, op cit, p 235
56 Ibid, p 242
57 McManners, op cit, pp 130, 157
58 *The Guardian*, 26 September 2000
59 'Doc', op cit, p 163
60 Ibid, p 164
61 Ibid, p 166
62 Ibid, p 167
63 Middlebrook, op cit, p 165
64 McManners, op cit, pp 206–8
65 Middlebrook, op cit, p 232

8. The Modern Navy
1   Broadsheet, 1983
2   Ibid
3   Denis Barker, *Ruling the Waves*,
    London, 1986, p 298
4   Ibid, p 313
5   Ibid p 208
6   Ibid p 296
7   Broadsheet, 1984
8   Barker, op cit, p 323
9   Christopher Terrill, *Shipmates – Inside*
    the Royal Navy Today, London, 2005,
    p 22
10 Barker, op cit, p 320
11 Terrill, op cit, p 75
12 Barker, op cit, p 316
13 Terrill, op cit, p 74

14 Barker, op cit, pp 317–18
15 Terrill, op cit, p 180
16 *Navy News*, March 2001
17 MoD report, *Board of Enquiry into the*
    Grounding of HMS Nottingham, 2002
18 Barker, op cit, p 50
19 *Hansard*, 2 April 1996
20 *The Independent*, 20 August 1997
21 Barker, op cit, pp 51-2
22 Christopher Terrill, *HMS Brilliant – in*
    a Ship's Company, London, 1996,
    p 202
23 Terrill, *Shipmates*, p 202
24 National Archives, ADM 1/12133
25 National Archives, 69/689
26 Broadsheet, 1988
27 *The Times*, 25July 2005
28 *Naval Review*, 1989, p 40
29 Ibid, April 1992, p 165
30 Terrill, op cit, p 102
31 Ibid, p 157
32 Ibid, p 102
33 *Naval Review*, p 115
34 Broadsheet, 2001–2 p 58
35 Ibid, 1998–9, p 47
36 Ibid, 2001–2, p 57
37 Ibid, 1997–8, p 88
38 *Navy News*, June 1998
39 Ibid, November 1999
40 Website: www.proud2serve.net
41 *Navy News*, September 1996
42 Ibid, February 1997
43 Broadsheet, 1997–8, p 96
44 Terrill, op cit, p 68
45 Ibid, p 47
46 *Navy News*, July 1998
47 Barker, op cit, p 47
48 Rick Jolly, *Jackspeak*, London, 2000,
    preface
49 Barker, op cit, p 216
50 Ibid, p 52
51 Terrill, op cit pp 70-2
52 Broadsheet, 1999/2000, pp 57–8
53 *Navy News*, March 2001
54 Ibid, July 1998

9. After the Cold War
1   Broadsheet, 1997, pp 50–1
2   Christopher Terrill, *HMS Brilliant – in*
    a Ship's Company, London, 1996, p 80
3   Broadsheet, 1997–8, p 48
4   *Navy News*, July 1993
5   Broadsheet, 2001–2, p 32
6   *Navy News*, June 1998
7   Broadsheet, 1998–9, p 45
8   *Navy News*, January 2003
9   Broadsheet, 1999/2000, pp 53–6

10   Ibid, pp 59–60
11   *Navy News*, November 2005
12   Broadsheet, 1983
13   Denis Barker, *Ruling the Waves*, London, 1986, p 389
14   Terrill, op cit, p 63
15   Idem
*1*6   *Naval Review*, 2000, pp 301–3
17   *Navy News*, March 2005
18   Terrill, op cit, p 57
19   Broadsheet, 1997–8, p 80
20   *Navy News*, July 1998
21   Broadsheet, 1999/2000, p 29
22   Ibid, pp 19, 89
23   *Navy News*, October 1998
24   Ibid, September 2001
25   Broadsheet, 2003–4, pp 19, 20
26   Terrill, op cit, p 35
27   Ibid, pp 54–5
28   *Navy News*, September 2001
29   Terrill, op cit, p 92
30   Ibid, p 132
31   Richard S. J. Gough, *The Weapon Director*, 2003, p 85
32   Ibid, p 85
33   http://www.d19.onthefirm.co.uk
34   *Navy News*, September 2001
35   Terrill, op cit, p 33
36   Ibid. p 40
37   Ibid, p 41
38   Ibid, p 70
39   Broadsheet, 2001–2, pp 45, 46
40   Terrill, op cit, p 139
41   Ibid, p 156
42   Ibid, p 81
43   Barker, p 198
44   Ibid, p 203
45   Terrill, op cit, p 206
46   Barker, op cit, p 205
47   Terrill, op cit, p 173
48   Ibid, p 180
49   *Navy News*, November 2005
50   Broadsheet 2000–1, p 57
51   Website: The Brodie Family, Mike Brodie, *My Gulf War Diary*
52   MOD net, Nursing Times, http://www.nursingtimes.net/
53   Christopher Terrill, *Shipmates – Inside the Royal Navy Today*, London, 2005, p 91
54   Gough, op cit, p 65
55   *Navy News*, February 2002
56   Terrill, *HMS Brilliant*, p 96
57   *Navy News*, November 2009

BIBLIOGRAPHY

General and Miscellaneous History

Allport. Alan, *Demobbed: Coming Home After the Second World War*, Yale, 2010

Kynaston, David, *Austerity Britain, 1945–51*, London, 2007

— *Family Britain, 1951–57*, London, 2010

Longmate, Norman, *How We Lived Then*, London, 2002

Mackenzie, S. P., *British War Films*, London, 2001

Mitchell, B. R., *Abstract of British Historical Statistics,* Cambridge, 1962

Royle, Trevor, *The Best Years of their Lives: The National Service Experience 1945–63*, London, 1986

Taylor, A. J. P., *English History 1914–1945*, Oxford, 1975

Vernon, Phillip E., and John B. Parry, *Personnel Selection in the British Forces*, London, 1949

Contemporary Works, World War II and After

Bolster, David, *Roll on my Twelve*, London, 1945

Burgess, Robert, and Roland Blackburn, *We Joined the Navy*, London, 1943

Divine, A. D., *Destroyers War*, London, 1942

Fernald, John, *Destroyer from America*, London, 1942

'Officer's Aide Memoire' in B. Lavery, ed, *The Royal Navy Officer's Pocket Book*, London, 2007

O'Conor, Rory, *Running a Big Ship*, Portsmouth, 1937

Swaffer, Hannen, *What Would Nelson Do?*, London, 1946

Modern Journalism, Television Series, etc.

Barker, Denis, *Ruling the Waves*, London, 1986

Flack, Jeremy, *Today's Royal Navy in Colour*, London, 1995

Terrill, Christopher, *HMS* Brilliant – *in a Ship's Company*, London, 1996

— *Shipmates – Inside the Royal Navy Today*, London, 2005

Naval History etc

Arthur, Max, Lost Voices of the Royal Navy, London, 2005

Bailey, Chris Howard, *The Royal Naval Museum Book of the Battle of the Atlantic*, Stroud, 1994

Barnett, Corelli, *Engage the Enemy More Closely*, London, 1991

Beaver, Paul, *Encyclopaedia of the Modern Royal Navy*, Cambridge, 1982

Brown, Malcolm, and Patricia Meehan, *Scapa Flow*, London, 1968

Buxton, Ian, *To Sail No More*, Liskeard, 1997

Cammel Laird, *HMS* Renown, nd, *c*.1969, Birkenhead

Campbell, John, *Naval Weapons of World War Two*, London, 1985

Chief Polaris Executive, *Polaris and the Royal Navy*, London, 1966

Connell, G. G., *Jack's War*, London, 1985

'Doc', *100 Year History of the Sick Berth Branch,* Portsmouth, 1984

Eadon, Stuart, ed, *Kamikaze: The Story of the British Pacific Fleet*, 1995

Friedman, Norman, *British Carrier Aviation*, London, 1998

Glenton, Bill, *Mutiny in Force X*, London, 1986

Gretton, Peter, *Crisis Convoy*, London, 1974

Grove, Eric, *Vanguard to Trident*, London, 1987

Hawkins, Ian, ed, *Destroyer*, London, 2003

Jolly, Rick, *Jackspeak*, London, 2000

Ladd, James D., *By Sea By Land,* London, 1998

Lavery, B., *Hostilities Only*, London, 2004

— *Shield of Empire*, Edinburgh, 2007

— *Churchill's Navy*, London, 2006

— *Able Seamen*, 2011

Leggett, Eric, *The Corfu Incident*, London, 1974

Lennox Kerr, J., and David James, *Wavy Navy, by Some Who Served*, London, 1950

Lund, Paul, and Harry Ludlam, *The War of the Landing Craft*, Slough, 1976

MacDermott, Brian, *Ships Without Names*, London, 1992

McKee, Alexander, *Black Saturday*, London, 1960

McManners, Hugh, *Forgotten Voices of the Falklands*, London, 2007

Marriott, Leo, *Modern Combat Ships 4: Type 22*, Shepperton,1986

Middlebrook, Martin, *Operation Corporate*, London, 1985,

Moore, J. E., ed, *The Impact of Polaris*, Huddersfield, 1999

Nailor, Peter, *The Nassau Connection*, London, 1988

Nethercoate-Bryant, Keith, *Submarine Memories*, Hadley, 1994

Phillipson, David, *Band of Brothers: Boy Seamen in the Royal Navy.* Stroud, 2003

Roskill, S. W., *The War at Sea*, 4 vols, London, 1954–61

Rossiter, Mike, *Sink the* Belgrano, London, 2008

Royal Institution of Naval Architects, *British Warship Design*, London, 1983

Schofield, B. B., *Navigation and Direction: The Story of HMS* Dryad, Havant, 1977

Wellings, Joseph, *On His Majesty's Service,* ed Hattendorf, Newport, Rhode Island, 1983

Wells, John G., *Whaley: The Story of HMS* Excellent, Portsmouth, 1980

Wingate, John, *HMS* Belfast, Windsor, 1972

Winton, John, *Sink the* Haguro, London, 1979

Second World War Memoirs and Biography

Brown, John L., *Dairy of a Matelot, 1942–45*, Lowesmoor, Worcester, 1991

Bull, Peter, *To Sea in a Sieve*, London, 1956

Callaghan, James, *Time and Chance,* London, 1987

Cox, Vivian A., *Seven Christmases*, Sevenoaks, 2010

Crossley, R. 'Mike', *They Gave me a Seafire*, Shrewsbury, 2001

Davies, John W., *Jack, The Sailor with the Navy Blue Eyes,* Bishop Auckland, 1995

Davis, John, *Lower Deck*, London, 1945

— *The Stone Frigate,* London, 1947

Fuller, Roy, *Vamp Till Ready*, London, 1982

Gritten, John, *Full Circle: The Log of the Navy's No 1 Conscript*, Dunfermline, 2003

Guinness, Alec, *Blessings in Disguise*, London, 1987

Holt, F. S., *A Banker all at Sea*, Newtown, Australia, 1983

Jones, Albert H., *No Easy Choices*, Upton on Severn, 1999

Jones, Tristan, *Heart of Oak*, 1984, reprinted Shrewsbury, 1997

Kellet, Fred, *A Flower for the Sea, a Fish for the Sky*, Dellwood, 1995

Kimberley, Ken, *Heavo, Heavo, Lash up and Stow*, Kettering, 1999

Luscombe, George, *Total Germany*, Edinburgh, 1999

Macdonald, Sir Roderick, *The Figurehead*, Bishop Auckland, 1993

Zeigler, Phillip, *Mountbatten*, London, 1985

Macintyre, Donald, *U-Boat Killer*, London, 2002

Mallalieu, J. P. W., *Very Ordinary Seaman,* London, 1944

— *On Larkhill*, London, 1983

Melly, George, *Rum, Bum and Concertina*, London, 1977

Monsarrat, Nicholas, *Corvette Command*, London, 1975 edition

— *Three Corvettes*, London, 2000

Oram, H. P. K., *The Rogue's Yarn*, London, 1993
Putt, S. Gorley, *Men Dressed as Seamen*, London, 1943
Rayner, D. A., *Escort – The Battle of the Atlantic*, London, 1955
Palmer, John, *Luck on my Side*, Barnsley, 2002
Read, Piers Paul, *Alec Guinness*, London, 2004
Reynolds, L. C., *Motor Gunboat 658*, London, 2002
Scott, Peter, *The Battle of the Narrow Seas*, 1945
Whelan, John, *Home is the Sailor*, London, 1957
Winn, Godfrey, *Home from the Sea*, London, 1946

Memoirs, post war
Cobbold, Peter M., *The National Service Sailor*, Wivenhoe, 1993
Feasey, Geoff, *Very Ordinary Officer*, Fisher, Australia
Frank, Leslie, *Yangtse River Incident*, Uckfield, 2006
Gough, Richard S. J., *The Weapon Director*, 2003
La Niece, P. G. , *Not a Nine to Five Job,* Yalding, 1992
Payne, Michael, *When I was on the* Tartar, Stroud, 1999
Rosenthal, Jack, *An Autobiography in Six Acts*, London, 2005
Sherringham, Denis, *Swing the Lamp, Jack Dusty*, Thorpe Bay, 1998

Manuscripts
Imperial War Museum, documents
Mass Observation Archive, University of Sussex, Report Nos 886–7
National Archives, various series especially Adm 1 and Adm 116, which
    are best approached by keyword search

Annuals
Brassey's Naval Annual (to 1949), *Brassey's Annual – The Armed
    Forces Yearbook* (1950–73), *Royal United Services Institute and
    Brassey's Defence Yearbook* (from 1974)
Broadsheet, Ministry of Defence naval magazine

Newspapers and Journals
Navy News, from 1954
Naval Review
Shipping World and Shipbuilder

Official Publications
Admiralty, *Royal Naval Handbook of Field Training*, London, 1920
Admiralty, BR 224/45, *Gunnery Pocket Book*, 1945
Admiralty, *Engineering Manual for His Majesty's Fleet*, BR 16, 1939

Admiralty, *First Aid in the Royal Navy*, BR 25, 1943

Admiralty, *The Gunnery Pocket Book*, BR 224/45, 1945

Admiralty, *Machinery Handbook*, BR 77, 1941

Admiralty, *Manual of Seamanship*, Vol. I, 19—, Vol. II, 1932

Admiralty, *Manual of Navigation*, Vol. I, Vol. III, 1938

Admiralty, *Notes for Medical Officers on Entry into the Royal Navy*, BR 767, 1943

Admiralty, *Manual for Officers' Stewards*, BR 97, 1932

Admiralty, *A Seaman's Pocket Book*, BR 827, 1943

Admiralty, *Training of Artificer Apprentices*, BR 91, 1936

Admiralty, *The Treatment of Battle Casualties Afloat*, BR 1443 (42), 1942

Admiralty Manual of Seamanship, 1967

BR 1927(52), *Naval Airman Branch Qualifying Courses*

MoD report, *Board of Enquiry into the Grounding of HMS* Nottingham, 2002

Hansard for Parliamentary debates

Websites

Diesel Weasel website

Onthefirm

Brodie family

INDEX